W9-AJM-202

MILESTONES TO AMERICAN LIBERTY:

THE FOUNDATIONS OF THE REPUBLIC

MILTON MELTZER

Milestones to American Liberty:

NEW YORK, ESTABLISHED 1834

the Foundations of the Republic

THOMAS Y. CROWELL COMPANY

Designed by Laurel Wagner
Library of Congress Catalog Card No. 61-17771
Manufactured in the United States of America
3 4 5 6 7 8 9 10

For my mother and father

Preface

IF THE PAST has any use beyond the pleasure of entertainment it is to help us make our decisions today. Few of us are at commanding positions, but even as the most private of citizens we constantly face intellectual and moral decisions that are often as grave for ourselves as the choices a President or a Supreme Court must make for the country. Indeed, among these papers is one in which a great writer reasoned that men must serve the state with their consciences and be prepared to resist its wrongs at the risk of being treated as an enemy by it. He went to jail once on that account, and now, more than a hundred years later, men and women are making the same moral decision at the same cost. These latter-day Thoreaus are trying to make the country see that when we said all men are endowed by their Creator with certain unalienable rights, we meant it, for then and forever.

Several of these papers are obviously indispensable to any collection of basic American documents. Many others are included which show some aspect of our developing national character, and are worth reading for the freshness or the passion of their utterance. The human voice, speaking up for freedom and equality, can here be heard in what would seem the most unlikely places: an old colonial law affecting education; the resolution of a local congregation on slavery; the constitution of a tiny rural cooperative society or the charter of a newborn union, the speech of an Indian chief to a President or a fishpeddler to a judge; the report of a spinster lady to a legislature or the advice of a philosopher to a graduation assembly.

In these, together with the state papers, the court decisions, and the presidential addresses, you will find an America that is on the side of change, of progress, of betterment of the human condition. Between our Declaration of Independence and the cry for freedom now going up in many parts of the world there is a gap of almost two hundred years in time, but if we know and cherish our past, there should be no gap in our understanding.

Each document is introduced and illustrated to help refresh the reader's memory of the men and events out of which the statement came. The commentary and captions are, of course, subjective, representing the author's own interpretation of the past. Exigencies of space meant the abridgement of some documents, but in such cases the vital passages are given and the omissions indicated.

The papers are not grouped by subject but arranged chronologically. Sometimes facsimiles are used to show the document in its first form and occasionally rough drafts are reproduced. An index, a reading list, and various historical charts in the appendices should also be of value to the general reader as well as the student.

For the many courtesies extended by library staffs and picture collections I wish to express my gratitude. Special thanks are due Anne Coldewey for aid in preparing the final manuscript.

Contents

MILESTONES TO AMERICAN LIBERTY

THE FOUNDATIONS OF THE REPUBLIC

We do solemnly covenant ourselves into a civill body politick

The threat of James I to "harry them out of the land" sent a little band of religious dissenters from England to Holland in 1608. They were known as "Separatists" because they wished to cut all ties with the Established Church. In 1620, some of them, known now as the Pilgrims, joined with a larger group in England to set sail on the Mayflower *for the New World. A joint stock company financed their venture.*

In November they sighted Cape Cod and decided to land an exploring party at Plymouth Harbor. But a rebellious "undesirable lot" picked up at Southhampton and London troubled the Pilgrim leaders, and to control their actions forty-one of the Pilgrims drew up the Mayflower Compact, which was signed in the cabin before going ashore. As they had done in religious matters, they bound themselves under civil conditions to frame "just and equal laws." The voluntary agreement to govern themselves was America's first written constitution.

IN THE NAME of God, Amen. We whose names are under-writen, the loyall subjects of our dread soveraigne Lord, King James, by the grace of God, of Great Britaine, Franc, and Ireland king, defender of the faith, etc., haveing undertaken, for the glorie of God, and advancemente of the Christian faith, and honour of our king and countrie, a voyage to plant the first colonie in the Northerne parts of Virginia, doe by these presents solemnly and mutualy in the presence of God, and one of another, covenant and combine our selves togeather into a civill body politick, for our better ordering and preservation and furtherance of the ends aforesaid; and by vertue hearof to enacte, constitute, and frame such just and equall lawes, ordinances, acts, constitutions, and offices, from time to time, as shall be thought most meete and convenient for the generall good of the Colonie, unto which we promise all due submission and obedience. In witnes wherof we have hereunder subscribed our names at Cap-Codd the 11. of November, in the year of the raigne of our soveraigne lord, King James, of England, France, and Ireland the eighteenth, and of Scotland the fiftie fourth. An°: Dom. 1620.

—*Bradford's* History of Plimoth Plantation, *1630*

RELATION OR
Iournall of the beginning and proceedings
of the Engliſh Plantation ſetled at *Plimoth* in NEW
ENGLAND, by certaine Engliſh Aduenturers both
Merchants and others.

With their difficult paſſage, their ſafe ariuall, their
ioyfull building of, and comfortable planting them-
ſelues in the now well defended Towne
of NEW PLIMOTH.

AS ALSO A RELATION OF FOVRE
ſeuerall diſcoueries ſince made by ſome of the
ſame Engliſh Planters there reſident.

I. In a iourney to PVCKANOKICK *the habitation of the Indians greateſt King* Maſſaſoyt *: as alſo their meſſage, the anſwer and entertainment they had of him.*

II. In a voyage made by ten of them to the Kingdome of Nawſet, *to ſeeke a boy that had loſt himſelfe in the woods : with ſuch accidents as befell them in that voyage.*

III. In their iourney to the Kingdome of Namaſchet, *in defence of their greateſt King* Maſſaſoyt, *againſt the* Narrohiggonſets, *and to reuenge the ſuppoſed death of their Interpreter* Tiſquantum.

IIII. Their voyage to the Maſſachuſets, *and their entertainment there.*

With an anſwer to all ſuch obiections as are any way made
againſt the lawfulneſſe of Engliſh plantations
in thoſe parts.

LONDON,
Printed for *Iohn Bellamie*, and are to be ſold at his ſhop at the two
Greyhounds in Cornhill neere the Royall Exchange. 1622.

Mourt's Relation, issued in London in 1622, was the earliest book to be published about Plymouth Colony.

In ye name of God Amen. We whose names are underwriten
the loyall subjects of our dread soueraigne Lord King James
by ye grace of God, of great Britaine, Franc, & Ireland king
defender of ye faith, &c.
Haueing undertaken, for ye glorie of God, and aduancemente
of ye Christian faith and honour of our king & countrie, a voyage to
plant ye first Colonie in ye Northerne parts of Virginia. Doe
by these presents solemnly & mutualy in ye presence of God, and
one of another, couenant, & combine our selues togeather into a
Ciuill body politick; for our better ordering, & preseruation & fur=
therance of ye ends aforesaid; and by vertue hearof to enacte,
constitute, and frame shuch just & equall lawes, ordinances,
Acts, constitutions, & offices, from time to time, as shall be thoug
most meete & conuenient for ye generall good of ye Colonie: unto
which we promise all due submission and obedience. In witnes
wherof we haue hereunder subscribed our names at Cap=
Codd ye ·11· of Nouember, in ye year of ye raigne of our soueraigne
Lord king James of England, France, & Ireland ye eighteen
and of Scotland ye fiftie fourth. Ano Dom. 1620

The Mayflower Compact, from the original manuscript of William Bradford's *History of Plimoth Plantation*, 1630. A Pilgrim father, Bradford was elected Governor of the colony in 1621 and served many terms. His complete *History* was not published until 1856.

An engraving of the *Mayflower* at sea. She sailed from England on September 16, 1620, carrying 101 passengers. In the first winter at Plymouth, disease killed half the settlers.

A print depicting the landing of the Pilgrims at Plymouth in December, 1620. A majority of the settlers were not members of the Pilgrim sect, including Captain Miles Standish, hired as the military leader.

Every person shall enjoy justice and law

Massachusetts Bay Colony was founded at Boston in 1630 by Puritans who hoped to establish in the New World an ideal commonwealth in which their "purified" church could prosper. With them they brought a charter from King Charles I which soon became a constitution for the colony. By 1640 over twenty-five thousand refugees were making their home in Massachusetts, now the largest of the English settlements in America.

The Puritan leaders were interested neither in freedom of worship for others nor in a free system of goverment. "Democracy," patriarch John Cotton said, was "not fit government either for church or commonwealth." But against the rigid rule of the church fathers the town meetings soon rebelled. Under pressure from the settlers the Puritans appointed the Reverend Nathaniel Ward of Ipswich to draw up the Massachusetts Body of Liberties. The law code was adopted by the General Court. It dealt with matters of religion—providing capital punishment for those who refused to profess faith in God—as well as with the secular questions of land, trade, and property. But the document's greatest importance was its restatement of certain human rights whose origin lay as far back as Magna Carta.

First clause of the *Body of Liberties,* from the original manuscript.

A Coppie of the Liberties of the Massachusets Colonie in New England

1 No mans life shall be taken away, no mans honour or good name shall be stayned, no mans person shall be arested, restrayned, banished, dismembred, nor any wayes punished, no man shall be deprived of his wife or children, no mans goods or estaite shall be taken away from him, nor any way indamaged under Coulor of law, or Countenance of Authoritie, unlesse it be by vertue or equitie of some expresse law of the Country warranting the same, established by a generall Court & sufficiently published, or in case of the defect of a law in any parteculer case by the word of god. And in Capitall cases, or in cases concerning dismembring or banishment, according to that word to be judged by the Generall Court.

(10)

oath shall be taken of the keeper, that it was without his default, and it ſhall be accepted: but if the beaſt be torne in pieces, and a peece be brought for witneſſe, it excuſeth the keeper.

Chap. VII.

Of Crimes.

AND firſt, of ſuch as deſerve capitall puniſhment, or cutting off from a mans people, whether by death or baniſhment.

Blaſphemy. Lev. 24. 11 to 16. 1 Firſt, Blaſphemy which is a curſing of God by Atheiſme or the like, to be puniſhed with death.

Idolatry. 2 Idolatry to be puniſhed with death.

Witchcraft. Ex. 22. 18. 3 Witchcraft which is fellowſhip by covenant with a familiar Spirit to be puniſhed with death.

Conſulters with witches. Lev. 19. 31. 20. 27. 4 Conſulters with Witches not to be tollerated, but either to be cut off by death, or by baniſhment.

Hereſie. Deut. 13. 10. 15, 16. 5 Hereſie which is the maintenance of ſome wicked errors, overthrowing the foundation of Chriſtian Religion, which obſtinacy if it be joyned with endeavour, to ſeduce others thereunto to be puniſhed with death: becauſe ſuch an Hereticke no leſſe than an Idolater ſeeketh to thruſt the ſoules of men from the Lord their God.

Falſe worſhip. Ex. 32. 27, 28 6 To worſhip God in a molten or graven Image, to be puniſhed with death.

Scandalous livers. 1 Cor. 5. 5 7 Such members of the Church, as doe wilfully reject to walke after due admonition, and conviction, the Churches eſtabliſhment, and their chriſtian admonition and cenſures, ſhall be cut off by baniſhment.

Revilers of Religion. 8 Whoſoever ſhall revile the Religion and Worſhip of God, and the Government of the Church as it is now eſtabliſhed, to be cut off by baniſhment.

Wilfull perjury. 9 Wilfull perjury, whether before the judgement ſeat or in private conference, to be puniſhed with death.

Raſh perjury. 10 Raſh perjury whether in publike or in private, to be puniſhed with baniſhmet, juſt it is that ſuch a mans name ſhould be cut off from his people, who prophans ſo groſly the name of God before his people

Sabbath breakers. Num. 15. 32 11 Profaning of the Lords day, in a careleſſe and ſcornefull neglect or contempt thereof to be puniſhed with death.

12 To

This page from John Cotton's *An Abstract of the Lawes of New England,* London, 1641, shows how harshly the theocracy wished to punish offenses against it. Not this code, however, but the somewhat more merciful *Body of Liberties,* was finally adopted by Massachusetts.

1. NO MAN'S LIFE shall be taken away, no man's honour or good name shall be stayned, no man's person shall be arrested, restrayned, banished, dismembred, nor any ways punished, no man shall be deprived of his wife or children, no man's goods or estaite shall be taken away from him, nor any way indammaged under Colour of law, of Coutenance of Authoritie, unless it be by virtue or equitie of some expresse law of the Country warranting the same, established by a general Court and sufficiently published, or in case of a defect of law in any partecular case by the word of god. And in Capitall cases, or in cases concerning dismembring or banishment, according to that word to be judged by the Generall Court.

2. Every person within this jurisdiction, whether Inhabitant or Forreiner, shall enjoy the same justice and law that is generall for the plantation, which we constitute and execute one toward another without partialitie or delay.

A schoolmaster of the early seventeenth century. There were public and private schools throughout New England. Reading, writing, arithmetic, and religion were taught, under a severe discipline.

Train up your children in learning and labor

With houses built, living provided for, churches reared, and civil governments established, "the next thing we longed for and looked after," wrote an anonymous Puritan in 1643, "was to advance learning and perpetuate it to Posterity." Five years after its founding, Boston had a school. Puritans took education seriously, for their faith called for every man to study the Scriptures for himself. With towns to support them and a large number of university graduates in the colony, schools soon flourished. In 1642 the Massachusetts General Court adopted a law obliging all parents to see that their children learned to read and to practice some trade. In 1647 another Act called for free public schools throughout the colony, a goal that took some time to achieve. "Amid all these privations and dangers," Horace Mann said two hundred years later, was "conceived the magnificent idea, not only of a universal, but of a free education, for the whole people."

THIS Co^rt, taking into consideration the great neglect of many parents & masters in training up their children in learning & labo^r, & other implyments which may be proffitable to the common wealth, do hereupon order and decree, that in euery towne ye chosen men appointed for managing the prudentiall affajres of the same shall henceforth stand charged with the care of the redresse of this evill, so as they shalbee sufficiently punished by fines for the neglect thereof, upon presentment of the grand iury, or other information or complaint in any Court within this iurisdiction; and for this end they, or the greater numbe^r of them, shall have power to take account from time to time of all parents and masters, and of their children, concerning their calling and implyment of their children, especially of their ability to read & understand the principles of religion & the capitall lawes of this country, and to impose fines upon such as shall refuse to render such accounts to them when they shall be required; and they shall have power, with consent of any Court or the magistrate, to put forth apprentices the children of such as they shall [find] not to be able & fitt to employ and bring them up. They shall take . . . that

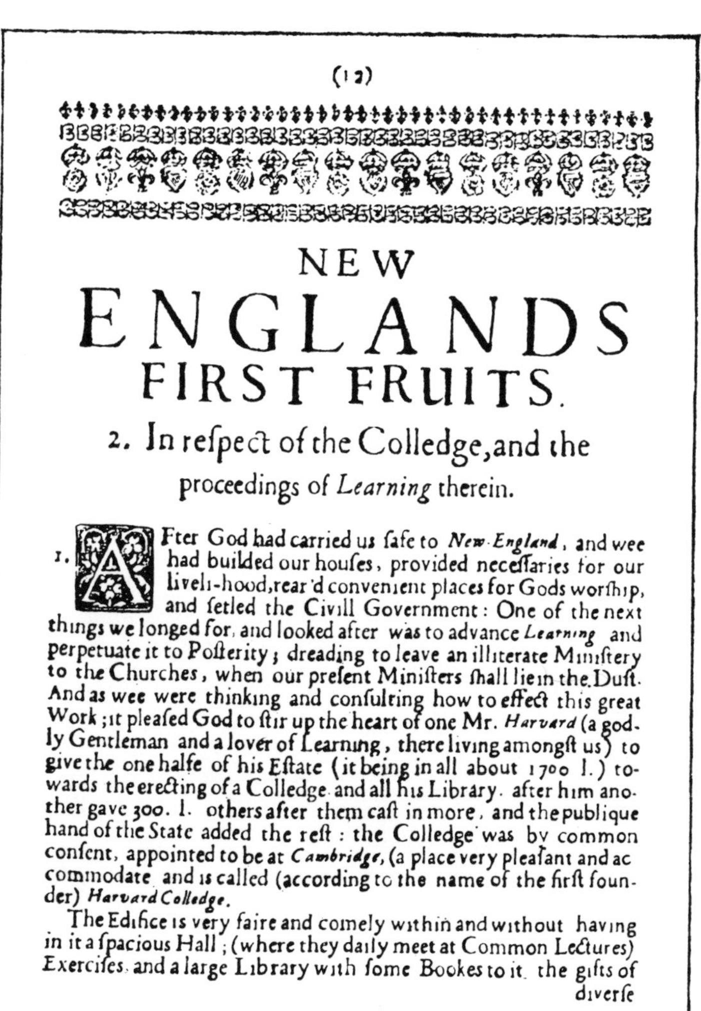

(12)

NEW ENGLANDS FIRST FRUITS.

2. In respect of the Colledge, and the proceedings of *Learning* therein.

1. After God had carried us safe to *New-England*, and wee had builded our houses, provided necessaries for our liveli-hood, rear'd convenient places for Gods worship, and setled the Civill Government: One of the next things we longed for, and looked after was to advance *Learning* and perpetuate it to Posterity; dreading to leave an illiterate Ministery to the Churches, when our present Ministers shall lie in the Dust. And as wee were thinking and consulting how to effect this great Work; it pleased God to stir up the heart of one Mr. *Harvard* (a godly Gentleman and a lover of Learning, there living amongst us) to give the one halfe of his Estate (it being in all about 1700 l.) towards the erecting of a Colledge, and all his Library: after him another gave 300. l. others after them cast in more, and the publique hand of the State added the rest: the Colledge was by common consent, appointed to be at *Cambridge*, (a place very pleasant and accommodate) and is called (according to the name of the first founder) *Harvard Colledge*.

The Edifice is very faire and comely within and without, having in it a spacious Hall; (where they daily meet at Common Lectures) Exercises, and a large Library with some Bookes to it, the gifts of diverse

First page of a London pamphlet (1643) showing Puritan concern for education. The founding of Harvard College is described.

Spiritual

MILK

FOR

BOSTON BABES

In either ENGLAND.

Drawn out of the Breasts of both *TESTAMENTS* for their souls *nourishment*

But may be of like use to any Children

By JOHN COTTON, *B. D.* *late Teacher to the Church of* Boston *in* New-England.

CAMBRIDG

Printed by *S. G.* for *Hezekiah Usher* at Boston in *New-England*

1656

Title page of Reverend John Cotton's catechism. After serving 21 years as vicar of a church in Boston, England, he became teacher to the church of Boston, New England. His catechism, used for over 150 years, was adapted for the *New England Primer.*

boyes and girles be not suffered to converse together, so as may occasion any wanton, dishonest, or immodest behavio^{r}; & for their better performance of this trust committed to them, they may divide the towne amongst them, appointing to every of the said townesmen a certaine number of families to have special oversight of. They are also to provide that a sufficient quantity of materialls, as hemp, flaxe, ec^{ra}, may be raised in their severall townes, & tooles & implements provided for working out the same; & for their assistance in this so needfull and beneficiall imploym^{t}, if they meete wth any difficulty or opposition wch they cannot well master by their own power, they may have reco^{r}se to some of the ma^{trats}, who shall take such course for their help & incuragm^{t} as the occasion shall require according to iustice; & the said townesmen, at the next Co^{r}t in those limits, after the end of their year, shall give a briefe account in writing of their proceedings herein, provided that they have bene so required by some Co^{r}t or magistrate a month at least before; & this order continew for two yeares, & till the Co^{r}t shall take further order.

God requireth not a uniformity of religion

Young Roger Williams left his native England when the government made life for the religious dissenters too miserable to endure. Arrived in Boston in 1631, the learned Puritan minister found the Massachusetts authorities just as hostile to dissent. That civil government should have no power in spiritual matters was one of the "strange opinions" he voiced. From this heretical attack upon the alliance of church and state Williams moved into the political realm, charging that King James has no right to give grants and patents to land that belonged to the Indians. Tried in 1635 as a dangerous agitator, he was banished from the colony.

In exile, Williams founded Providence and the colony of Rhode Island, where he pioneered the practice of both religious liberty and political democracy. From The Bloudy Tenent of Persecution, *a pamphlet he printed in England, is taken Williams's argument for complete religious toleration.*

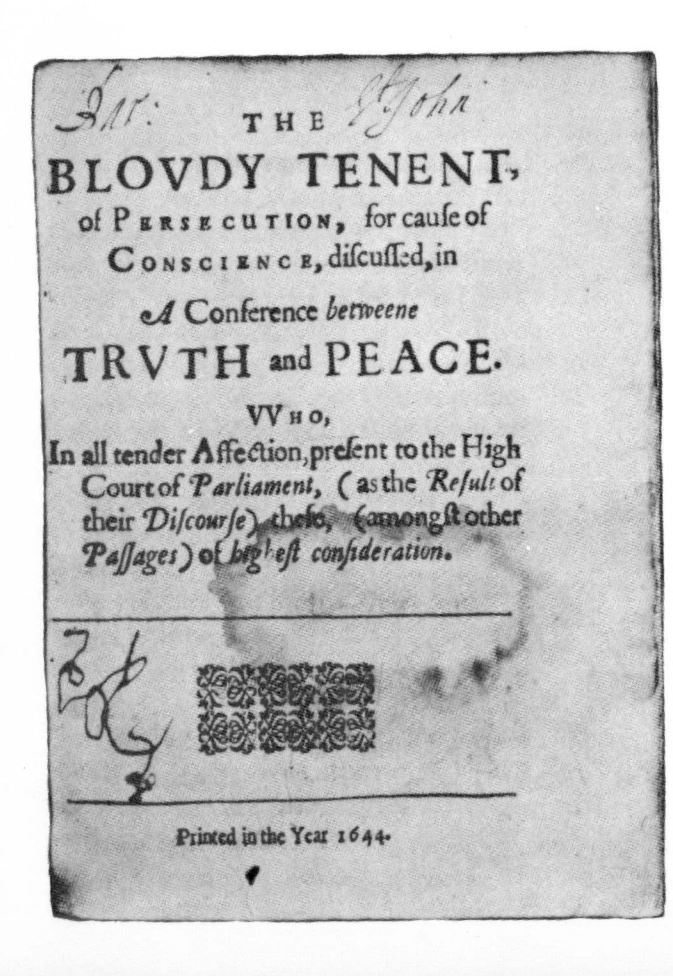

THE
BLOVDY TENENT,
of PERSECUTION, for cause of
CONSCIENCE, discussed, in
A Conference *betweene*
TRVTH and PEACE.
VVHO,
In all tender Affection, present to the High
Court of *Parliament*, (as the *Result* of
their *Discourse*) these, (amongst other
Passages) of highest *consideration.*

Printed in the Year 1644.

In this book Roger Williams argued that all individuals and religious bodies—Jews, Catholics, Protestants, pagans—had the natural right of religious liberty. The pamphlet was written in England when Williams had returned to frustrate the attempt of Massachusetts to take away the colony on the Narragansett. He won a charter for Rhode Island on March 14, 1644.

FIRST, that the blood of so many hundred thousand souls of Protestants and Papists, spilt in the wars of present and former ages, for their respective consciences, is not required nor accepted by Jesus Christ the Prince of Peace.

Secondly, pregnant scriptures and arguments are throughout the work proposed against the doctrine of persecution for cause of conscience.

Thirdly, satisfactory answers are given to scriptures, and objections produced by Mr. Calvin, Beza, Mr. Cotton, and the ministers of the New English churches and others former and later, tending to prove the doctrine of persecution for cause of conscience.

Fourthly, the doctrine of persecution for cause of conscience is proved guilty of all the blood of the souls crying for vengeance under the altar.

Fifthly, all civil states with their officers of justice in their respective constitutions and administrations

Puritan Boston would not suffer the beliefs of the Quakers who, like Roger Williams, advocated separation of church and state, and whipped them, tied to the cart's tail, through the streets.

are proved essentially civil, and therefore not judges, governors, or defenders of the spiritual or Christian state and worship.

Sixthly, it is the will and command of God that (since the coming of his Son the Lord Jesus) a permission of the most paganish, Jewish, Turkish, or antichristian consciences and worships, be granted to all men in all nations and countries; and they are only to be fought against with that sword which is only (in soul matters) able to conquer, to wit, the sword of God's Spirit, the Word of God.

Seventhly, the state of the Land of Israel, the kings and people thereof in peace and war, is proved figurative and ceremonial, and no pattern nor president for any kingdom or civil state in the world to follow.

Eighthly, God requireth not a uniformity of religion to be enacted and enforced in any civil state; which enforced uniformity (sooner or later) is the greatest occasion of civil war, ravishing of conscience, persecution of Christ Jesus in his servants, and of the hypocrisy and destruction of millions of souls.

When banishment from Massachusetts was ordered for Williams, he escaped before the authorities could seize him. The Indians befriended him in his flight through the winter woods to the Narragansett country. He studied their language, visited them in their wigwams, won their affection. Their example of tolerance deepened his own love of liberty.

Roger Williams, the man who established the New World's principle of religious liberty. He was the son of a London merchant, and a graduate of Pembroke College, Cambridge. He died in 1683.

John Cotton, a leader of the Puritan theocracy against whom Williams rebelled.

Ninthly, in holding an enforced uniformity of religion in a civil state, we must necessarily disclaim our desires and hopes of the Jew's conversion to Christ.

Tenthly, an enforced uniformity of religion throughout a nation or civil state, confounds the civil and religious, denies the principles of Christianity and civility, and that Jesus Christ is come in the flesh.

Eleventhly, the permission of other consciences and worships than a state professeth only can (according to God) procure a firm and lasting peace (good assurance being taken according to the wisdom of the civil state for uniformity of civil obedience from all forts).

Twelfthly, lastly, true civility and Christianity may both flourish in a state or kingdom, notwithstanding the permission of divers and contrary consciences, either of Jew or Gentile.

We are against the traffic of men

At Jamestown, Virginia, in 1619, a Dutch ship unloaded the first cargo of Africans to reach the American colonies. The Negro slaves proved easier and cheaper to import for labor than white indentured workers. Each African, at this time, cost the slave trader about $25, and brought $150 in the American market. Later the selling price was much higher, and the trade in "black gold" became a fabulously profitable business for many nations.

Slavery spread North and South in the English colonies and the struggle to overthrow it went with it. To make the Negro free became for many the test of American democracy. Among the first to protest against the institution of slavery were those who felt trading in men was not consistent with their religion. On February 18, 1688, a monthly meeting of Mennonites in Germantown, Pennsylvania, adopted this resolution.

THESE ARE the reasons why we are against the traffic of men-body, as followeth: Is there any that would be done or handled at this manner? viz., to be sold or made a slave for all the time of his life? How fearful and faint-hearted are many at sea, when they see a strange vessel, being afraid it should be a Turk, and they should be taken, and sold for slaves into Turkey. Now, what is this better done, than Turks do? Yea, rather is it worse for them, which they say are Christians; for we do hear that the most part of such negers are brought are brought hither against their will and consent, and that many of them are stolen. Now, though they be black, we cannot conceive there is more liberty to have them slaves, as it is to have other white ones. There is a saying, that we should do all men like as we will be done ourselves; making no difference of what generation, descent, or colour they are. And those who steal or rob men, and those who buy or purchase them, are they not all alike? Here is liberty of conscience, which is right and reasonable; here ought to be likewise liberty of the body, except of

Slaves were at first used from one end to the other of the American colonies. The South, however, became the greatest slave market because its ever-growing plantations of rice, cotton, tobacco, and sugar cane sorely needed manpower. This print depicts a slave auction in colonial New York where, as in all the Northern states, slavery was extinguished not long after the upheaval of the American Revolution.

A captive in Africa awaiting sale to traders who gathered slaves at the coast for export to the Americas. In the eighteenth century alone some seven million Africans were converted into merchandise.

evil-doers, which is another case. But to bring men hither, or to rob or sell them against their will, we stand against. . . . Ah, do consider according to Christianity! . . . Pray, what thing in the world can be done worse towards us, than if men should rob or steal us away, and sell us for slaves to strange countries; separating husbands from wives and children. Being now this is not done in the manner we would be done at; therefore, we contradict, and are against this traffic of men-body. And we who profess that it is not lawful to steal, must likewise, avoid to purchase such things as are stolen, but rather help to stop this robbing and stealing. . . .

Now consider well this thing, if it is good or bad. And in case you find it to be good to handle these blacks in that manner, we desire and require you hereby lovingly, that you may inform us herein, which at this time was never done, viz., that Christians have such a liberty to do so. To the end we shall be satisfied on this point and satisfy likewise our good friends and acquaintances in our native country, to whom it is a terror, or fearful thing, that men should be handled so in Pennsylvania.

This is from our meeting at Germantown, held ye 18th of the 2nd month, 1688, to be delivered to the monthly meeting at Richard Worrell's.

Garret Henderich, Derick Op De Graeff, Francis Daniel Pastorius, Abram Op De Graeff.

Plan of a slave ship, showing how a black cargo was packed for the voyage across the Atlantic. Every foot of space was used. The chained slaves were stacked like logwood; one out of five, it was estimated, died along the bloody sea lane.

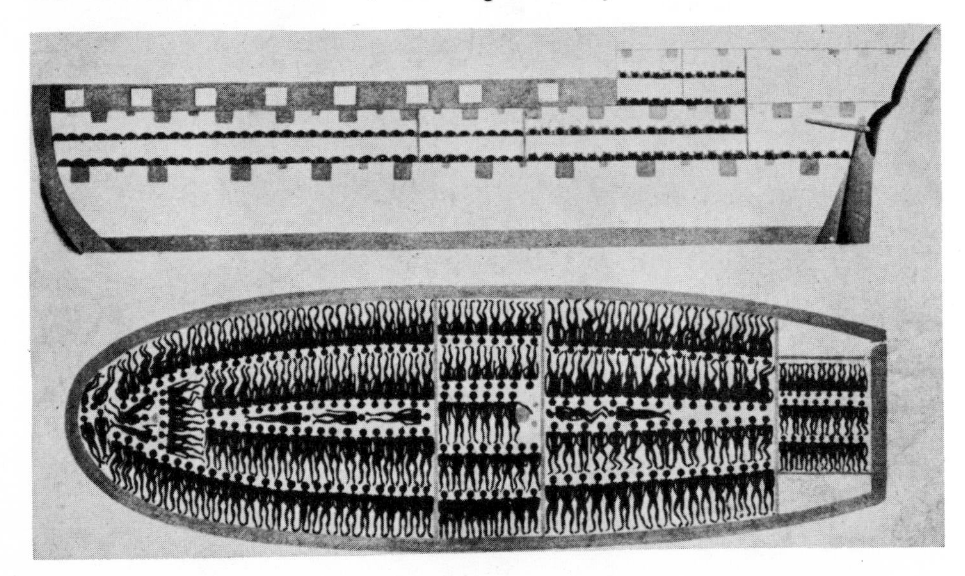

The Governor's Council ordered Zenger's "seditious" papers to be publicly burned, but it was hard to find a willing hand. The sheriff's slave had to do it.

The right of exposing and opposing arbitrary power by speaking and writing truth

The trial of John Peter Zenger, said Gouverneur Morris, was "the morning star of that liberty which subsequently revolutionized America." Zenger arrived in New York as a German lad of thirteen, and was apprenticed to a colonial printer. In the 1730's the opposition to the tyrannical royal governor, William Cosby, chose Zenger to publish the New-York Weekly Journal *as their weapon in the political battle. In 1734 Zenger was charged with seditious libel and a high bail arbitrarily set. But jail did not keep the printer from getting out his paper.*

When his trial came up in the Spring, his attorneys were disbarred. Secretly they secured the help of aged Andrew Hamilton, one of the most distinguished lawyers in the colonies. In a surprise appearance at the trial Hamilton made a stirring appeal for "the Liberty—both of exposing and opposing arbitrary Power . . . by speaking and writing Truth."

The jury brought in a swift acquittal. An excerpt from the report of the trial follows.

THE

TRIAL

OF

John Peter Zenger,

OF

NEW-YORK, PRINTER;

Who was Tried and Acquitted,

For PRINTING and PUBLISHING a LIBEL against the Government,

WITH

The PLEADINGS and ARGUMENTS on both Sides.

Ita CUIQUE *eveniat, ut de* REPUBLICA *meruit.* CIC.

LONDON:

Printed for P. BROWN, in *Fleet-Street*. MDCCLII.

[Price One Shilling and Sixpence.]

The report of the Zenger trial, published in London.

IT IS TRUE in Times past it was a Crime to speak Truth, and in that terrible Court of Star-Chamber, many worthy and brave Men suffered for so doing; and yet even in that Court, and in those bad Times, a great and good Man durst say, what I hope will not be taken amiss of me to say in this Place, *to wit, the Practice of Informations for Libels is a Sword in the Hands of a wicked king and* [of] *an arrand Coward to cut down and destroy the innocent; the one cannot, because of his high station, and the other dares not, because of his Want of Courage, revenge himself in another Manner.*

Mr. ATTORNEY, Pray Mr. HAMILTON, have a Care what you say, don't go too far neither, I don't like those Liberties.

Mr. HAMILTON, Sure, Mr. Attorney, you won't make any Applications; all Men agree that we are governed by the best of Kings, and I cannot see the Meaning of Mr. Attorney's Caution. . . . May it please Your Honour, I was saying, That notwithstanding all the Duty and Reverence claimed by Mr. Attorney to Men in Authority, they are not exempt from observing the Rules of common Justice, either in their private or publick Capacities; the Laws of our Mother Country know no Exception. . . .

I hope to be pardon'd, Sir, for my Zeal upon this Occasion: It is an old and wise Caution, *That when our Neighbour's House is on Fire, We ought to take Care of our own.* For tho', blessed be God, I live in a Government where Liberty is well understood, and freely enjoy'd; yet Experience has shewn us all (I'm sure it has to me) that a bad Precedent in one Government, is soon set up for an Authority in another; and therefore I cannot but think it mine, and every Honest Man's Duty, that (while we pay all due Obedience to Men in Authority) we ought at the same Time to be upon our Guard against Power, wherever we apprehend that it may effect Ourselves or our Fellow-Subjects.

I am truly very unequal to such an Undertaking on many Accounts. And you see I labour under the Weight of many Years, and am born down with great Infirmities of Body; yet Old and Weak as I am, I should think it my Duty, if required, to go to the utmost Part of the land, where my Service cou'd be of any Use in assisting to quench the flame of Prosecutions upon Informations, set on Foot by the Government, to deprive a People of the Right of Remonstrating (and complaining too) of the arbitrary Attempts of Men in Power. Men who injure and oppress the People under their Administration provoke them to cry out and complain; and then make that very Complaint the foundation for new Oppressions and Prosecutions. . . . But to conclude; the Question before the Court and you, Gentlemen of the Jury, is not of small nor private Concern, it is not the Cause of a poor Printer, nor of *New York* alone, which you are now trying; No! It may in its Consequence, affect every Freeman that lives under a British Government on the Main of *America.* It is the best Cause. It is the Cause of Liberty; and I make no Doubt but your upright Conduct, this Day, will not only entitle you to the Love and Esteem of your Fellow-Citizens; but every Man, who prefers Freedom to a Life of Slavery, will bless and honour You, as Men who have baffled the Attempt of Tyranny; and by an impartial and uncorrupt Verdict, have laid a noble Foundation for securing to ourselves, our Posterity, and our Neighbours, That to which Nature and the Laws of our Country have given us a Right,—the Liberty—both of exposing and opposing arbitrary Power (in these Parts of the World, at least) by speaking and writing Truth.

The trial over, and his acquittal won, Zenger announces the victory for a free press.

XCIII.

THE

New-York Weekly JOURNAL.

Containing the freſheſt Advices, Foreign, and Domeſtick.

MUNDAY Auguſt 18th, 1735.

To my Subſcribers and Benefactors.

Gentlemen;

I Think my ſelf in Duty bound to to make publick Acknowledgment for the many Favours received at your Hands, which I do in this Manner return you my hearty Thanks for. I very ſoon intend to print my Tryal at Length, that the World may ſee how unjuſt my Sufferings have been, ſo will only at this Time give this ſhort Account of it.

On *Munday* the 4*th* Inſtant my Tryal for Printing Parts of my Journal *No.* 13. and 23. came on, in the Supreme Court of this Province, before the moſt numerous Auditory of People, I may with Juſtice ſay, that ever were ſeen in that Place at once; my Jury ſworn were,

1 *Harmanus Rutgers*,
2 *Stanley Holms*,
3 *Edward Man*,
4 *John Bell*,
5 *Samuel Weaver*,
6 *Andrew Marſchalk*,
7 *Egbert Van Borſen*,
8 *Thomas Hunt*,
9 *Benjamin Hildrith*,
10 *Abraham Kitaltaſs*,
11 *John Goelet*,
12 *Hercules Wendover*,

John Chambers, Eſq; had been appointed the Term before by the Court as my Council, in the Place of *James Alexander* and *William Smith*, who were then ſilenced on my Account, and to Mr. *Chambers*'s Aſſiſtance came *Andrew Hamilton*, Eſq; of *Philadelphia* Barreſter at Law; when Mr Attorney offered the Information and the Proofs, Mr. *Hamilton* told him, he would acknowledge my Printing and Publiſhing the Papers in the Information, and ſave him the Trouble of that Proof, and offered to prove the Facts of thoſe Papers true, and had Witneſſes ready to prove every Fact; he long inſiſted on the Liberty of Making Proof thereof, but was over-ruled therein. Mr. Attorney offered no Proofs of my Papers being *falſe*, *malicious* and *ſeditious*, as they were charged to be, but inſiſted that they were Lybels tho' true. There were many Arguments and Authorities on this point, and the Court were of Opinion with Mr. Attorney on that Head: But the Jury having taken the Information out with them, they returned in about Ten Minutes, and found me *Not Guilty*; upon which there were immediately three Hurra's of many Hundreds of People in the preſence of the Court, before the Verdict was returned. The next Morning my Diſcharge was moved for and granted, and ſufficient was ſub-

Patrick Henry addressing the Virginia Assembly on May 29, 1765. Proposing several resolutions against Britain's colonial policy, he made the famous "If this be treason" speech.

1775 Patrick Henry: Speech

Give me liberty, or give me death!

Among the delegates to the First Continental Congress when it met at Philadelphia in September, 1774, was Patrick Henry of Virginia. A leading lawyer of his colony, he was known in the House of Burgesses as a resounding spokesman for the western frontier. In 1765, while introducing resolutions asserting that Virginians could be taxed only by their own assembly, his speech had closed with the ringing lines . . . "Caesar had his Brutus—Charles the First, his Cromwell—and George the Third may profit by their example. If this be treason, make the most of it."

At Philadelphia, the Continental Congress proclaimed a Declaration of Grievances against British policies and pledged a commercial boycott to pressure repeal of Parliamentary acts violating American rights. The radicals were in the majority at Philadelphia; wavering citizens were pressed to decide what course to take. Some hoped for conciliation and compromise with the British. Others felt no concessions should be made, but pleaded against the use of force.

The New Englanders gathered their arms and summoned the people to drill for their defense. On March 23, 1775, Patrick Henry spoke to the Virginia Convention in favor of resolutions to raise militia to resist British policy. The oration, pieced together from later accounts, is one of the most famous in our history.

Patrick Henry. The revolutionary orator and statesman began his career as a storekeeper and farmer, became a lawyer, a legislator, and finally, Governor of Virginia. Late in life his politics switched from Republican to Federalist.

MR. PRESIDENT, it is natural to men to indulge in the illusions of hope. We are apt to shut our eyes against a painful truth—and listen to the song of that siren, till she transforms us into beasts. Is this the part of wise men, engaged in a great and arduous struggle for liberty? Are we disposed to be of the number of those who, having eyes, see not, and having ears, hear not, the things which so nearly concern their temporal salvation? For my part, whatever anguish of spirit it may cost, I am willing to know the whole truth; to know the worst and to provide for it.

I have but one lamp by which my feet are guided, and that is the lamp of experience. I know of no way of judging of the future but by the past. And judging by the past, I wish to know what there has been in the conduct of the British ministry for the last ten years to justify those hopes with which gentlemen have been pleased to solace themselves and the house? Is it that insidious smile with which our petition has been lately received? Trust it not, sir; it will prove a snare to your feet. Suffer not yourself to be betrayed with a kiss. Ask yourself how this gracious reception of our petition comports with those warlike preparations which cover our waters and darken our land. Are fleets and armies necessary to a work of love and reconciliation? Have we shown ourselves so unwilling to be reconciled that force must be called in to win back our love? Let us not deceive ourselves, sir. These are the implements of war and subjugation—the last arguments to which kings resort. I ask gentlemen, sir, what means this martial array if its purpose be not to force us to submission? Can gentlemen assign any other possible motive for it? Has Great Britain any enemy in this quarter of the world, to call for this accumulation of navies and armies? No, sir, she has none. They are meant for us; they can be meant for no other. They are sent over to bind and rivet upon us those chains which the British ministry have been so long forging.

And what have we to oppose to them? Shall we try argument? Sir, we have been trying that for the last ten years. Have we anything new to offer upon the subject? Nothing. We have the subject up in every light of which it is capable; but it has been all in vain. Shall we resort to entreaty and humble supplication? What terms shall we find which have not been already exhausted? Let us not, I beseech you, sir, deceive ourselves longer. Sir, we have done everything that could be done to avert the storm which is now coming on. We have petitioned—we have remonstrated—we have supplicated—we have prostrated ourselves before the throne, and have implored its interposition to arrest the tyrannical hands of the ministry and parliament. Our petitions have been slighted; our remonstrances have produced additional violence and insult; our supplications have been disregarded; and we have been spurned with contempt from the foot of the throne. In vain, after these things, may we indulge the fond hope of peace and reconciliation.

There is no longer any room for hope. If we wish to be free—if we mean to preserve inviolate those inestimable privileges for which we have been so long contending—if we mean not basely to abandon the noble struggle in which we have been so long engaged, and which we have pledged ourselves never to abandon until the glorious object of our contest shall be obtained—we must fight!—I repeat it, sir, we must fight; an appeal to arms and to the God of Hosts is all that is left us!

They tell us, sir, that we are weak—unable to cope with so formidable an adversary. But when shall we be stronger? Will it be the next week or the next year? Will it be when we are totally disarmed, and when a British guard shall be stationed in every house? Shall we gather strength by irresolution and inaction? Shall we acquire the means of effectual resistance by lying supinely on our backs and hugging the delusive phantom of hope, until our enemy shall have bound us hand and foot? Sir, we are not weak, if we make a proper use of those forces which the God of nature hath placed in our power. Three millions of people armed in the holy cause of liberty, and in such a country as that which we possess, are invincible by any force which our enemy can send against us. Besides, sir, we shall not fight our battles alone. There is a just God who presides over the destinies of nations, and who will raise up friends to fight our battles for us. The battle, sir, is not to the strong alone; it is to the vigilant, the active, the brave. Besides, sir, we have no election. If we were base enough to desire it, it is now too late to retire from the contest. There is no retreat but in submission and slavery! Our chains are forged. Their clanking may be heard on the plains of Boston! The war is inevitable—and let it come! I repeat it sir, let it come!

It is vain, sir, to extenuate the matter. Gentlemen may cry, peace, peace—but there is no peace. The war is actually begun! The next gale that sweeps from the north will bring to our ears the clash of resounding arms! Our brethren are already in the field! Why stand we here idle? What is it that gentlemen wish? What would they have? Is life so dear, or peace so sweet, as to be purchased at the price of chains and slavery? Forbid it, Almighty God! I know not what course others may take; but as for me, give me liberty, or give me death!

All men have certain inherent rights

The colonial Americans began to experiment with making their own governments when they created committees of correspondence, conventions, and assemblies. As they fought a revolution against a government which denied them precious rights, they struggled to create new governments which would guarantee them against tyranny and oppression. Their experience taught them governments cannot be given unlimited trust. Power uncurbed tends to be despotic.

The philosophy of the men engaged in making States stood upon two principles: governments derive their powers from the people, and these powers are subject to definition and limitation. Representative bodies therefore met to design a structure of government. First to be framed was the Virginia Constitution. After forcing the royal governor to flee, the revolutionary assembly met in convention in May and June, 1776, declared their colony's independence, and adopted a State constitution.

From George Mason the convention accepted, with slight modifications, a draft of a bill of rights. Affecting political thought not only of American statesmen but of European as well, its influence was vast. It gave the force of fundamental law to the individual citizen's inherent rights and liberties. Now he was armed against arbitrary authority.

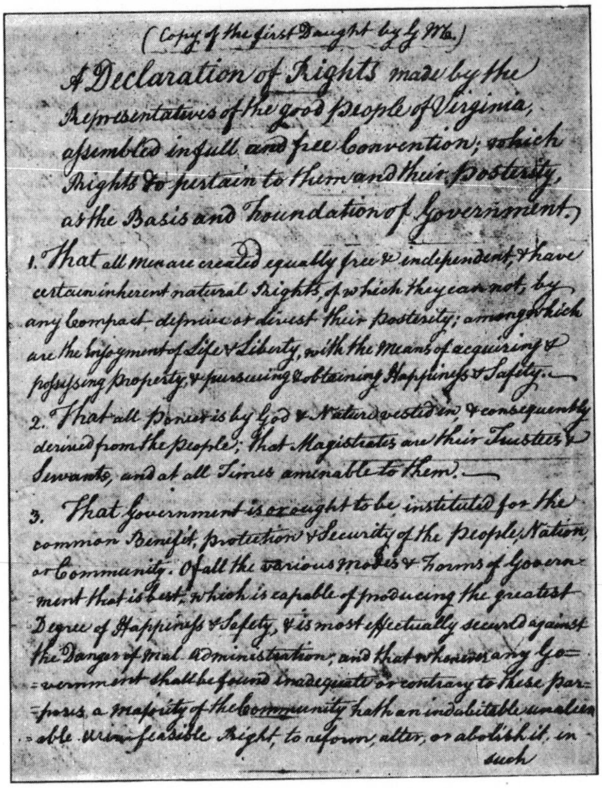
(Copy of the first Draught by G Ma)

A Declaration of Rights made by the Representatives of the good people of Virginia, assembled in full and free Convention; which Rights do pertain to them and their posterity, as the Basis and Foundation of Government.

1. That all Men are created equally free & independent, & have certain inherent natural Rights, of which they can not, by any Compact, deprive or divest their posterity; among which are the Enjoyment of Life & Liberty, with the Means of acquiring & possessing property, & pursuing & obtaining Happiness & Safety.

2. That all Power is by God & Nature vested in, & consequently derived from the people; that Magistrates are their Trustees & Servants, and at all Times amenable to them.

3. That Government is or ought to be instituted for the common Benefit, protection & Security of the people, Nation, or Community. Of all the various Modes & Forms of Government that is best, which is capable of producing the greatest Degree of Happiness & Safety, & is most effectually secured against the Danger of mal administration; and that whenever any Government shall be found inadequate or contrary to these purposes, a Majority of the Community hath an indubitable unalienable & indefeasible Right, to reform, alter, or abolish it, in such

A page from the first draft of the Bill of Rights adopted by the Virginia Convention on June 12, 1776.

A DECLARATION OF RIGHTS made by the representatives of the good people of Virginia, assembled in full and free convention; which rights do pertain to them and their posterity, as the basis and foundation of government.

1. That all men are by nature equally free and independent, and have certain inherent rights, of which, when they enter into a state of society, they cannot, by any compact, deprive or divest their posterity; namely, the enjoyment of life and liberty, with the means of acquiring and possessing property, and pursuing and obtaining happiness and safety.

2. That all power is vested in, and consequently derived from, the people; that magistrates are their trustees and servants, and at all times amenable to them.

3. That government is, or ought to be, instituted for the common benefit, protection, and security of the people, nation, or community; of all the various modes and forms of government, that is best which is capable of producing the greatest degree of happiness and safety, and is most effectually secured against the danger of maladministration; and that when any government shall be found inadequate or contrary to these purposes, a majority of the com-

George Mason, who drafted Virginia's Bill of Rights, the model for all the states. Mason, an aristocrat, owned Gunston Hall and a 5,000-acre plantation. He was one of America's greatest civil libertarians. His influence was strongly felt in the drafting of the national Bill of Rights as well, especially in the Second, Third, and Fourth Amendments.

munity hath an indubitable, inalienable, and indefeasible right to reform, alter, or abolish it, in such manner as shall be judged most conducive to the public weal.

4. That no man, or set of men, are entitled to exclusive or separate emoluments or privileges from the community, but in consideration of public services; which, not being descendible, neither ought the offices of magistrate, legislator, or judge to be hereditary.

5. That the legislative and executive powers of the State should be separate and distinct from the judiciary; and, that the members of the two first may be restrained from oppression by feeling and participating the burdens of the people, they should, at fixed periods, be reduced to a private station, return into that body from which they were originally taken, and the vacancies be supplied by frequent, certain, and regular elections, in which all, or any part of the former members, to be again eligible or ineligible, as the laws shall direct.

6. That elections of members to serve as representatives of the people, in assembly, ought to be free; and that all men, having sufficient evidence of

permanent common interest with, and attachment to, the community, have the right of suffrage, and cannot be taxed or deprived of their property for public uses, without their own consent, or that of their representatives so elected, nor bound by any law to which they have not, in like manner, assented for the public good.

7. That all power of suspending laws, or the execution of laws, by any authority without consent of the representatives of the people, is injurious to their rights, and ought not to be exercised.

8. That in all capital or criminal prosecutions a man hath a right to demand the cause and nature of his accusation, to be confronted with the accusers and witnesses, to call for evidence in his favor, and to a speedy trial by an impartial jury of twelve men of his vicinage, without whose unanimous consent he cannot be found guilty; nor can he be compelled to give evidence against himself; that no man be deprived of his liberty, except by the law of the land or the judgment of his peers.

9. That excessive bail ought not to be required, nor excessive fines imposed, nor cruel and unusual punishments inflicted.

10. That general warrants, whereby an officer or messenger may be commanded to search suspected places without evidence of a fact committed, or to seize any person or persons not named, or whose offence is not particularly described and supported by evidence, are grievous and oppressive, and ought not to be granted.

11. That in controversies respecting property, and in suits between man and man, the ancient trial by jury is preferable to any other, and ought to be held sacred.

12. That the freedom of the press is one of the great bulwarks of liberty, and can never be restrained but by despotic governments.

13. That a well-regulated militia, composed of the body of the people trained to arms, is the proper, natural, and safe defence of a free State; that standing armies, in time of peace, should be avoided as dangerous to liberty; and that in all cases the military should be under strict subordination to, and governed by, the civil power.

14. That the people have a right to uniform government; and, therefore, that no government separate from, or independent of the government of Virginia, ought to be erected or established within the limits thereof.

15. That no free government, or the blessings of liberty, can be preserved to any people, but by a firm adherence to justice, moderation, temperance, frugality, and virtue, and by frequent recurrence to fundamental principles.

16. That religion, or the duty which we owe to our Creator, and the manner of discharging it, can be directed only by reason and conviction, not by force or violence; and therefore all men are equally entitled to the free exercise of religion, according to the dictates of conscience; and that it is the mutual duty of all to practise Christian forbearance, love, and charity towards each other.

Th Jefferson

Thomas Jefferson, only thirty-three when he drafted the Declaration of Independence, is here portrayed by John Trumbull in a detail from the large painting in the United States Capitol.

We pledge our Lives, our Fortunes and our sacred Honor

The shots fired from behind the stone walls at Lexington and Concord in April, 1775, had begun the war against Britain. Yet some voices in the Continental Congress still spoke for a compromise that would reunite the colonials with the mother country. By the next summer, however, the smoke of the guns had smothered that hope. One June 10, 1776, Thomas Jefferson, John Adams, Benjamin Franklin, Roger Sherman and Robert R. Livingston were appointed a committee to draft a declaration in support of the Richard Henry Lee Resolution of Independence.

Given the responsibility by the committee, Jefferson wrote the "Rough Draft" between June 10 and June 28. It began with a statement of governmental principles, went on to indict the Crown for its violations of those principles, and concluded with a declaration that the colonies were now free and independent.

On July 4 Congress approved the Declaration. Without dissent the thirteen states had established a revolutionary government and created a new nation in the family of nations, founded on an eloquent philosophy of democracy.

WHEN in the Course of human events, it becomes necessary for one people to dissolve the political bands which have connected them with another, and to assume among the powers of the earth, the separate and equal station to which the Laws of Nature and of Nature's God entitle them, a decent respect to the opinions of mankind requires that they should declare the causes which impel them to the separation.—We hold these truths to be self-evident, that all men are created equal, that they are endowed by their Creator with certain unalienable Rights, that among these are Life, Lib-

IN CONGRESS, JULY 4, 1776.

A DECLARATION

BY THE REPRESENTATIVES OF THE

UNITED STATES OF AMERICA,

IN GENERAL CONGRESS ASSEMBLED.

WHEN in the Course of human Events, it becomes necessary for one People to dissolve the Political Bands which have connected them with another, and to assume among the Powers of the Earth, the separate and equal Station to which the Laws of Nature and of Nature's God entitle them, a decent Respect to the Opinions of Mankind requires that they should declare the causes which impel them to the Separation.

We hold these Truths to be self-evident, that all Men are created equal, that they are endowed by their Creator with certain unalienable Rights, that among these are Life, Liberty, and the Pursuit of Happiness—That to secure these Rights, Governments are instituted among Men, deriving their just Powers from the Consent of the Governed, that whenever any Form of Government becomes [illegible]

The first printing of the Declaration, ordered by Congress on July 4, was made that night by John Dunlap. The broadside was wafered into a blank space left for it in the Rough Journal of Congress. This is a portion of that first official copy.

erty and the pursuit of Happiness.—That to secure these rights, Governments are instituted among Men, deriving their just powers from the consent of the governed,—That whenever any Form of Government becomes destructive of these ends, it is the Right of the People to alter or to abolish it, and to institute new Government, laying its foundation on such principles and organizing its powers in such form, as to them shall seem most likely to effect their Safety and Happiness. Prudence, indeed, will dictate that Governments long established should not be changed for light and transient causes; and accordingly all experience hath shewn, that mankind are more disposed to suffer, while evils are sufferable, than to right themselves by abolishing the forms to which they are accustomed. But when a long train of abuses and usurpations, pursuing invariably the same Object evinces a design to reduce

George III, target of the Declaration's indictment, in a silhouette made by his daughter, Princess Elizabeth.

them under absolute Despotism, it is their right, it is their duty, to throw off such Government, and to provide new Guards for their future security.—Such has been the patient sufferance of these Colonies; and such is now the necessity which constrains them to alter their former Systems of Government. The history of the present King of Great Britain is a history of repeated injuries and usurpations, all having in direct object the establishment of an absolute Tyranny over these States. To prove this, let Facts be submitted to a candid world.—He has refused his Assent to Laws, the most wholesome and necessary for the public good.—He has forbidden his Governors to pass Laws of immediate and pressing importance, unless suspended in their operation till his Assent should be obtained; and when so suspended, he has utterly neglected to attend to them.—He has refused to pass other Laws for the accommodation of large districts of people, unless those people would relinquish the right of Representation in the Legislature, a right inestimable to them and formidable to tyrants only.—He has called together legislative bodies at places unusual, uncomfortable, and distant from the depository of their Public Records, for the sole purpose of fatiguing them into compliance with his measures.—He has dissolved Representative Houses repeatedly, for opposing with many firmness his invasions on the rights of the people.—He has refused for a long time, after such dissolutions, to cause others to be elected; whereby the Legislative Powers, incapable of Annihilation, have returned to the People at large for their exercise; the State remaining in the mean time exposed to all the dangers of invasion from without, and convulsions within.—He has endeavoured to prevent the population of these States; for that purpose obstructing the Laws of Naturalization of Foreigners; refusing to pass others to encourage their migration hither, and raising the conditions of new Appropriations of Lands.—He has obstructed the Administration of Justice, by refusing his Assent to Laws for establishing Judiciary Powers.—He has made Judges dependent on his Will alone, for the tenure of their offices, and the amount and payment of their salaries.—He has erected a multitude of New Offices, and sent hither swarms of Officers to harass our People, and eat out their substance.—He has kept among us, in times of peace, Standing Armies without the Consent of our legislatures.—He has affected to render the Military independent of and superior to the Civil Power.—He has combined with others to subject us to a jurisdiction foreign to our constitution, and unacknowledged by our laws; giving his Assent to their acts of pretended Legislation:—For quartering large bodies of armed troops among us:—For protecting them, by a mock Trial, from punishment for any Murders which they should commit on the Inhabitants of these States:—For cutting off our Trade with all parts of the world:—For imposing Taxes on us without our Consent:—For depriving us in many cases, of the benefits of Trial by Jury:—For transporting us beyond Seas to be tried for pretended offences:—For abolishing the free System of English Laws in a neighbouring Province, establishing therein an Arbitrary government, and enlarging its Boundaries so as to render it at once an example and fit instrument for introducing the same absolute rule into these Colonies:—For taking away our Charters, abolishing our most valuable Laws, and altering fundamentally the Forms of our Governments:—For suspending our own Legislatures, and declaring themselves invested with Power to legislate for us in all cases whatsoever.—He has abdicated Government here, by declaring us out of his Protection and waging War against us.—He has plundered our seas, ravaged our Coasts, burnt our towns, and destroyed the Lives of our people.—He

The broadsides blazoning the Declaration streamed out from Philadelphia on July 5. As the post riders reached towns and army posts the Declaration was read to the excited crowds.

The Liberty Bell.

is at this time transporting large Armies of foreign Mercenaries to compleat the works of death, desolation and tyranny, already begun with circumstances of Cruelty & perfidy scarcely paralleled in the most barbarous ages, and totally unworthy the Head of a civilized nation.—He has constrained our fellow Citizens taken Captive on the high Seas to bear Arms against their Country, to become the executioners of their friends and Brethren, or to fall themselves by their Hands.—He has excited domestic insurrections amongst us, and has endeavoured to bring on the inhabitants of our frontiers, the merciless Indian Savages, whose known rule of warfare, is an undistinguished destruction of all ages, sexes and conditions.—In every stage of these Oppressions We have Petitioned for Redress in the most humble terms: Our repeated Petitions have been answered only by repeated injury. A Prince, whose character is thus marked by every act which may define a Tyrant, is unfit to be the ruler of a free People.—Nor have We been wanting in attention to our British brethren. We have warned them from time to time of attempts by their legislature to extend an unwarrantable jurisdiction over us. We have reminded them of the circumstances of our emigration and settlement here. We have appealed to their native justice and magnanimity, and we have conjured them by the ties of our common kindred to disavow these usurpations, which, would inevitably interrupt our connections and correspondence. They too have been deaf to the voice of justice and of consanguinity. We must, therefore, acquiesce in the necessity, which denounces our Separation, and hold them, as we hold the rest of mankind, Enemies in War, in Peace Friends.—

We, therefore, the Representatives of the United States of America, in General Congress, Assembled, appealing to the Supreme Judge of the world for the rectitude of our intentions, do, in the Name, and by Authority of the good People of these Colonies, solemnly publish and declare, That these United Colonies are, and of Right ought to be Free and Independent States; that they are Absolved from all Allegiance to the British Crown, and that all political connection between them and the State of Great Britain, is and ought to be totally dissolved; and that as Free and Independent States, they have full Power to levy War, conclude Peace, contract Alliances, establish Commerce, and to do all other Acts and Things which Independent States may of right do.—And for the support of this Declaration, with a firm reliance on the Protection of Divine Providence, we mutually pledge to each other our Lives, our Fortunes and our sacred Honor.

Resolved That these united colonies are and of right
ought to be free and independant states;
that they are absolved from all allegiance
to the british crown and that all political
connection between them and the state of
great Britain is and ought to be totally
dissolved

On July 2, 1776, Congress adopted this resolution of Richard Henry Lee of Virginia, declaring "That these United Colonies are, and of right ought to be, free . . ." It was the act cutting the tie with the mother country. Jefferson's Declaration was to be the document announcing the great event.

A Declaration by the Representatives of the UNITED STATES OF AMERICA, in General Congress assembled.

When in the course of human events it becomes necessary for ~~a~~ one people to dissolve the political bands which have connected them with another, and to [illegible] assume among the powers of the earth the separate and equal ~~equal & independant~~ station to which the laws of nature & of nature's god entitle them, a decent respect to the opinions of mankind requires that they should declare the causes which impel them to ~~the~~ the separation.

We hold these truths to be self-evident; ~~sacred & undeniable~~; that all men are created equal ~~& independant~~; that they are endowed by their creator with ~~equal rights, some of which are~~ [inherent &] certain inalienable rights; that among ~~which~~ these are ~~the preservation of~~ life, & liberty, & the pursuit of happiness; that to secure these ~~ends~~ rights, governments are instituted among men, deriving their just powers from the consent of the governed; that whenever any form of government ~~shall~~ becomes destructive of these ends, it is the right of the people to alter or to abolish it, & to institute new government, laying it's foundation on such principles & organising it's powers in such form, as to them shall seem most likely to effect their safety & happiness. prudence indeed will dictate that governments long established should not be changed for light & transient causes: and accordingly all experience hath shewn that mankind are more disposed to suffer while evils are sufferable, than to right themselves by abolishing the forms to which they are accustomed. but when a long train of abuses & usurpations [begun at a distinguished period, &] pursuing invariably the same object, evinces a design to ~~subject~~ reduce them under absolute Despotism ~~to arbitrary power~~, it is their right, it is their duty, to throw off such government & to provide new guards for their future security. such has been the patient sufferance of these colonies; & such is now the necessity which constrains them to [expunge] alter their former systems of government. the history of ~~his~~ the present king of Great Britain ~~majesty~~ is a history of [unremitting] repeated injuries and usurpations, [among which, appears no solitary fact ~~[illegible]~~ to contradict the uniform tenor of the rest, ~~all of which~~ but all have] in direct object the establishment of an absolute tyranny over these states. to prove this, let facts be submitted to a candid world, [for the truth of which we pledge a faith yet unsullied by falsehood]

Dr. Franklin's handwriting

Mr. Adams's handwriting

The "Rough Draft" of the Declaration of Independence, submitted by Jefferson to Franklin and Adams. It contains alterations made by the three men.

[*New Hampshire*] Josiah Bartlett, Wm Whipple, Matthew Thornton, [*Massachusetts Bay*] Saml Adams, John Adams, Robt Treat Paine, Elbridge Gerry; [*Rhode Island*] Step. Hopkins, William Ellery; [*Connecticut*] Roger Sherman, Samel Huntington, Wm Williams, Oliver Wolcott; [*New York*] Wm Floyd, Phil. Livingston, Frans Lewis, Lewis Morris; [*New Jersey*] Richd Stockton, Jno Witherspoon, Fras Hopkinson, John Hart, Abra Clark; [*Pennsylvania*] Robt Morris, Benjamin Rush, Benja Franklin, John Morton, Geo Clymer, Jas Smith, Geo. Taylor, James Wilson, Geo. Ross; [*Delaware*] Cæsar Rodney, Geo Read, Tho M:Kean; [*Maryland*] Samuel Chase, Wm Paca, Thos Stone, Charles Carroll of Carrollton; [*Virginia*] George Wythe, Richard Henry Lee, Th Jefferson, Benja Harrison, Thos Nelson jr., Francis Lightfoot Lee, Carter Braxton; [*North Carolina*] Wm Hooper, Joseph Hewes, John Penn; [*South Carolina*] Edward Rutledge, Thos Heyward Junr, Thomas Lynch Junr, Arthur Middleton; [*Georgia*] Button Gwinnett, Lyman Hall, Geo Walton.

The familiar signatures at the foot of the engrossed Declaration. Most of the members of Congress present signed the parchment on August 2, 1776; the others added their names later. John Hancock is said to have written his name bold so that John Bull could read it without his glasses.

These are the times that try men's souls

The *American* CRISIS.

NUMBER I.

By the Author of COMMON SENSE.

THESE are the times that try men's souls: The summer soldier and the sunshine patriot will, in this crisis, shrink from the service of his country; but he that stands it NOW, deserves the love and thanks of man and woman. Tyranny, like hell, is not easily conquered; yet we have this consolation with us, that the harder the conflict, the more glorious the triumph. What we obtain too cheap, we esteem too lightly:---'Tis dearness only that gives every thing its value. Heaven knows how to set a proper price upon its goods; and it would be strange, indeed, if so celestial an article as FREEDOM should not be highly rated. Britain, with an army to enforce her tyranny, has declared, that she has a right (*not only to* TAX, but) "to "BIND *us in* ALL CASES WHATSOEVER," and if being *bound in that manner* is not slavery, then is there not such a thing as slavery upon earth. Even the expression is impious, for so unlimited a power can belong only to GOD.

WHETHER the Independence of the Continent was declared too soon, or delayed too long, I will not now enter into as an argument; my own simple opinion is, that had it been eight months earlier, it would have been much better. We did not make a proper use of last winter, neither could we, while we were in a dependent state. However, the fault, if it were one, was all our own; we have none to blame but ourselves*. But no great deal is lost yet; all that Howe has been doing for this month past is rather a ravage than a conquest, which the spirit of the Jersies a year ago would have quickly repulsed, and which time and a little resolution will soon recover.

I have as little superstition in me as any man living, but

my

* "The present winter" (meaning the last) "is worth an "age if rightly employed, but if lost, or neglected, the whole "Continent will partake of the evil; and there is no punish-"ment that man does not deserve, be he who, or what, or "where he will, that may be the means of sacrificing a season "so precious and useful." COMMON SENSE.

The Crisis appeared first in the *Pennsylvania Journal* of December 19, 1776. On the 23rd, it was published as a pamphlet. This is the title page of the first printing.

From the astounding success of his Common Sense *Tom Paine plunged promptly into the middle of the battle. Six months after publication of his pamphlet the Congress adopted the Declaration of Independence. It was cause and effect, said George Washington. Paine joined the tattered remnants of the Commander's army and retreated with them to the Delaware early in December, 1776. The army dwindled from disease and dissertion. Morale fled in the December frosts.*

Washington appealed to Paine to strike again the fire that had kindled independence. Out of Paine's passionate faith came the first number of The Crisis, *"These are the times that try men's souls. . . ." Read to the troops, it stiffened the will to win. Published in pamphlet form, it renewed public zeal for America's high mission. Excerpts from* The Crisis *follow.*

THESE are the times that try men's souls. The summer soldier and the sunshine patriot will, in this crisis, shrink from the service of their country; but he that stands it *now,* deserves the love and thanks of man and woman. Tyranny, like hell, is not easily conquered; yet we have this consolation with us, that the harder the conflict, the more glorious the triumph. What we obtain too cheap, we esteem too lightly: it is dearness only that gives every thing its value. Heaven knows how to put a proper price upon its goods; and it would be strange indeed if so celestial an article as FREEDOM should not be highly rated. Britain, with an army to enforce her tyranny, has declared that she has a right (*not only to* TAX) but "to BIND *us in* CASES WHATSOEVER," and if being *bound in that manner,* is not slavery, then there is not such a thing as slavery upon earth. Even the expression is impious; for so unlimited a power can belong only to God.

Whether the independence of the continent was declared too soon, or delayed too long, I will not now enter into as an argument; my own simple opinion is, that had it been eight months earlier, it would have been much better. We did not make a proper use of last winter, neither could we, while we were in a dependent state. However, the fault, if it were one, was all our own; we have none to blame but ourselves. But no great deal is lost yet. All that Howe has been doing for this month past, is rather a ravage than a conquest, which the spirit of the Jerseys, a year ago, would have quickly repulsed, and which time and a little resolution will soon recover.

I have as little superstition in me as any man living, but my secret opinion has ever been, and still is, that God Almighty will not give up a people to military destruction, or leave them unsupportedly to perish, who have so earnestly and so repeatedly sought to avoid the calamities of war, by every decent method which wisdom could invent. Neither have I so much of the infidel in me, as to suppose that He has relinquished the government of the world, and given us up to the care of devils; and as I do not, I cannot see on what grounds the king of Britain can look up to heaven for help against us: a common murderer, a highwayman, or a housebreaker, has as good a pretence as he.

'Tis surprising to see how rapidly a panic will sometimes run through a country. All nations and ages have been subject to them. Britain has trembled like an ague at the report of a French fleet of flat bottomed boats; and in the fourteenth century the whole English army, after ravaging the kingdom of France, was driven back like men petrified with fear; and this brave exploit was performed by a few broken forces collected and headed by a

A few days after *The Crisis* came from Paine's pen, Washington's troops, in a desperate move, crossed the icy Delaware. It was Christmas Day, 1776. The next day, at Trenton, Washington's men defeated the Hessians. The victory was the answer to those who had begun to believe the American cause was lost.

woman, Joan of Arc. Would that heaven might inspire some Jersey maid to spirit up her countrymen, and save her fair fellow sufferers from ravage and ravishment! Yet panics, in some cases, have their uses; they produce as much good as hurt. Their duration is always short; the mind soon grows through them, and acquires a firmer habit than before. But their peculiar advantage is, that they are the touchstones of sincerity and hypocrisy, and bring things and men to light, which might otherwise have lain forever undiscovered. In fact, they have the same effect on secret traitors, which an imaginary apparition would have upon a private murderer. They sift out the hidden thoughts of man, and hold them up in public to the world. Many a disguised Tory has lately shown his head, that shall penitentially solemnize with curses the day on which Howe arrived upon the Delaware. . . .

I shall conclude this paper with some miscellaneous remarks on the state of our affairs; and shall begin with asking the following question, Why is it that the enemy have left the New England provinces, and made these middle ones the seat of war? The answer is easy: New England is not infested with Tories, and we are. I have been tender in raising the cry against these men, and used numberless arguments to show them their danger, but it will not do to sacrifice a world either to their folly or their baseness. The period is now arrived, in which either they or we must change our sentiments, or one or both must fall. And what is a Tory? Good God! what is he? I should not be afraid to go with a hundred whigs against a thousand Tories, were they to attempt to get into arms. Every Tory is a coward; for servile, slavish, self-interested fear is the foundation of Toryism; and a man under such influence, though he may be cruel, never can be brave.

But, before the line of irrecoverable separation be drawn between us, let us reason the matter together: Your conduct is an invitation to the enemy, yet not one in a thousand of you has heart enough to join him. Howe is as much deceived by you as the American cause is injured by you. He expects you will all take up arms, and flock to his standard, with muskets on your shoulders. Your opinions are of no use to him, unless you support him personally, for 'tis soldiers, and not Tories, that he wants.

I once felt all that kind of anger, which a man ought to feel, against the mean principles that are held by the Tories: a noted one, who kept a tavern at Amboy, was standing at his door, with as pretty a child in his hand, about eight or nine years old, as ever I saw, and after speaking his mind as freely as he thought was prudent, finished with this unfatherly expression, *"Well! give me peace in my day."* Not a man lives on the continent but fully believes that a separation must some time or other finally take place, and a generous parent should have said, *"If there must be trouble, let it be in my day, that my child may have peace"*; and this single reflection, well applied, is sufficient to awaken every man to duty. Not a place upon earth might be so happy as America. Her situation is remote from all the wrangling world, and she has nothing to do but to trade with them. A man can distinguish himself between temper and principle, and I am as confident, as I am that God governs the world, that America will never be happy till she gets clear of foreign dominion. Wars, without ceasing, will break out till that period arrives, and the continent must in the end be conqueror; for though the flame of liberty may sometimes cease to shine, the coal can never expire. . . .

Thomas Paine

Thomas Paine, in the only known life portrait, painted about 1805 by John Wesley Jarvis. The English-born spokesman for the American Revolution came penniless to America in 1774. A letter of introduction from Benjamin Franklin, the London agent of the colonies, won the thirty-seven-year-old failure a job with the *Pennsylvania Magazine*. From writing articles on "Cupid & Hymen" he turned to *Common Sense*, a smashing argument for independence which sold 120,000 copies in the first three months of 1776.

Tom Paine's revolutionary propaganda did not stop with the American victory. This British cartoon lampoons Paine's defense of republican government and the early French Revolution, as expressed in his *The Rights of Man.* The pamphlet was suppressed by the British and Paine, then in France, was tried for treason and outlawed.

All men shall be free in matters of religion

"The care of every man's soul belongs to himself." So ran one of the "Notes on Religion" Thomas Jefferson jotted down a few months after drafting the Declaration of Independence. What were the implications of religion for the development of democracy? If religion and government were woven together, could man's inherent liberties be protected? The concept of separation of Church and State had been introduced over a hundred years earlier by Roger Williams and William Penn. In 1776 Virginia disestablished the Anglican Church by suspending payment of tithes. The next year Jefferson drafted a bill to establish religious freedom as part of a revised code of laws designed to transform Virginia from a royalist into a democratic State. Introduced into the General Assembly in 1779, when Jefferson was Governor, the bill met bitter attack and was shelved. But the battle for passage—"the severest contest in which I have ever been engaged," Jefferson said—was won six years later. In January, 1786, while Jefferson was in France, his friends succeeded in putting the bill through. "It is honorable for us to have produced the first legislature who has had the courage to declare that the reason of man may be trusted with the formation of his own opinions," Jefferson wrote. All citizens, regardless of race or creed, were protected in their freedom of conscience. On Jefferson's tomb are engraved the three contributions to mankind he valued most: the Declaration of Independence, the founding of the University of Virginia, and the Statute of Religious Liberty.

1. WELL aware that Almighty God hath created the mind free; that all attempts to influence it by temporal punishments or burdens, or by civil incapacitations, tend only to beget habits of hypocrisy and meanness, and are a departure from the plan of the Holy Author of our religion, who being Lord both of body and mind, yet chose not to propagate it by coercions on either, as was his Almighty power to do; that the impious presumption of legislators and rulers, civil as well as ecclesiastical, who being themselves but fallible and uninspired men, have assumed dominion over the faith of others, setting up their own opinions and modes of thinking as the only true and infallible, and as such endeavoring to impose them on others, hath established and maintained false religions over the greatest part of the world, and through all time; that to compel a man to furnish contributions of money for the propagation of opinions which he disbelieves, is sinful and tyrannical; that even the forcing him to support this or that teacher of his own religious persuasion, is depriving him of the comfortable liberty of giving his contributions to the particular pastor whose morals he would make his pattern, and whose powers he feels most persuasive to righteousness, and is withdrawing from the ministry those temporary rewards, which proceeding from an approbation of their personal conduct, are an additional incitement to earnest and unremitting labors for the instruction of mankind; that our civil rights have no dependence on our religious opinions, any more than our opinions in physics or geometry; that therefore the proscribing any citizen as unworthy the public confidence by laying upon him an incapacity of being called to offices of trust and emolument, unless he profess or renounce this or that religious opinion, is depriving him injuriously of those privileges and advantages to which in common with his fellow-citizens he has a natural right; that it tends only to corrupt the principles of that religion it is meant to encourage, by bribing with a monopoly of worldly honors and emoluments, those who will externally profess and conform to it; that though indeed these are criminal who do not withstand such temptation, yet neither are those innocent who lay the bait in their way; that to suffer the civil magistrate to intrude his powers into the field of opinion, and to restrain the profession or propagation of principles on supposition of their ill tendency, is a dangerous fallacy, which at once destroys all religious liberty, because he being of course judge of that tendency will make his opinions the rule of judgment, and approve or condemn the sentiments of others only as they shall square with or differ from his own;

George Wythe, the "faithful and beloved Mentor" of Jefferson at William and Mary, joined his law pupil in submitting the bill for religious freedom to the Virginia House of Delegates in 1779. Wythe was a signer of the Declaration of Independence, helped draft the Constitution, and established the first professorship in law in the United States. With George Mason and James Madison he was one of the devoted trio who supported Jefferson in transforming the royal colony of Virginia into a democratic commonwealth.

that it is time enough for the rightful purposes of civil government, for its officers to interfere when principles break out into overt acts against peace and good order; and finally, that truth is great and will prevail if left to herself, that she is the proper and sufficient antagonist to error, and has nothing to fear from the conflict, unless by human interposition disarmed of her natural weapons, free argument and debate, errors ceasing to be dangerous when it is permitted freely to contradict them.

2. *Be it therefore enacted by the General Assembly,* That no man shall be compelled to frequent or support any religious worship, place or ministry whatsoever, nor shall be enforced, restrained, molested, or burthened in his body or goods, nor shall otherwise suffer on account of his religious opinions or belief; but that all men shall be free to profess, and by argument to maintain, their opinion in matters of religion, and that the same shall in no wise diminish, enlarge or affect their civil capacities.

3. And though we well know that this Assembly, elected by the people for the ordinary purposes of legislation only, have no power to restrain the acts of succeeding Assemblies, constituted with powers equal to our own, and that therefore to declare this act to be irrevocable would be of no effect in law, yet as we are free to declare, and do declare, that the rights hereby asserted are of the natural rights of mankind, and that if any act shall hereafter be passed to repeal the present or to narrow its operation, such act will be an infringement of natural right.

C H A P. LXXXII.

A BILL for establishing religious freedom.

SECTION I. WELL aware that the opinions and belief of men depend not on their own will, but follow involuntarily the evidence proposed to their minds; that Almighty God hath created the mind free, and manifested his supreme will that free it shall remain by making it altogether insusceptible of restraint; that all attempts to influence it by temporal punishments, or burthens, or by civil incapacitations, tend only to beget habits of hypocrisy and meanness, and are a departure from the plan of the holy author of our religion, who being lord both of body and mind, yet chose not to propagate it by coercions on either, as was in his Almighty power to do, but to extend it by its influence on reason alone; that the impious presumption of legislators and rulers, civil as well as ecclesiastical, who, being themselves but fallible and uninspired men, have assumed dominion over the faith of others, setting up their own opinions and modes of thinking as the only true and infallible, and as such endeavoring to impose them on others, hath established and maintained false religions over the greatest part of the world and through all time: That to compel a man to furnish contributions of money for the propagation of opinions which he disbelieves and abhors, is sinful and tyrannical; that even the forcing him to support this or that teacher of his own religious persuasion, is depriving him of the comfortable liberty of giving his contributions to the particular pastor whose morals he would make his pattern, and whose powers he feels most persuasive to righteousness; and is withdrawing from the ministry those temporary rewards, which proceeding from an approbation of their personal conduct, are an additional incitement to earnest and unremitting labours for the instruction of mankind; that our civil rights have no dependance on our religious opinions, any more than our opinions in physics or geometry; that therefore the proscribing any citizen as unworthy the public confidence by laying upon him an incapacity of being called to offices of trust and emolument, unless he profess or renounce this or that religious opinion, is depriving him injuriously of those privileges and advantages to which, in common with his fellow citizens, he has a natural right; that it tends also to corrupt the principles of that very religion it is meant to encourage, by bribing, with a monopoly of worldly honours and emoluments, those who will externally profess and conform to it; that though indeed these are criminal who do not withstand such temp- [illegible] neither [illegible] the bait in their way [illegible] the opinions of [illegible] are not the [illegible]

An early printed draft of the Virginia Statute of Religious Liberty, which established the principle of separation of church and state and the right of the individual to his own opinion in matters of religion.

An ORDINANCE for the GOVERNMENT of the TERRITORY of the UNITED STATES, North-West of the RIVER OHIO.

The Ordinance of 1787, announced in a broadside. The antislavery Article Six was a last-minute addition, supported equally by southern and northern states.

1787 Northwest Ordinance

On an equal footing

Under the Articles of Confederation, drafted in 1781, Congress prepared to deal with the problem of the West. England's had been among the more enlightened colonial policies of the European nations, but still the Americans had not been treated as equals. What would the new Revolutionary government do with the Western lands? The Peace of 1783 had recognized the States' claims to the territories. Most of the States soon ceded those claims to the central government. In deciding the fate of the lands north of the Ohio and east of the Mississippi, Congress worked out an enlightened law that provided for their evolution into states, guaranteed political equality with the original states, and protected the frontiersmen against governmental tyranny. It also barred slavery forever in the region north of the Ohio. On July 13, the famous Northwest Ordinance of 1787 was adopted.

BE IT ORDAINED by the United States in Congress assembled . . .

[SEC. 9.] So soon as there shall be five thousand free male inhabitants, of full age, in the district, upon giving proof thereof to the governor, they shall receive authority, with time and place, to elect representatives from their counties or townships to represent them in the general assembly: *Provided,* That, for every five hundred free male inhabitants, there shall be one representative, and so on, progressively, with the number of free male inhabitants, shall the right of representation increase, until the number of representatives shall amount to twenty-five; after which the number and proportion of representatives shall be regulated by the legislature. . . .

[SEC. 13.] And, for extending the fundamental principles of civil and religious liberty, which form the basis whereon these republics, their laws and constitutions are erected; to fix and establish those principles as the basis of all laws, constitutions, and governments, which forever hereafter shall be formed in the said territory: to provide, also, for the establishment of States, and permanent government therein, and for their admission to a share in the Federal councils on an equal footing with the original States, at as early periods as may be consistent with the general interest:

[SEC. 14.] It is hereby ordained and declared by the authority aforesaid, That the following articles shall be considered as articles of compact between

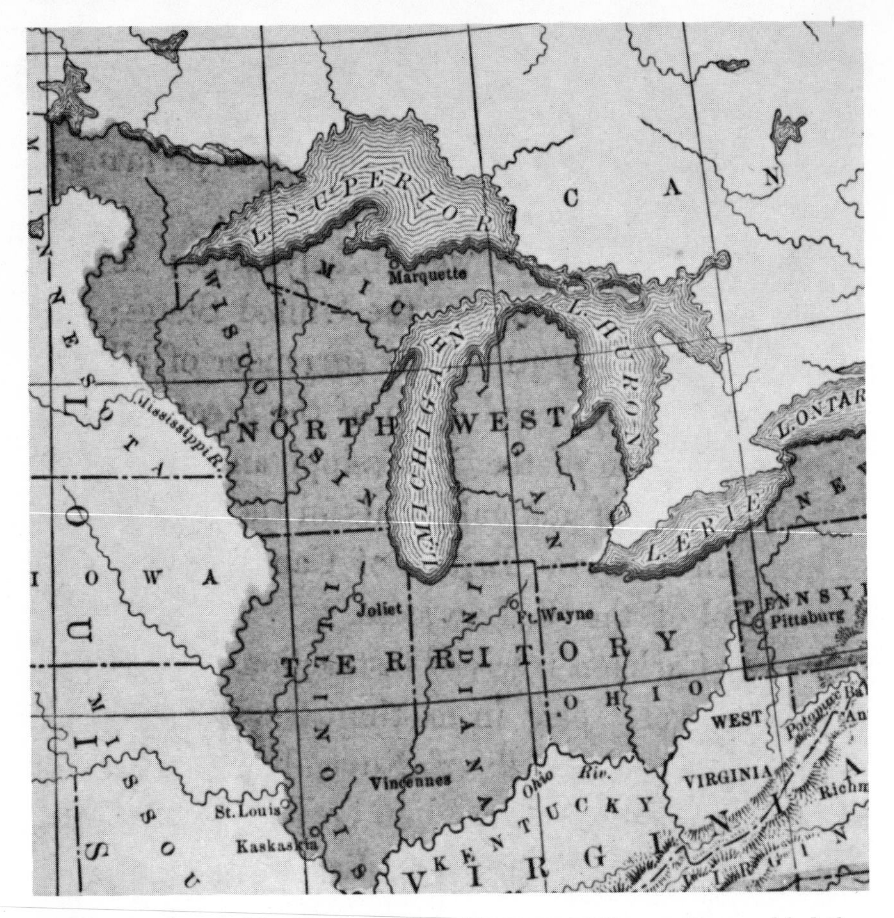

Western lands ceded by Virginia, Massachusetts, and Connecticut enabled the Confederation to organize the Northwest Territory and plan for forming it into states of the union. Ohio, Indiana, Illinois, Wisconsin, and Michigan were carved out of it.

the original States and the people and States in the said territory, and forever remain unalterable, unless by common consent, to wit:

Article I

No person, demeaning himself in a peaceable and orderly manner, shall ever be molested on account of his mode of worship or religious sentiments, in the said territory.

Article II

The inhabitants of the said territory shall always be entitled to the benefits of the writs of *habeas corpus*, and of the trial by jury; of a proportionate representation of the people in the legislature, and of judicial proceedings according to the course of the common law. All persons shall be bailable, unless for capital offences, where the proof shall be evident, or the presumption great. All fines shall be moderate; and no cruel or unusual punishments shall be inflicted. No man shall be deprived of his liberty or property, but by the judgment of his peers, or the law of the land, and, should the public exigencies make it necessary, for the common preservation, to take any person's property, or to demand his particular services, full compensation shall be made for the same. And, in the just preservation of rights and property, it is understood and declared, that no law ought ever to be made or have force in the said territory, that shall, in any manner whatever, interfere with or affect private contracts or engagements, *bona fide,* and without fraud previously formed.

Article III

Religion, morality, and knowledge being necessary to good government and the happiness of mankind, schools and the means of education shall forever be encouraged. The utmost good faith shall always be observed towards the Indians; their lands and property shall never be taken from them without their consent; and, in their property, rights, and liberty, they shall never be invaded or disturbed unless in just and lawful wars authorized by Congress; but laws founded in justice and humanity shall from time to time be made, for preventing wrongs being done to them, and for preserving peace and friendship with them.

Article IV

The said territory, and the States which may be formed therein, shall forever remain a part of this Confederacy of the United States of America, subject to the Articles of Confederation, and to such alterations therein as shall be constitutionally made; and to all the acts and ordinances of the United States in Congress assembled, conformable thereto.

Article V

There shall be formed in the said territory, not less than three nor more than five States . . . And, whenever any of the said States shall have sixty thousand free inhabitants therein, such State shall be admitted, by its delegates, into the Congress of the United States, on an equal footing with the original States, in all respects whatever; and shall be at liberty to form a permanent constitution and State government: *Provided,* the constitution and government, so to be formed, shall be republican, and in conformity to the principles contained in these articles, and, so far as it can be consistent with the general interest of the confederacy, such admission shall be allowed at an earlier period, and when there may be a less number of free inhabitants in the State than sixty thousand.

Article VI

There shall be neither slavery nor involuntary servitude in the said territory, otherwise than in the punishment of crimes, whereof the party shall have been duly convicted: *Provided, always,* That any person escaping into the same, from whom labor or service is lawfully claimed in any one of the original States, such fugitive may be lawfully reclaimed, and conveyed to the person claiming his or her labor or service as aforesaid . . .

Done by the United States, in Congress assembled, the 13th day of July, in the year of our Lord 1787, and of their sovereignty and independence the twelfth.

Marietta, a frontier village in the Ohio part of the Northwest Territory, founded by Revolutionary veterans. This print depicts the Campus Martius stockade in 1788.

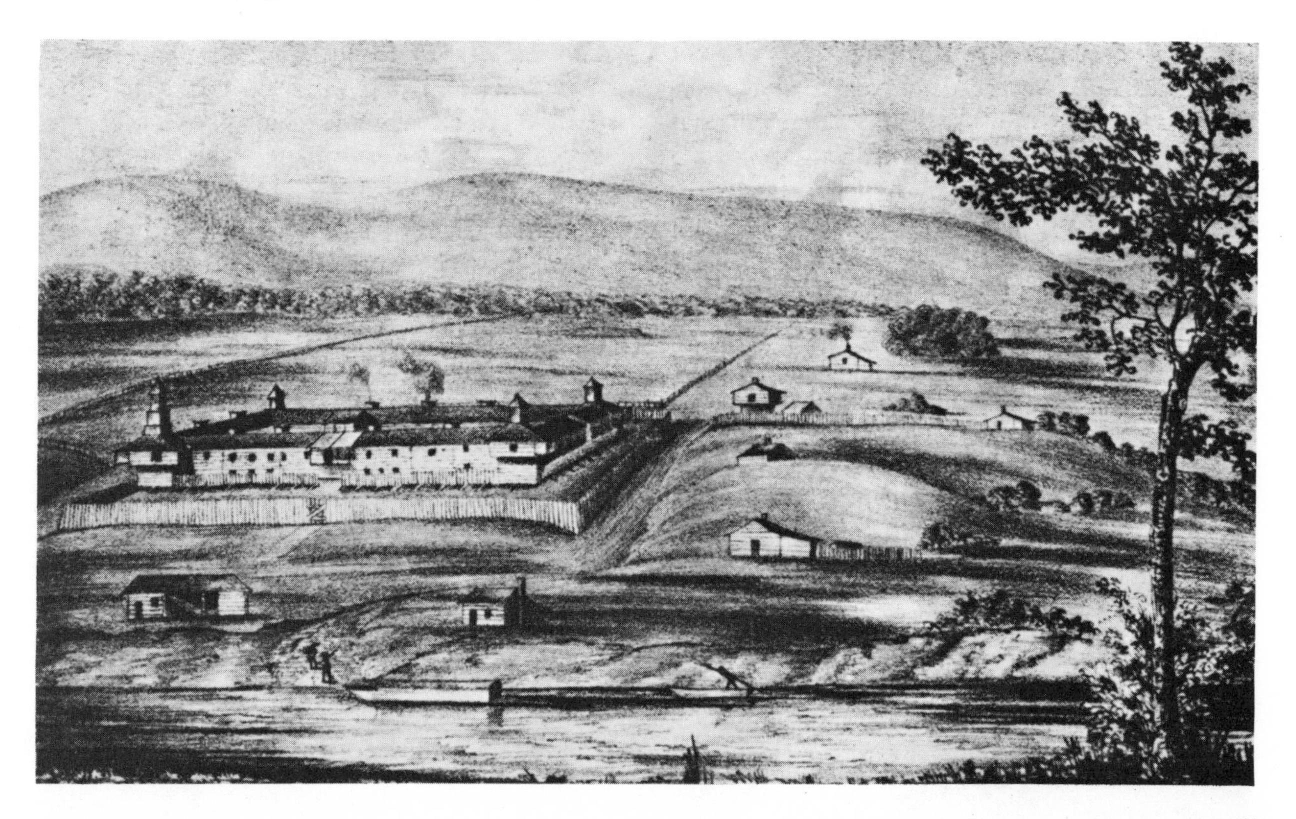

We the People of the United States, in Order to form a more perfect Union, establish Justice, insure domestic Tranquility, provide for the common defence, promote the general Welfare, and secure the Blessings of Liberty to ourselves and our Posterity, do ordain and establish this Constitution for the United States of America.

Article I

Section 1. All legislative Powers herein granted shall be vested in a Congress of the United States, which shall consist of a Senate and House of Representatives.

Section 2. The House of Representatives shall be composed of Members chosen every second Year by the People of the several States, and the Electors

We the people of the United States

The young republic which rose triumphantly out of the Revolutionary War now faced the task of self-government. The machinery at hand was the Articles of Confederation, adopted in 1781. This system rapidly proved too weak and inadequate. The states quarreled among themselves over boundary lines, over tariffs, over court decisions, and hard times deepened the bitterness. A strong central authority was badly needed to coordinate interests and ensure order.

In February, 1789, the Congress issued a call for a convention to revise the Articles of Confederation. The delegates wisely tossed aside the old constitution and wrote a completely new one. From their deliberations came a Constitution which Gladstone called "the most wonderful work ever struck off at a given time by the brain and purpose of man." Its wisdom, its practical ingenuity and its vitality armed the new nation for a turbulent future.

The Constitution was drafted by 55 delegates meeting in secret sessions. Missing at the deliberations were the fiery radicals who had raised the first flag of rebellion. These —spokesmen for the farmers, artisans, mechanics and small businessmen—feared the proposed strong central government would rob the majority of Americans of their new-won freedom. In the struggle for the necessary approval of nine of the 13 states, the Federalist papers played a large role. John Jay (left), James Madison (right) and Alexander Hamilton wrote the 85 brilliant essays which did much to organize the educated and propertied classes in support of the new government.

WE THE PEOPLE of the United States, in Order to form a more perfect Union, establish Justice, insure domestic Tranquility, provide for the common defence, promote the general Welfare, and secure the Blessings of Liberty to ourselves and our Posterity, do ordain and establish this Constitution for the United States of America.

Article I

Section 1. All legislative Powers herein granted shall be vested in a Congress of the United States, which shall consist of a Senate and House of Representatives.

Section 2. The House of Representatives shall be composed of Members chosen every second Year by the People of the several States, and the Electors in each State shall have the Qualifications requisite for Electors of the most numerous Branch of the State Legislature.

This cartoon appeared in *The Independent Chronicle and Commercial Advertiser* on June 26, 1788, to mark New Hampshire's ratification of the Constitution. With the ninth state in, the Constitution became effective. On March 4, 1789, it was declared in force.

The Ninth PILLAR erected !

" The Ratification of the Conventions of nine States, shall be sufficient for the establishment of this Constitution, between the States so ratifying the same." *Art.* vii.

INCIPIENT MAGNI PROCEDERE MENSES.

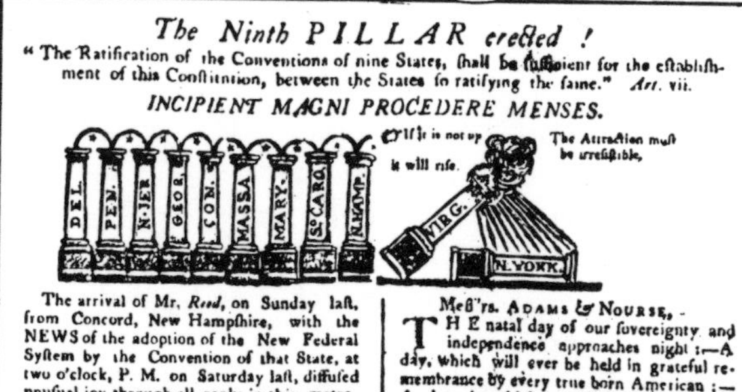

The arrival of Mr. *Reed*, on Sunday last, from Concord, New Hampshire, with the NEWS of the adoption of the New Federal System by the Convention of that State, at two o'clock, P. M. on Saturday last, diffused unusual joy through all ranks in this metropolis,—as by this great event, the Federal Edifice is reared, and the future good government of the States in general secured to the people. On the question for adoption, the decision appeared as follows:

For the Constitution, 57
Against it, 46
—
Majority, 11

Mr. *Reed* was honoured with dispatches from His Excellency John Sullivan, Esquire, President of New-Hampshire Convention, to His Excellency Governour Hancock—the contents of which follows.—

CONCORD, June 21, 1788.

SIR,

I HAVE the honor to inform your Excellency by favour of Mr. Reed, who is obliging enough to forward this Letter, that the Convention of this State have this Moment adopted the New Constitution. Yeas, 57; Nays, 46. The Amendments recommended, nearly the same as in your State.

With every Sentiment of respectful Attachment, I have the Honour to be,

Your Excellency's
most obedient Servant,
JOHN SULLIVAN.

"Gov. Hancock."

The bells in the several churches, on Monday morning, testified to the pleasure which filled the breast of every citizen, on this pleasing event.

The inhabitants of Roxbury also testified their extreme pleasure on the arrival of this important intelligence, by the same demonstrations of joy.

Extract of a letter from a gentleman of the first information, dated Petersburgh, June 9, 1788, received per a vessel in 5 days from Norfolk

"I have been attending the debates of

Mess'rs. Adams & Nourse,

THE natal day of our sovereignty and independence approaches nigh:—A day, which will ever be held in grateful remembrance by every true born American:—A day, in which our illustrious heroes and patriots nobly shook off the galling shackles of vassalage, and fettered tyranny at the shrine of liberty. To the honour of Boston, be it spoken, that its inhabitants, not content only with celebrating the anniversary with festivity and mirth; but call upon one of their fellow citizens, publicly to recite the causes which led to the late revolution, and recapitulate the zeal and indefatigable perseverance of our illustrious Chiefs in obtaining the acquisition. The youth of this town, that they might not be remiss in case of an emergency, have devoted much of their time to become disciplinarians in the art of war; and their frequent military exhibitions have carried strong convictions of their proficiency: And although the institution of JULY ORATIONS was to keep alive the flame of patriotism, and no one is denied access to the assembly, yet the young militairs, to their great disappointment and mortification, were excluded the last year, by reason of the *Parade*. Can patriotism ever be nurtur'd in a more grateful soil, than in the breasts of those who stand ever ready to guard the precious legacy left to them by their fathers?—And must they be again deprived of these pleasures, and excluded from hearing the addresses of a person, who has borne so conspicuous a part in military matters for some time past?—Justice forbid! In deference to the opinions of those who superintend the affairs of that day, I would observe, that the Old-South Meeting-House, would be more convenient than the Chapel-Church,—and there can be no impropriety in allotting a gallery for the *then* parading companies, as their being embodied together in that manner, in their uniforms, would not only add brilliancy to the assembly, but be productive of great satisfaction to

MANY.

On May 25, 1787, the Federal Convention began its sessions in the State House in Philadelphia—now called Independence Hall. Washington and Franklin were the most eminent and respected of the delegates. Over half were lawyers; planters and merchants and a few physicians and professors made up the rest of the 55. On September 17, after a sultry summer of debate, the state delegations voted approval of the draft.

No Person shall be a Representative who shall not have attained to the Age of twenty five Years, and been seven Years a Citizen of the United States, and who shall not, when elected, be an Inhabitant of that State in which he shall be chosen.

Representatives and direct Taxes shall be apportioned among the several States which may be included within this Union, according to their respective Numbers, which shall be determined by adding to the whole Number of free Persons, including those bound to Service for a Term of Years, and excluding Indians not taxed, three fifths of all other Persons. The actual Enumeration shall be made within three Years after the first Meeting of the Congress of the United States, and within every subsequent Term of ten Years, in such Manner as they shall by Law direct. The Number of Repre-

As head of the State of Pennsylvania, Benjamin Franklin was host to the Constitutional Convention when it met in Philadelphia in May, 1787. Now eighty-one, the veteran diplomat was dean of the delegates as they worked to revise the Articles of Confederation which he had helped draw up in 1776. With Washington, Franklin shared the task of conciliating the delegates, holding them together for the great task of creating the Constitution.

sentatives shall not exceed one for every thirty Thousand, but each State shall have at Least one Representative; and until such enumeration shall be made, the State of New Hampshire shall be entitled to chuse three, Massachusetts eight, Rhode-Island and Providence Plantations one, Connecticut five, New-York six, New Jersey four, Pennsylvania eight, Delaware one, Maryland six, Virginia ten, North Carolina five, South Carolina five, and Georgia three.

When vacancies happen in the Representation from any State, the Executive Authority thereof shall issue Writs of Election to fill such Vacancies.

The House of Representatives shall chuse their Speaker and other Officers; and shall have the sole Power of Impeachment.

Section 3. The Senate of the United States shall be composed of two Senators from each State, chosen by the Legislature thereof, for six Years; and each Senator shall have one Vote.

Immediately after they shall be assembled in Consequence of the first Election, they shall be divided as equally as may be into three Classes. The Seats of the Senators of the first Class shall be vacated at the Expiration of the second Year, of the second Class at the Expiration of the fourth Year, and of the third Class at the Expiration of the sixth Year, so that one third may be chosen every second Year; and if Vacancies happen by Resignation, or otherwise, during the Recess of the Legislature of any State, the Executive thereof may make temporary Appointments until the next Meeting of the Legislature, which shall then fill such Vacancies.

No Person shall be a Senator who shall not have attained to the Age of thirty Years, and been nine Years a Citizen of the United States, and who shall not, when elected, be an Inhabitant of that State for which he shall be chosen.

The Vice President of the United States shall be President of the Senate, but shall have no Vote, unless they be equally divided.

The Senate shall chuse their other Officers, and also a President pro tempore, in the Absence of the Vice President, or when he shall exercise the Office of President of the United States.

The Senate shall have the sole Power to try all Impeachments. When sitting for that Purpose, they shall be on Oath or Affirmation. When the President of the United States is tried, the Chief Justice shall preside: And no Person shall be convicted without the Concurrence of two thirds of the Members present.

Judgment in Cases of Impeachment shall not extend further than to removal from Office, and disqualification to hold and enjoy any Office of honor, Trust or Profit under the United States: but the Party convicted shall nevertheless be liable and subject to Indictment, Trial, Judgment and Punishment, according to Law.

Section 4. The Times, Places and Manner of holding Elections for Senators and Representatives, shall be prescribed in each State by the Legislature thereof; but the Congress may at any time by Law make or alter such Regulations, except as to the Places of chusing Senators.

The Congress shall assemble at least once in every Year, and such Meeting shall be on the first Monday in December, unless they shall by Law appoint a different Day.

Section 5. Each House shall be the Judge of the Elections, Returns and Qualifications of its own Members, and a Majority of each shall constitute a Quorum to do Business; but a smaller Number may adjourn from day to day, and may be authorized to compel the Attendance of absent Members, in such Manner, and under such Penalties as each House may provide.

Each House may determine the Rules of its Proceedings, punish its Members for disorderly Behaviour, and, with the Concurrence of two thirds, expel a Member.

Each House shall keep a Journal of its Proceedings, and from time to time publish the same, excepting such Parts as may in their Judgment require Secrecy; and the Yeas and Nays of the Members of either House on any question shall, at the Desire of one fifth of those Present, be entered on the Journal.

Neither House, during the Session of Congress, shall, without the Consent of the other, adjourn for more than three days, nor to any other Place than that in which the two Houses shall be sitting.

Section 6. The Senators and Representatives shall receive a Compensation for their Services, to be ascertained by Law, and paid out of the Treasury of the United States. They shall in all Cases, except Treason, Felony and Breach of the Peace, be privileged from Arrest during their Attendance at the Session of their respective Houses, and in going to and returning from the same; and for any Speech or Debate in either House, they shall not be questioned in any other Place.

No Senator or Representative shall, during the Time for which he was elected, be appointed to any civil Office under the Authority of the United States which shall have been created, or the Emoluments whereof shall have been encreased during such time; and no Person holding any Office under the United States, shall be a Member of either House during his Continuance in Office.

Section 7. All Bills for raising Revenue shall originate in the House of Representatives; but the Senate may propose or concur with Amendments as on other Bills.

Every Bill which shall have passed the House of Representatives and the Senate, shall, before it become a Law, be presented to the President of the United States; If he approve he shall sign it, but if not he shall return it, with his Objections to that House in which it shall have originated, who shall enter the Objections at large on their Journal, and proceed to reconsider it. If after such Reconsideration two thirds of that House shall agree to pass the Bill, it shall be sent, together with the Objections, to the other House, by which it shall likewise be reconsidered, and if approved by two thirds of that House, it shall become a Law. But in all such Cases the Votes of both Houses shall be determined by Yeas and Nays, and the Names of the Persons voting for and against the Bill shall be entered on the Journal of each House respectively. If any Bill shall not be returned by the President within ten Days (Sundays excepted) after it shall have been presented to him, the Same shall be a Law, in like Manner as if he had signed it, unless the Congress by their Adjournment prevent its Return, in which Case it shall not be a Law.

Every Order, Resolution, or Vote to which the Concurrence of the Senate and House of Representatives may be necessary (except on a question of Adjournment) shall be presented to the President of the United States; and before the Same shall take Effect, shall be approved by him, or being disapproved by him, shall be repassed by two thirds of the Senate and House of Representatives, according to the Rules and Limitations prescribed in the Case of a Bill.

Eight days after the adoption of the Declaration of Independence, a Congressional committee appointed to prepare a plan of confederation for the thirteen colonies brought in its report. After more than a year of intermittent debate the articles were adopted by Congress and on November 17, 1777, sent to each state for ratification. Above is the title page of the first printing of the Articles of Confederation. Not until March 1, 1781, was ratification complete; less than ten years later the Articles were replaced by the Constitution.

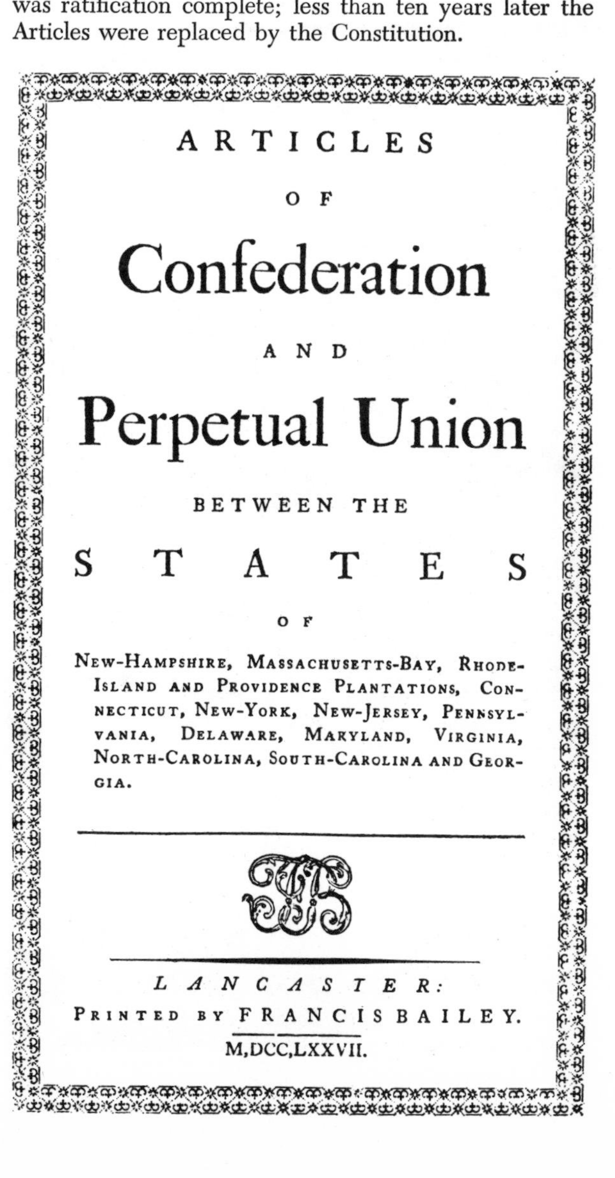
ARTICLES

OF

Confederation

AND

Perpetual Union

BETWEEN THE

STATES

OF

NEW-HAMPSHIRE, MASSACHUSETTS-BAY, RHODE-ISLAND AND PROVIDENCE PLANTATIONS, CONNECTICUT, NEW-YORK, NEW-JERSEY, PENNSYLVANIA, DELAWARE, MARYLAND, VIRGINIA, NORTH-CAROLINA, SOUTH-CAROLINA AND GEORGIA.

LANCASTER:

PRINTED BY FRANCIS BAILEY.

M,DCC,LXXVII.

Section 8. The Congress shall have Power To lay and collect Taxes, Duties, Imposts and Excises, to pay the Debts and provide for the common Defence and general Welfare of the United States; but all Duties, Imposts and Excises shall be uniform throughout the United States;

To borrow Money on the credit of the United States;

To regulate Commerce with foreign Nations, and among the several States, and with the Indian Tribes;

To establish an uniform Rule of Naturalization, and uniform Laws on the subject of Bankruptcies throughout the United States;

To coin Money, regulate the Value thereof, and of foreign Coin, and fix the Standard of Weights and Measures;

To provide for the Punishment of counterfeiting the Securities and current Coin of the United States;

To establish Post Offices and post Roads;

To promote the Progress of Science and useful Arts, by securing for limited Times to Authors and Inventors the exclusive Right to their respective Writings and Discoveries;

To constitute Tribunals inferior to the supreme Court;

To define and punish Piracies and Felonies committed on the high Seas, and Offences against the Law of Nations;

To declare War, grant Letters of Marque and Reprisal, and make Rules concerning Captures on Land and Water;

To raise and support Armies, but no Appropriation of Money to that Use shall be for a longer Term than two Years;

To provide and maintain a Navy;

To make Rules for the Government and Regulation of the land and naval Forces;

Heavy taxes and private debt produced widespread distress among the Massachusetts farmers after the Revolution. They vainly petitioned their conservative legislature for relief. By the fall of 1786 men were ready to take up arms against their state. Led by Daniel Shays, a thousand farmers attacked the Springfield arsenal in January, 1787, but militia (above), financed by Boston merchants, threw them back. Although the uprising was crushed, it helped broaden support for a new constitution to create a stronger central government.

[5]

or cauſe, the court ſhall nevertheleſs proceed to pronounce judgment. The judgment ſhall be final and concluſive. The proceedings ſhall be tranſmitted to the Preſident of the Senate, and ſhall be lodged among the public records for the ſecurity of the parties concerned. Every commiſſioner ſhall, before he ſit in judgment, take an oath, to be adminiſtered by one of the judges of the ſupreme or ſuperior court of the State where the cauſe ſhall be tried, "well "and truly to hear and determine the matter in queſtion, according to the "beſt of his judgment, without favour, affection, or hope of reward."

Strike out

Sect. 3. All controverſies concerning lands claimed under different grants of two or more States, whoſe juriſdictions, as they reſpect ſuch lands, ſhall have been decided or adjuſted ſubſequent to ſuch grants, or any of them, ſhall, on application to the Senate, be finally determined, as near as may be, in the ſame manner as is before preſcribed for deciding controverſies between different States.

Strike out

X.

Sect. 1. The Executive Power of the United States ſhall be veſted in a ſingle perſon. His ſtile ſhall be, "The Preſident of the United States of America;" and his title ſhall be, "His Excellency." He ſhall be elected by joint ballot by the Legiſlature.+ He ſhall hold his office during the term of ſeven years; but ſhall not be elected a ſecond time.

+ to which election a majority of the votes of the members present shall be required

Sect. 2. He ſhall, from time to time, give information to the Legiſlature ~~to the Legiſlature~~ of the State of the Union: and ~~he may~~ recommend to their conſideration ſuch meaſures as he ſhall judge neceſſary, and expedient: he may convene them on extraordinary occaſions. and In caſe of diſagreement between the two Houſes, with

A printed draft of the Constitution, showing George Washington's annotations on part of page five.

To provide for calling forth the Militia to execute the Laws of the Union, suppress Insurrections and repel Invasions;

To provide for organizing, arming, and disciplining, the Militia, and for governing such Part of them as may be employed in the Service of the United States, reserving to the States respectively, the Appointment of the Officers, and the Authority of training the Militia according to the discipline prescribed by Congress;

To exercise exclusive Legislation in all Cases whatsoever, over such District (not exceeding ten Miles square) as may, by Cession of particular States, and the Acceptance of Congress, become the Seat of the Government of the United States, and to exercise like Authority over all Places purchased by the Consent of the Legislature of the State in which the Same shall be, for the Erection of Forts, Magazines, Arsenals, dock-Yards, and other needful Buildings;—And

To make all Laws which shall be necessary and proper for carrying into Execution the foregoing Powers, and all other Powers vested by this Constitution in the Government of the United States, or in any Department or Officer thereof.

Section 9. The Migration or Importation of such Persons as any of the States now existing shall think proper to admit, shall not be prohibited by the Congress prior to the Year one thousand eight hundred and eight, but a Tax or duty may be imposed on such Importation, not exceeding ten dollars for each Person.

The Privilege of the Writ of Habeas Corpus shall not be suspended, unless when in Cases of Rebellion or Invasion the public Safety may require it.

No Bill of Attainder or ex post facto Law shall be passed.

No Capitation, or other direct, Tax shall be laid, unless in Proportion to the Census or Enumeration herein before directed to be taken.

No Tax or Duty shall be laid on Articles exported from any State.

No Preference shall be given by any Regulation of Commerce or Revenue to the Ports of one State over those of another: nor shall Vessels bound to, or from, one State, be obliged to enter, clear, or pay Duties in another.

No Money shall be drawn from the Treasury, but in Consequence of Appropriations made by Law; and a regular Statement and Account of the Receipts

CONGRESS OF THE UNITED STATES.

In the HOUSE *of* REPRESENTATIVES,

Monday, 24th Auguſt, 1789,

RESOLVED, BY THE SENATE AND HOUSE OF REPRESENTATIVES OF THE UNITED STATES OF AMERICA IN CONGRESS ASSEMBLED, two thirds of both Houſes deeming it neceſſary, That the following Articles be propoſed to the Legiſlatures of the ſeveral States, as Amendments to the Conſtitution of the United States, all or any of which Articles, when ratified by three fourths of the ſaid Legiſlatures, to be valid to all intents and purpoſes as part of the ſaid Conſtitution—Viz.

ARTICLES in addition to, and amendment of, the Conſtitution of the United States of America, propoſed by Congreſs, and ratified by the Legiſlatures of the ſeveral States, purſuant to the fifth Article of the original Conſtitution.

ARTICLE THE FIRST.

After the firſt enumeration, required by the firſt Article of the Conſtitution, there ſhall be one Repreſentative for every thirty thouſand, until the number ſhall amount to one hundred, after which the proportion ſhall be ſo regulated by Congreſs, that there ſhall be not leſs than one hundred Repreſentatives, nor leſs than one Repreſentative for every forty thouſand perſons, until the number of Repreſentatives ſhall amount to two hundred, after which the proportion ſhall be ſo regulated by Congreſs, that there ſhall not be leſs than two hundred Repreſentatives, nor leſs than one Repreſentative for every fifty thouſand perſons.

ARTICLE THE SECOND.

No law varying the compenſation to the members of Congreſs, ſhall take effect, until an election of Repreſentatives ſhall have intervened.

ARTICLE THE THIRD.

Congreſs ſhall make no law eſtabliſhing religion or prohibiting the free exerciſe thereof, nor ſhall the rights of Conſcience be infringed.

ARTICLE THE FOURTH.

The Freedom of Speech, and of the Preſs, and the right of the People peaceably to aſſemble, and conſult for their common good, and to apply to the Government for a redreſs of grievances, ſhall not be infringed.

The original Joint Resolution of Congress, September 25, 1787, known as the Bill of Rights, was signed by Augustus Muhlenberg, Speaker of the House, and John Adams, President of the Senate. It proposed twelve constitutional amendments, of which ten were ratified by the requisite three-fourths of the States. These became part of the fundamental law of the land on December 15, 1791, when Virginia's ratification made the first ten amendments a part of the Constitution. Strong objections to the Constitution itself, which omitted specific guarantees of personal rights and liberties, were satisfied with the adoption of a written bill of rights. Above is the first page of the Senate's working draft of the bill, showing editing of articles three and four, which were later to evolve into the First Amendment.

and Expenditures of all public Money shall be published from time to time.

No Title of Nobility shall be granted by the United States: And no Person holding any Office of Profit or Trust under them, shall, without the Consent of the Congress, accept of any present, Emolument, Office, or Title, of any kind whatever, from any King, Prince or foreign State.

Section 10. No State shall enter into any Treaty, Alliance, or Confederation; grant Letters of Marque and Reprisal; coin Money; emit Bills of Credit; make any Thing but gold and silver Coin a Tender in Payment of Debts; pass any Bill of Attainder, ex post facto Law, or Law impairing the Obligation of Contracts, or grant any Title of Nobility.

No State shall, without the Consent of the Congress, lay any Imposts or Duties on Imports or Exports, except what may be absolutely necessary for executing it's inspection Laws: and the net Produce of all Duties and Imposts, laid by any State on Imports or Exports, shall be for the Use of the Treasury of the United States; and all such Laws shall be subject to the Revision and Controul of the Congress.

No State shall, without the Consent of Congress, lay any Duty of Tonnage, keep Troops, or Ships of War in time of Peace, enter into any Agreement or Compact with another State, or with a foreign Power, or engage in War, unless actually invaded, or in such imminent Danger as will not admit of delay.

> "SINCE the earliest days philosophers have dreamed of a country where the mind and spirit of man would be free; where there would be no limits to inquiry; where men would be free to explore the unknown and to challenge the most deeply rooted beliefs and principles. Our First Amendment was a bold effort to adopt this principle—to establish a country with no legal restrictions of any kind upon the subjects people could investigate, discuss and deny. The Framers knew, better perhaps than we do today, the risks they were taking. They knew that free speech might be the friend of change and revolution. But they also knew that it is always the deadliest enemy of tyranny. With this knowledge they still believed that the ultimate happiness and security of a nation lies in its ability to explore, to change, to grow and ceaselessly to adapt itself to new knowledge born of inquiry free from any kind of governmental control over the mind and spirit of man. Loyalty comes from love of good government, not fear of a bad one."
>
> *Justice Hugo L. Black, February 17, 1960*

ARTICLE II

Section 1. The executive Power shall be vested in a President of the United States of America. He shall hold his Office during the Term of four Years, and, together with the Vice President, chosen for the same Term, be elected, as follows

Each State shall appoint, in such Manner as the Legislature thereof may direct, a Number of Electors, equal to the whole Number of Senators and Representatives to which the State may be entitled in the Congress: but no Senator or Representative, or Person holding an Office of Trust or Profit under the United States, shall be appointed an Elector.

The Electors shall meet in their respective States, and vote by Ballot for two Persons, of whom one at least shall not be an Inhabitant of the same State with themselves. And they shall make a List of all the Persons voted for, and of the Number of Votes for each; which List they shall sign and certify, and transmit sealed to the Seat of the Government of the United States, directed to the President of the Senate. The President of the Senate shall, in the Presence of the Senate and House of Representatives, open all the Certificates, and the Votes shall then be counted. The Person having the greatest Number of Votes shall be the President, if such Number be a Majority of the whole Number of Electors appointed; and if there be more than one who have such Majority, and have an equal Number of Votes, then the House of Representatives shall immediately chuse by Ballot one of them for President; and if no person have a Majority, then from the five highest on the List the said House shall in like Manner chuse the President. But, in chusing the President, the Votes shall be taken by States, the Representation from each State having one Vote; A quorum for this Purpose shall consist of a Member or Members from two thirds of the States, and a Majority of all the States shall be necessary to a Choice. In every Case, after the Choice of the President, the Person having the greatest Number of Votes of the Electors shall be the Vice President. But if there should remain two or more who have equal Votes, the Senate shall chuse from them by Ballot the Vice President.

The Congress may determine the Time of chusing the Electors, and the Day on which they shall give their Votes; which Day shall be the same throughout the United States.

No Person except a natural born Citizen, or a

Citizen of the United States, at the time of the Adoption of this Constitution, shall be eligible to the Office of President; neither shall any Person be eligible to that Office who shall not have attained to the Age of thirty five Years, and been fourteen Years a Resident within the United States.

In Case of the Removal of the President from Office, or of his Death, Resignation, or Inability to discharge the Powers and Duties of the said Office, the Same shall devolve on the Vice President, and the Congress may by Law provide for the Case of Removal, Death, Resignation or Inability, both of the President and Vice President, declaring what Officer shall then act as President, and such Officer shall act accordingly, until the Disability be removed, or a President shall be elected.

The President shall, at stated Times, receive for his Services, a Compensation, which shall neither be encreased nor diminished during the Period for which he shall have been elected, and he shall not receive within that Period any other Emolument from the United States, or any of them.

Before he enter on the Execution of his Office, he shall take the following Oath or Affirmation:—"I do solemnly swear (or affirm) that I will faithfully execute the Office of President of the United States, and will to the best of my Ability, preserve, protect and defend the Constitution of the United States."

Section 2. The President shall be Commander in Chief of the Army and Navy of the United States, and of the Militia of the several States, when called into the actual Service of the United States; he may require the Opinion, in writing, of the principal Officer in each of the executive Departments, upon any Subject relating to the Duties of their respective Offices, and he shall have Power to grant Reprieves and Pardons for Offences against the United States, except in Cases of Impeachment.

He shall have Power, by and with the Advice and Consent of the Senate, to make Treaties, provided two thirds of the Senators present concur; and he shall nominate, and by and with the Advice and Consent of the Senate, shall appoint Ambassadors, other public Ministers and Consuls, Judges of the supreme Court, and all other Officers of the United States, whose Appointments are not herein otherwise provided for, and which shall be established by Law: but the Congress may by Law vest the Appointment of such inferior Officers, as they think proper, in the President alone, in the Courts of Law, or in the Heads of Departments.

The President shall have Power to fill up all Vacancies that may happen during the Recess of the Senate, by granting Commissions which shall expire at the End of their next Session.

Section 3. He shall from time to time give to the Congress Information of the State of the Union, and recommend to their Consideration such Measures as he shall judge necessary and expedient; he may, on extraordinary Occasions, convene both Houses, or either of them, and in Case of Disagreement between them, with Respect to the Time of Adjournment, he may adjourn them to such Time as he shall think proper; he shall receive Ambassadors and other public Ministers; he shall take Care that the Laws be faithfully executed, and shall Commission all the Officers of the United States.

Section 4. The President, Vice President and all civil Officers of the United States, shall be removed from Office on Impeachment for, and Conviction of, Treason, Bribery, or other high Crimes and Misdemeanors.

Article III

Section 1. The judicial Power of the United States, shall be vested in one supreme Court, and in such inferior Courts as the Congress may from time to time ordain and establish. The Judges, both of the supreme and inferior Courts, shall hold their Offices during good Behaviour, and shall, at stated Times, receive for their Services, a Compensation, which shall not be diminished during their Continuance in Office.

Section 2. The judicial Power shall extend to all Cases, in Law and Equity, arising under this Constitution, the Laws of the United States, and Treaties made, or which shall be made, under their Authority;—to all Cases affecting Ambassadors, other public Ministers and Consuls;—to all Cases of admiralty and maritime Jurisdiction;—to Controversies to which the United States shall be a Party; —to Controversies between two or more States;— between a State and Citizens of another State;—between Citizens of different States,—between Citizens of the same State claiming Lands under Grants of different States, and between a State, or the Citizens thereof, and foreign States, Citizens or Subjects.

In all Cases affecting Ambassadors, other public Ministers and Consuls, and those in which a State shall be Party, the supreme Court shall have original Jurisdiction. In all the other Cases before mentioned, the supreme Court shall have appellate Jurisdiction, both as to Law and Fact, with such Exceptions, and under such Regulations as the Congress shall make.

The Trial of all Crimes, except in Cases of Impeachment, shall be by Jury; and such Trial shall be held in the State where the said Crimes shall have been committed; but when not committed within any State, the Trial shall be at such Place or Places as the Congress may by Law have directed. *Section 3.* Treason against the United States, shall consist only in levying War against them, or in adhering to their Enemies, giving them Aid and Comfort. No person shall be convicted of Treason unless on the Testimony of two Witnesses to the same overt Act, or on Confession in open Court.

The Congress shall have Power to declare the Punishment of Treason, but no Attainder of Treason shall work Corruption of Blood, or Forfeiture except during the Life of the Person attainted.

Article IV

Section 1. Full Faith and Credit shall be given in each State to the public Acts, Records, and judicial Proceedings of every other State. And the Congress may by general Laws prescribe the Manner in which such Acts, Records and Proceedings shall be proved, and the Effect thereof.

Section 2. The Citizens of each State shall be entitled to all Privileges and Immunities of Citizens in the several States.

A Person charged in any State with Treason, Felony, or other Crime, who shall flee from Justice, and be found in another State, shall on Demand of the executive Authority of the State from which he fled, be delivered up, to be removed to the State having Jurisdiction of the Crime.

No Person held to Service or Labour in one State, under the Laws thereof, escaping into another, shall, in Consequence of any Law or Regulation therein, be discharged from such Service or Labour, but shall be delivered up on Claim of the Party to whom such Service or Labour may be due.

Section 3. New States may be admitted by the Congress into this Union; but no new State shall be formed or erected within the Jurisdiction of any other State; nor any State be formed by the Junction of two or more States, or Parts of States, without the Consent of the Legislatures of the States concerned as well as of the Congress.

The Congress shall have Power to dispose of and make all needful Rules and Regulations respecting the Territory or other Property belonging to the United States; and nothing in this Constitution shall be so construed as to Prejudice any Claims of the United States, or of any particular State.

Section 4. The United States shall guarantee to every State in this Union a Republican Form of Government, and shall protect each of them against Invasion; and on Application of the Legislature, or of the Executive (when the Legislature cannot be convened) against domestic Violence.

Article V

The Congress, whenever two thirds of both Houses shall deem it necessary, shall propose Amendments to this Constitution, or, on the Application of the Legislatures of two thirds of the several States, shall call a Convention for proposing Amendments, which, in either Case, shall be valid to all Intents and Purposes, as Part of this Constitution, when ratified by the Legislatures of three fourths of the several States, or by Conventions in three fourths thereof, as the one or the other Mode of Ratification may be proposed by the Congress; Provided that no Amendment which may be made prior to the Year One thousand eight hundred and eight shall in any Manner affect the first and fourth Clauses in the Ninth Section of the first Article; and that no State, without its Consent, shall be deprived of it's equal Suffrage in the Senate.

Article VI

All Debts contracted and Engagements entered into, before the Adoption of this Constitution, shall be as valid against the United States under this Constitution, as under the Confederation.

This Constitution, and the Laws of the United States which shall be made in Persuance thereof; and all Treaties made, or which shall be made, under the Authority of the United States, shall be the supreme Law of the Land; and the Judges in every State shall be bound thereby, any Thing in the Constitution or Laws of any State to the Contrary notwithstanding.

The Senators and Representatives before mentioned, and the Members of the several State Legislatures, and all executive and judicial Officers, both of the United States and of the several States, shall be bound by Oath or Affirmation, to support this Constitution; but no religious Test shall ever be required as a Qualification to any Office or public Trust under the United States.

Article VII

The Ratification of the Conventions of nine States, shall be sufficient for the Establishment of this Constitution between the States so ratifying the Same.

DONE in Convention by the Unanimous Consent of the States present the Seventeenth Day of September in the Year of our Lord one thousand seven hundred and Eighty seven and of the Independence of the United States of America the Twelfth IN WITNESS whereof We have hereunto subscribed our Names,

G° WASHINGTON—Presid^t
and deputy from Virginia

New Hampshire, John Langdon, Nicholas Gilman; Massachusetts, Nathaniel Gorham, Rufus King; Connecticut, Wm Saml Johnson, Roger Sherman; New York, Alexander Hamilton; New Jersey, Wil: Livingston, David Brearley, Wm Paterson, Jona: Dayton; Pensylvania, B Franklin, Thomas Mifflin, Robt Morris, Geo. Clymer, Thos Fitz-Simons, Jared Ingersoll, James Wilson, Gouv Morris; Delaware, Geo: Read, Gunning Bedford jun, John Dickinson, Richard Bassett, Jaco: Broom; Maryland, James McHenry, Dan of St Thos Jenifer, Danl Carroll; Virginia, John Blair, James Madison Jr; North Carolina, Wm Blount, Richd Dobbs Spaight, Hu Williamson; South Carolina, J. Rutledge, Charles Cotesworth Pinckney, Charles Pinckney, Pierce Butler; Georgia, William Few, Abr Baldwin.

Articles in addition to, and Amendment of the Constitution of the United States of America, proposed by Congress, and ratified by the Legislatures of the several States, pursuant to the fifth Article of the original Constitution.

[Amendments I-X ratified December 15, 1791.]

[Article I]

Congress shall make no law respecting an establishment of religion, or prohibiting the free exercise thereof; or abridging the freedom of speech, or of the press; or the right of the people peaceably to assemble, and to petition the government for a redress of grievances.

[Article II]

A well regulated Militia, being necessary to the security of a free State, the right of the people to keep and bear Arms, shall not be infringed.

[Article III]

No Soldier shall, in time of peace be quartered in any house, without the consent of the Owner, nor in time of war, but in a manner to be prescribed by law.

[Article IV]

The right of the people to be secure in their persons, houses, papers, and effects, against unreasonable searches and seizures, shall not be violated, and no Warrants shall issue, but upon probable cause, supported by Oath or affirmation, and particularly describing the place to be searched, and the persons or things to be seized.

[Article V]

No person shall be held to answer for a capital, or otherwise infamous crime, unless on a presentment or indictment of a Grand Jury, except in cases arising in the land or naval forces, or in the Militia, when in actual service in time of War or public danger; nor shall any person be subject for the same offence to be twice put in jeopardy of life or limb; nor shall be compelled in any criminal case to be a witness against himself, nor be deprived of life, liberty, or property, without due process of law; nor shall private property be taken for public use, without just compensation.

[Article VI]

In all criminal prosecutions, the accused shall enjoy the right to a speedy and public trial, by an impartial jury of the State and district wherein the crime shall have been committed, which district shall have been previously ascertained by law, and to be informed of the nature and cause of the accusation; to be confronted with the witnesses against him; to have compulsory process for obtaining witnesses in his favor, and to have the Assistance of Counsel for his defence.

[Article VII]

In Suits at common law, where the value in controversy shall exceed twenty dollars, the right of trial by jury shall be preserved, and no fact tried by a jury, shall be otherwise re-examined in any Court of the United States, than according to the rules of the common law.

[Article VIII]

Excessive bail shall not be required, nor excessive fines imposed, nor cruel and unusual punishments inflicted.

[Article IX]

The enumeration in the Constitution, of certain rights, shall not be construed to deny or disparage others retained by the people.

[Article X]

The powers not delegated to the United States by the Constitution, nor prohibited by it to the States, are reserved to the States respectively, or to the people.

[ARTICLE XI]
[Ratified January 8, 1798]

The Judicial power of the United States shall not be construed to extend to any suit in law or equity, commenced or prosecuted against one of the United States by Citizens of another State, or by Citizens or Subjects of any Foreign State.

[ARTICLE XII]
[Ratified September 25, 1804]

The Electors shall meet in their respective states, and vote by ballot for President and Vice-President, one of whom, at least, shall not be an inhabitant of the same state with themselves; they shall name in their ballots the person voted for as President, and in distinct ballots the person voted for as Vice-President, and they shall make distinct lists of all persons voted for as President, and of all persons voted for as Vice-President, and of the number of votes for each, which lists they shall sign and certify, and transmit sealed to the seat of the government of the United States, directed to the President of the Senate;—The President of the Senate shall, in the presence of the Senate and House of Representatives, open all the certificates and the votes shall then be counted;—The person having the greatest number of votes for President, shall be the President, if such number be a majority of the whole number of Electors appointed; and if no person have such majority, then from the persons having the highest numbers not exceeding three on the list of those voted for as President, the House of Representatives shall choose immediately, by ballot, the President. But in choosing the President, the votes shall be taken by states, the representation from each state having one vote; a quorum for this purpose shall consist of a member or members from two-thirds of the states, and a majority of all the states shall be necessary to a choice. And if the House of Representatives shall not choose a President whenever the right of choice shall devolve upon them, before the fourth day of March next following, then the Vice-President shall act as President, as in the case of the death or other constitutional disability of the President.—The person having the greatest number of votes as Vice-President, shall be the Vice-President, if such number be a majority of the whole number of Electors appointed, and if no person have a majority, then from the two highest numbers on the list, the Senate shall choose the Vice-President; a quorum for the purpose shall consist of two-thirds of the whole number of Senators, and a majority of the whole number shall be necessary to a choice. But no person constitutionally ineligible to the office of President shall be eligible to that of Vice-President of the United States.

[ARTICLE XIII]
[Ratified December 18, 1865]

Section 1. Neither slavery nor involuntary servitude, except as a punishment for crime whereof the party shall have been duly convicted, shall exist within the United States, or any place subject to their jurisdiction.
Section 2. Congress shall have power to enforce this article by appropriate legislation.

[ARTICLE XIV]
[Ratified July 28, 1868]

Section 1. All persons born or naturalized in the United States, and subject to the jurisdiction thereof, are citizens of the United States and of the State wherein they reside. No State shall make or enforce any law which shall abridge the privileges or immunities of citizens of the United States; nor shall any State deprive any person of life, liberty, or property, without due process of law; nor deny to any person within its jurisdiction the equal protection of the laws.
Section 2. Representatives shall be apportioned among the several States according to their respective numbers, counting the whole number of persons in each State, excluding Indians not taxed. But when the right to vote at any election for the choice of electors for President and Vice-President of the United States, Representatives in Congress, the Executive and Judicial officers of a State, or the members of the Legislature thereof, is denied to any of the male inhabitants of such State, being twenty-one years of age, and citizens of the United States, or in any way abridged, except for participation in rebellion, or other crime, the basis of representation therein shall be reduced in the proportion which the number of such male citizens shall bear to the whole number of male citizens twenty-one years of age in such State.
Section 3. No person shall be a Senator or Representative in Congress, or elector of President and Vice-President, or hold any office, civil or military, under the United States, or under any State, who, having previously taken an oath, as a member of Congress, or as an officer of the United States, or as a member of any State legislature, or as an executive or judicial officer of any State, to support the Constitution of the United States, shall have engaged in insurrection or rebellion against the same, or given aid or comfort to the enemies thereof. But Congress may by a vote of two-thirds of each House, remove such disability.

Section 4. The validity of the public debt of the United States, authorized by law, including debts incurred for payment of pensions and bounties for services in suppressing insurrection or rebellion, shall not be questioned. But neither the United States nor any State shall assume or pay any debt or obligation incurred in aid of insurrection or rebellion against the United States, or any claim for the loss of emancipation of any slave; but all such debts, obligations and claims shall be held illegal and void.
Section 5. The Congress shall have power to enforce, by appropriate legislation, the provisions of this article.

[ARTICLE XV]
[Ratified March 30, 1870]

Section 1. The right of citizens of the United States to vote shall not be denied or abridged by the United States or by any State on account of race, color, or previous condition of servitude.
Section 2. The Congress shall have power to enforce this article by appropriate legislation.

[ARTICLE XVI]
[Ratified February 25, 1913]

The Congress shall have power to lay and collect taxes on incomes, from whatever source derived, without apportionment among the several States, and without regard to any census or enumeration.

[ARTICLE XVII]
[Ratified May 31, 1913]

The Senate of the United States shall be composed of two Senators from each State, elected by the people thereof, for six years; and each Senator shall have one vote. The electors in each State shall have the qualifications requisite for electors of the most numerous branch of the State legislature.

When vacancies happen in the representation of any State in the Senate, the executive authority of such State shall issue writs of election to fill such vacancies: *Provided,* That the legislature of any State may empower the executive thereof to make temporary appointments until the people fill the vacancies by election as the legislature may direct.

This amendment shall not be so construed as to affect the election or term of any Senator chosen before it becomes valid as part of the Constitution.

[ARTICLE XVIII]
[Ratified January 29, 1919]

Section 1. After one year from the ratification of this article, the manufacture, sale, or transportation of intoxicating liquors within, the importation thereof into, or the exportation thereof from the United States and all territory subject to the jurisdiction thereof for beverage purposes is hereby prohibited.
Section 2. The Congress and the several States shall have concurrent power to enforce this article by appropriate legislation.
Section 3. This article shall be inoperative unless it shall have been ratified as an amendment to the Constitution by the legislatures of the several States, as provided in the Constitution, within seven years from the date of the submission hereof to the States by Congress.

[ARTICLE XIX]
[Ratified August 26, 1920]

The right of citizens of the United States to vote shall not be denied or abridged by the United States or by any States on account of sex.

The Congress shall have power to enforce this article by appropriate legislation.

[ARTICLE XX]
[Ratified February 6, 1933]

Section 1. The terms of the President and Vice President shall end at noon on the twentieth day of January, and the terms of Senators and Representatives at noon on the 3d day of January, of the years in which such terms would have ended if this article had not been ratified; and the terms of their successors shall then begin.
Section 2. The Congress shall assemble at least once in every year, and such meeting shall begin at noon on the 3d day of January, unless they shall by law appoint a different day.
Section 3. If, at the time fixed for the beginning of the term of the President, the President elect shall have died, the Vice President elect shall become President. If a President shall not have been chosen before the time fixed for the beginning of his term, or if the President elect shall have failed to qualify, then the Vice President elect shall act as President until a President shall have qualified; and the Congress may by law provide for the case wherein neither a President elect nor a Vice President elect shall have qualified, declaring who shall then act as President, or the manner in which one who is to act shall be selected, and such person shall act accordingly until a President or Vice President shall have qualified.
Section 4. The Congress may by law provide for the case of the death of any of the persons from whom the House of Representatives may choose a President whenever the right of choice shall have devolved upon them, and for the case of the death of

any of the persons from whom the Senate may choose a Vice President whenever the right of choice shall have devolved upon them.
Section 5. Sections 1 and 2 shall take effect on the 15th day of October following the ratification of this article.
Section 6. This article shall be inoperative unless it shall have been ratified as an amendment to the Constitution by the legislatures of three-fourths of the several States within seven years from the date of its submission.

[Article XXI]
[Ratified December 5, 1933]

Section 1. The eighteenth article of amendment to the Constitution of the United States is hereby repealed.
Section 2. The transportation or importation into any State, Territory or possession of the United States for delivery or use therein of intoxicating liquors, in violation of the laws thereof, is hereby prohibited.
Section 3. This article shall be inoperative unless it shall have been ratified as an amendment to the Constitution by convention in the several States, as provided in the Constitution, within seven years from the date of the submission thereof to the States by the Congress.

[Article XXII]
[Ratified February 26, 1951]

Section 1. No person shall be elected to the office of the President more than twice, and no person who has held the office of President, or acted as President, for more than two years of a term to which some other person was elected President shall be elected to the office of the President more than once. But this Article shall not apply to any person holding the office of President when this Article was proposed by the Congress, and shall not prevent any person who may be holding the office of President, or acting as President, during the term within which this Article becomes operative from holding the office of President or acting as President during the remainder of such term.
Section 2. This Article shall be inoperative unless it shall have been ratified as an amendment to the Constitution by the legislatures of three-fourths of the several States within seven years from the date of its submission to the States by the Congress.

1796 George Washington: Farewell Address

The name of Americans

No other political document has been so often cited in public debate as Washington's Farewell Address. Nearing the end of his second term in office, the President, now in his middle sixties, was tired of the political uproar occasioned by the division between the forces led by Jefferson and Hamilton. Washington had hoped to retire earlier, in 1793, but the country's need for his unifying leadership had pressured him into a second term. With the aid of notes prepared by James Madison and suggestions from Alexander Hamilton and John Jay, Washington completed a draft dated September 17, 1796, which was published to the American people in the Philadelphia Daily American Advertiser *on September 19.*

Washington's testament underlined the need for a strong national government, and warned against sectional rivalries, political factionalism, and "inveterate antipathies against particular nations and passionate attachments for others."

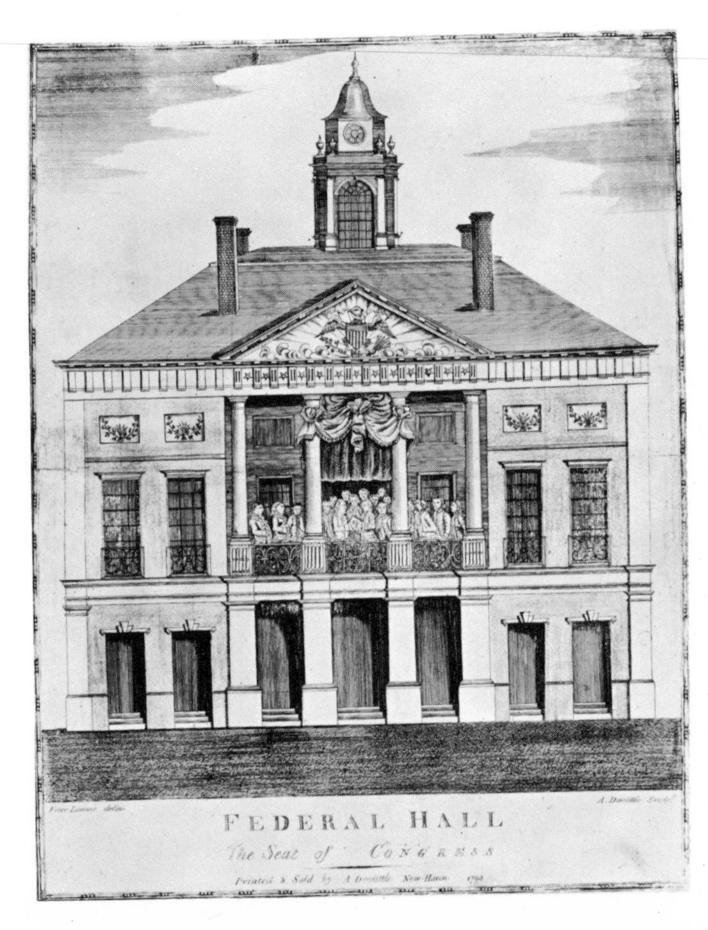

On April 30, 1789, George Washington was inaugurated as the first President of the United States. This contemporary drawing shows the oath of office being administered by Robert R. Livingston, Chancellor of New York, on the balcony of Federal Hall, at the corner of Broad and Wall Streets, in New York City. The engraving is by Amos Doolittle.

To the PEOPLE *of the* UNITED STATES:

FRIENDS and FELLOW-CITIZENS,

THE period for a new election of a Citizen, to adminiſter the executive government of the United States, being not far diſtant, and the time actually arrived, when your thoughts muſt be employed in deſignating the perſon, who is to be cloathed with that important truſt, it appears to me proper, eſpecially as it may conduce to a more diſtinct expreſſion of the public voice, that I ſhould now appriſe you of the reſolution I have formed, to decline being conſidered among the number of thoſe, out of whom a choice is to be made.

I beg you, at the ſame time, to do me the juſtice to be aſſured, that this reſolution has not been taken, without a ſtrict regard to all the conſiderations appertaining to the relation, which binds a dutiful citizen to his country; and that, in withdrawing the tender of ſervice which ſilence in my ſituation might imply, I am influenced by no diminution of zeal for your future intereſt; no deficiency of grateful reſpect for your paſt kindneſs; but am ſupported by a full conviction that the ſtep is compatible with both.

[illegible] acc[illegible] of, and continuance hither- [illegible] faults of [illegible] incompetent abilities will be conſigned to oblivion, as myſelf muſt ſoon be to the manſions of reſt.

Relying on its kindneſs in this as in other things, and actuated by that fervent love towards it, which is ſo natural to a man, who views in it the native ſoil of himſelf and his progenitors for ſeveral generations; I anticipate with pleaſing expectation that retreat, in which I promiſe myſelf to realize, without alloy, the ſweet enjoyment of partaking, in the midſt of my fellow Citizens, the benign influence of good laws under a free government—the ever favourite object of my heart, and the happy reward, as I truſt, of our mutual cares, labours and dangers.

G. WASHINGTON.

UNITED STATES,
17th September, 1796.

UNITED STATES, *September 17, 1796.*

Friends and Fellow-Citizens:

THE PERIOD for a new election of a citizen to administer the Executive Government of the United States being not far distant, and the time actually arrived when your thoughts must be employed in designating the person who is to be clothed with that important trust, it appears to me proper, especially as it may conduce to a more distinct expression of the public voice, that I should now apprise you of the resolution I have formed to decline being considered among the number of those out of whom a choice is to be made. . . .

A solicitude for your welfare which can not end but with my life, and the apprehension of danger natural to that solicitude, urge me on an occasion like the present to offer to your solemn contemplation and to recommend to your frequent review some sentiments which are the result of much reflection, of no inconsiderable observation, and which appear to me all important to the permanency of your felicity as a people. . . .

Interwoven as is the love of liberty with every

A portrait of Washington by Gilbert Stuart.

ligament of your hearts, no recommendation of mine is necessary to fortify or confirm the attachment.

The unity of government which constitutes you one people is also now dear to you. It is justly so, for it is a main pillar in the edifice of your real independence, the support of your tranquillity at home, your peace abroad, of your safety, of your prosperity, of that very liberty which you so highly prize. But as it is easy to foresee that from different causes and from different quarters much pains will be taken, many artifices employed, to weaken in your minds the conviction of this truth, as this is the point in your political fortress against which the batteries of internal and external enemies will be most constantly and actively (though often covertly and insidiously) directed, it is of infinite moment that you should properly estimate the immense value of your national union to your collective and individual happiness; that you should cherish a cordial, habitual, and immovable attachment to it; accustoming yourselves to think and speak of it as of the palladium of your political safety and prosperity; watching for its preservation with jealous anxiety; discountenancing whatever may suggest even a suspicion that it can in any event be abandoned, and indignantly frowning upon the first dawning of every attempt to alienate any portion of our country from the rest or to enfeeble the sacred ties which now link together the various parts.

For this you have every inducement of sympathy and interest. Citizens by birth or choice of a common country, that country has a right to concentrate your affections. The name of American, which belongs to you in your national capacity, must always exalt the just pride of patriotism more than any appellation derived from local discriminations. With slight shades of difference, you have the same religion, manners, habits, and political principles. You have in a common cause fought and triumphed together. The independence and liberty you possess are the work of joint councils and joint efforts, of common dangers, sufferings, and successes. . . .

While, then, every part of our country thus feels an immediate and particular interest in union, all the parts combined can not fail to find in the united mass of means and efforts greater strength, greater resource, proportionably greater security from external danger, a less frequent interruption of their peace by foreign nations, and what is of inestimable value, they must derive from union an exemption from those broils and wars between themselves which so frequently afflict neighboring countries not tied together by the same governments, . . . which opposite foreign alliances, attachments, and intrigues would stimulate and imbitter. Hence, likewise, they will avoid the necessity of those overgrown military establishments which, under any form of government, are inauspicious to liberty, and which are to be regarded as particularly hostile to republican liberty. In this sense it is that your union ought to be considered as a main prop of your liberty, and that the love of the one ought to endear to you the preservation of the other. . . .

Is there a doubt whether a common government can embrace so large a sphere? Let experience solve it. To listen to mere speculation in such a case were criminal. . . . It is well worth a fair and full experiment. . . .

Toward the preservation of your Government and the permanency of your present happy state, it is

Alexander Hamilton, pamphleteer and soldier in the Revolutionary cause, and the first Secretary of the Treasury. He helped Washington draft his political testament.

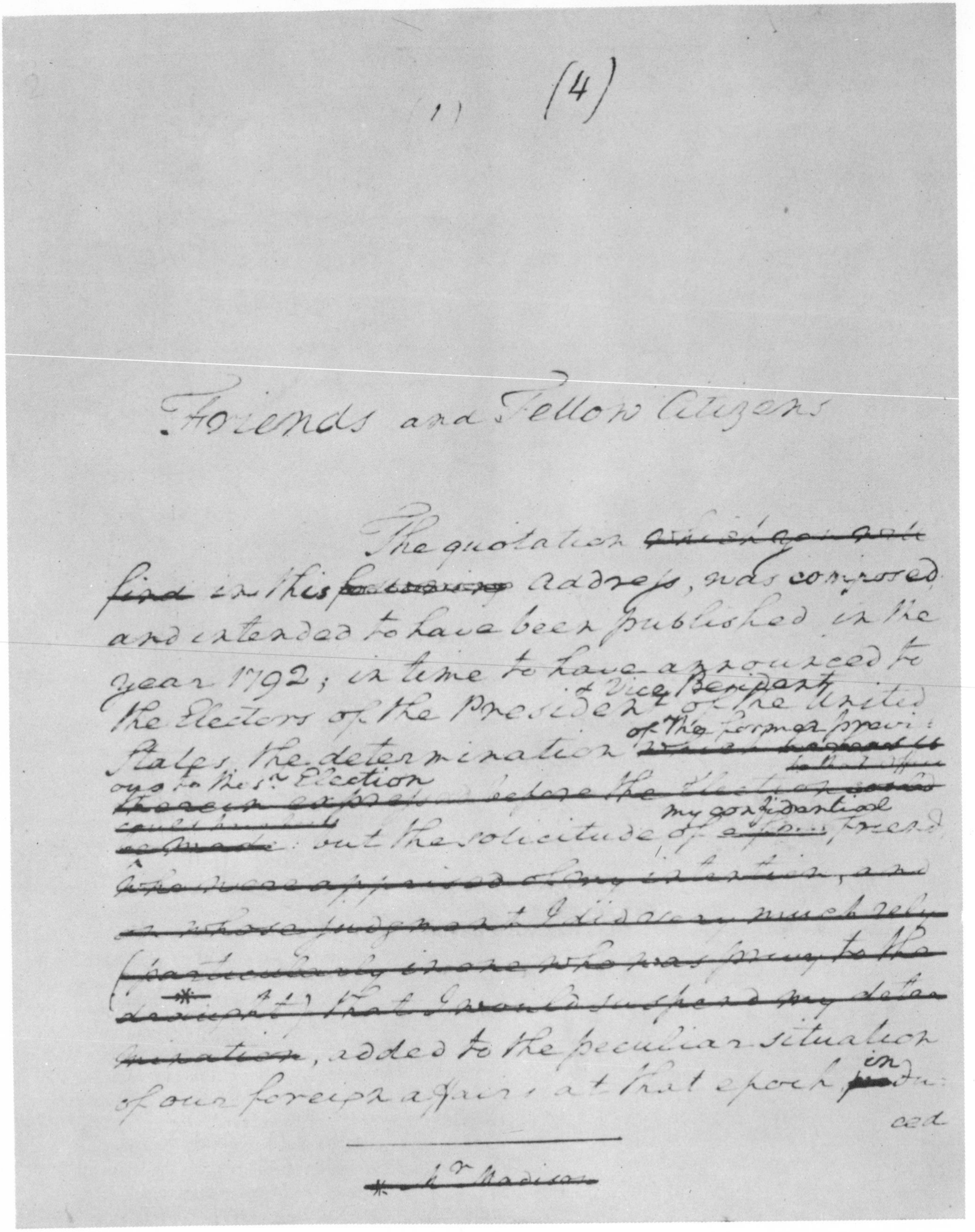

(4)

Friends and Fellow Citizens

The quotation ~~which you will find~~ in this ~~following~~ address, was composed and intended to have been published in the year 1792; in time to have announced to the Electors of the President & Vice President of the United States, the determination of the former previous to the 1st Election ~~which I had then in expectation before the Election could be made~~: but the solicitude of my confidential friends ~~who were apprised of my intention, and on whose judgment I did very much rely (particularly in one who was privy to the draught*)~~ that I would suspend my determination, added to the peculiar situation of our foreign affairs at that epoch, induced

~~* Mr Madison~~

A page from Washington's first draft of the Farewell Address.

requisite not only that you steadily discountenance irregular oppositions to its acknowledged authority, but also that you resist with care the spirit of innovation upon its principles, however specious the pretexts. . . . In all the changes to which you may be invited remember that time and habit are at least as necessary to fix the true character of governments as of other human institutions; that experience is the surest standard by which to test the real tendency of the existing constitution of a country; that facility in changes upon the credit of mere hypothesis and opinion exposes to perpetual change, from the endless variety of hypothesis and opinion; and remember especially that for the efficient management of your common interests in a country so extensive as ours a government of as much vigor as is consistent with the perfect security of liberty is indispensable. Liberty itself will find in such a goverment, with powers properly distributed and adjusted, its surest guardian. It is, indeed, little else than a name where the government is too feeble to withstand the enterprises of faction, to confine each member of the society within the limits prescribed by the laws, and to maintain all in the secure and tranquil enjoyment of the rights of person and property.

I have already intimated to you the danger of parties in the State, with particular reference to the founding of them on geographical discriminations. Let me now take a more comprehensive view, and warn you in the most solemn manner against the baneful effects of the spirit of party generally.

This spirit, unfortunately, is inseparable from our nature, having its root in the strongest passions of the human mind. It exists under different shapes in all governments, more or less stifled, controlled, or repressed; but in those of the popular form it is seen in its greatest rankness and is truly their worst enemy. . . .

It serves always to distract the public councils and enfeeble the public administration. It agitates the community with ill-founded jealousies and false alarms; kindles the animosity of one part against another; foments occasionally riot and insurrection. It opens the door to foreign influence and corruption, which find a facilitated access to the government itself through the channels of party passion. . . .

It is substantially true that virtue or morality is a necessary spring of popular government. . . . Promote, then, as an object of primary importance, institutions for the general diffusion of knowledge. In proportion as the structure of a government gives force to public opinion, it is essential that public opinion should be enlightened.

Observe good faith and justice toward all nations. Cultivate peace and harmony with all. Religion and morality enjoin this conduct. And can it be that good policy does not equally enjoin it? It will be worthy of a free, enlightened, and at no distant period a great nation to give to mankind the magnanimous and too novel example of a people always guided by an exalted justice and benevolence. . . . The experiment, at least, is recommended by every sentiment which ennobles human nature. Alas! is it rendered impossible by its vices?

In the execution of such a plan nothing is more essential than that permanent, inveterate antipathies against particular nations and passionate attachments for others should be excluded, and that in place of them just and amicable feelings toward all should be cultivated. The nation which indulges toward another an habitual hatred or an habitual fondness is in some degree a slave. It is a slave to its animosity or to its affection, either of which is sufficient to lead it astray from its duty and its interest. Antipathy in one nation against another disposes each more readily to offer insult and injury, to lay hold of slight causes of umbrage, and to be haughty and intractable when accidental or trifling occasions of dispute occur. . . .

So, likewise, a passionate attachment of one nation for another produces a variety of evils. Sympathy for the favorite nation, facilitating the illusion of an imaginary common interest in cases where no real common interest exists, and infusing into one the enmities of the other, betrays the former into a participation in the quarrels and wars of the latter without adequate inducement or justification. It leads also to concessions to the favorite nation of privileges denied to others, which is apt doubly to injure the nation making the concessions by unnecessarily parting with what ought to have been retained, and by exciting jealousy, ill will, and a disposition to retaliate in the parties from whom equal privileges are withheld; and it gives to ambitious, corrupted, or deluded citizens (who devote themselves to the favorite nation) facility to betray or sacrifice the interests of their own country without odium, sometimes even with popularity, . . .

Against the insidious wiles of foreign influence (I conjure you to believe me, fellow-citizens) the jealousy of a free people ought to be *constantly* awake, since history and experience prove that foreign influence is one of the most baneful foes of republican government. But that jealousy, to be useful, must be impartial, else it becomes the instrument of the very influence to be avoided, instead of a defense against it. Excessive partiality for one foreign nation and excessive dislike of another cause those whom they actuate to see danger only on one side, and serve to veil and even second the arts of influence on the other. . . .

Europe has a set of primary interests which to us have none or a very remote relation. Hence she must be engaged in frequent controversies, the causes of which are essentially foreign to our concerns. Hence, therefore, it must be unwise in us to implicate ourselves by artificial ties in the ordinary vicissitudes of her politics or the ordinary combinations and collisions of her friendships or enmities.

Our detached and distant situation invites and enables us to pursue a different course. If we remain one people, under an efficient government, the period is not far off when we may defy material injury from external annoyance; when we may take such an attitude as will cause the neutrality we may at any time resolve upon to be scrupulously respected; when belligerent nations, under the impossibility of making acquisitions upon us, will not lightly hazard the giving us provocation; when we may choose peace or war, as our interest, guided by justice, shall counsel.

Why forego the advantages of so peculiar a situation? Why quit our own to stand upon foreign ground? Why, by interweaving our destiny with that of any part of Europe, entangle our peace and

An old print commemorating Washington's brief retirement to Mount Vernon. He died two years later, on December 13, 1799.

prosperity in the toils of European ambition, rivalship, interest, humor, or caprice?

It is our true policy to steer clear of permanent alliances with any portion of the foreign world, so far, I mean, as we are now at liberty to do it; for let me not be understood as capable of patronizing infidelity to existing engagements. I hold the maxim no less applicable to public than to private affairs that honesty is always the best policy. I repeat, therefore, let those engagements be observed in their genuine sense. But in my opinion it is unnecessary and would be unwise to extend them.

Taking care always to keep ourselves by suitable establishments on a respectable defensive posture, we may safely trust to temporary alliances for extraordinary emergencies.

Harmony, liberal intercourse with all nations are recommended by policy, humanity, and interest. But even our commercial policy should hold an equal and impartial hand, neither seeking nor granting exclusive favors or preferences; consulting the natural course of things; diffusing and diversifying by gentle means the streams of commerce, but forcing nothing; establishing with powers so disposed, in order to give trade a stable course, to define the rights of our merchants, and to enable the Government to support them, conventional rules of intercourse, the best that present circumstances and mutual opinion will permit, but temporary and liable to be from time to time abandoned or varied as experience and circumstances shall dictate; constantly keeping in view that it is folly in one nation to look for disinterested favors from another; that it must pay with a portion of its independence for whatever it may accept under that character; that by such acceptance it may place itself in the condition of having given equivalents for nominal favors, and yet of being reproached with ingratitude for not giving more. There can be no greater error than to . . . calculate upon real favors from nation to nation. . . .

Though in reviewing the incidents of my Administration I am unconscious of intentional error, I am nevertheless too sensible of my defects not to think it probable that I may have committed many errors. Whatever they may be, I fervently beseech the Almighty to avert or mitigate the evils to which they may tend. I shall also carry with me the hope that my country will never cease to view them with indulgence, and that, after forty-five years of my life dedicated to its service with an upright zeal, the faults of incompetent abilities will be consigned to oblivion, as myself must soon be to the mansions of rest.

Relying on its kindness in this as in other things, and actuated by that fervent love toward it which is so natural to a man who views in it the native soil of himself and his progenitors for several generations, I anticipate with pleasing expectation that retreat in which I promise myself to realize without alloy the sweet enjoyment of partaking in the midst of my fellow-citizens the benign influence of good laws under a free government—the ever-favorite object of my heart, and the happy reward, as I trust, of our mutual cares, labors, and dangers.

The right of freely examining public characters and measures

As Washington's administration gave way to John Adams', the Federalists and Republicans were at each other's throats. Adams, the Federalist candidate, had defeated Jefferson by the narrow margin of three electoral votes, and the Republican leader, through a split in the Federalist ranks, became Vice-President. A state of undeclared war between revolutionary France and the United States rapidly developed. The struggle moved to an explosive point, and the Federalists saw in the troubles with France a chance to cripple the Jeffersonians. As new migrants entered the country, the Federalists feared their radical principles might infect American thought. Republican sympathy with the French was now labeled treason. With Congress in their control, the Federalists moved to strike down their "unpatriotic" political foes. In 1798 they passed the Alien and Sedition Acts, a series of four laws. One extended residence requirements for naturalized citizens from five years to fourteen. Two others gave the President power to deport any alien he thought a threat to the nation's security, and in time of war, to deport or arrest at will aliens of an enemy nation. The fourth measure punished with heavy fines or imprisonment anyone who would "write, print, utter, or publish" any "false, scandalous, or malicious" statements designed to bring disrepute upon the government, Congress, or the President.

Infuriated by this attack upon free speech and press, Jefferson drafted a resolution for Kentucky to pass while his friend Madison did the same for Virginia. These declared the Alien and Sedition laws unconstitutional on the principle that minorities and individuals are protected against their government by limitations written into the constitution. Among these is the First Amendment, safeguarding freedom of religion, of speech, and of the press.

The Kentucky and Virginia Resolutions helped rouse the opposition to the tyrannical measures of the Federalists and paved the way for a radical change of government two years later, when Jefferson came into power.

Kentucky Resolution

(November 16, 1798)

I. Resolved, that the several States composing the United States of America, are not united on the principle of unlimited submission to their general government; but that by compact under the style and title of a Constitution for the United States and of amendments thereto, they constituted a general government for special purposes, delegated to that government certain definite powers, reserving each State to itself, the residuary mass of right to their own self-government; and that whensoever the general government assumes undelegated powers, its acts are unauthoritative, void, and of no force: . . .

II. Resolved, that . . . [the Sedition Act] . . . (and all other acts which assume to create, define, or punish crimes other than those enumerated in the Constitution), are altogether void and of no force, and that the power to create, define, and punish such other crimes is reserved, and of right appertains solely and exclusively to the respective States. . . .

III. Resolved, that it is true as a general principle, and is also expressly declared by one of the amendments to the Constituiton that "the powers not delegated to the United States by the Constitution, nor prohibited by it to the States, are reserved to the States respectively or to the people;" . . . And

Vermont's Republican Congressman, Matthew Lyon, defends himself with a pair of tongs against a caning attack from Connecticut Federalist Roger Griswold. The 1798 cartoonist shows Congress amused at the brawl. Later, Lyon was convicted of sedition for criticizing President Adams in a letter, and spent four months in jail.

that . . . another and more special provision has been made by one of the amendments to the Constitution which expressly declares, that "Congress shall make no law respecting an establishment of religion, or prohibiting the free exercise thereof, or abridging the freedom of speech, or of the press," . . . That therefore [the Sedition Act], which does abridge the freedom of the press, is not law, but is altogether void and of no effect. . . .

Virginia Resolution

(December 24, 1798)

Resolved, That the General Assembly of Virginia doth unequivocally express a firm resolution to maintain and defend the Constitution of the United States, and the Constitution of this state, against every aggression either foreign or domestic; . . .

Matthew Lyon, whose Vermont constituents re-elected him to Congress from jail.

Gazette of the United States.

A NATIONAL PAPER, PUBLISHED WEDNESDAYS AND SATURDAYS BY JOHN FENNO, No. 34, NORTH FIFTH-STREET, PHILADELPHIA.

[No. 129 of Vol. IV.] SATURDAY, AUGUST 24, 1793. [Whole No. 451.]

National Gazette

By PHILIP FRENEAU.

Vol I. MONDAY, October 31, 1791. Numb. 1.

The *Federalist Gazette* of the United States, edited by John Fenno, was sponsored by Hamilton, while the opposition *National Gazette,* under the poet Philip Freneau (right), was Jefferson's voice. The papers were acidly partisan. All ten men convicted under the Sedition Act were Republican publishers or printers.

That the General Assembly doth particularly PROTEST against the palpable and alarming infractions of the Constitution in the two late cases of the "Alien and Sedition Acts," passed at the last session of Congress; the first of which exercises a power nowhere delegated to the federal government, and which, by uniting legislative and judicial powers to those of executive, subverts the general principles of free government, as well as the particular organization and positive provisions of the Federal Constitution: and the other of which acts exercises, in like manner, a power not delegated by the Constitution, but, on the contrary, expressly and positively forbidden by one of the amendments thereto,—a power which, more than any other, ought to produce universal alarm, because it is levelled against the right of freely examining public characters and measures, and of free communication among the people thereon, which has ever been justly deemed the only effectual guardian of every other right. . . .

A portrait of Thomas Jefferson.

Error of opinion may be tolerated

where reason is left free to combat it

1801 Thomas Jefferson: First Inaugural Address

An aquatint portrait of Jefferson after a drawing made in 1798 by Thaddeus Kosciusko, the Polish general who volunteered his military services to the Revolutionary army because he was devoted to the cause of liberty.

Thomas Jefferson, Secretary of State under Washington, had left the first President's Cabinet so that he could more freely organize resistance to Hamilton's policies. Elected Vice-President to John Adams, he continued his opposition to the Federalists and mustered sufficient support to win the Presidency in 1800. The new President, the popular champion of democracy, walked from his boarding house through the muddy village streets to the unfinished Capitol to deliver his inaugural address. It was a simple ceremony. In his speech Jefferson strove to restore harmony to the political scene. The principles he expressed, and the eloquent art with which he voiced them, made his address one of our great state papers.

DURING the contest of opinion through which we have passed, the animation of discussions and of exertions has sometimes worn an aspect which might impose on strangers unused to think freely and to speak and to write what they think; but this being now decided by the voice of the nation, announced according to the rules of the Constitution, all will, of course, arrange themselves under the will of the law, and unite in common efforts for the common good. All, too, will bear in mind

The acquisition of Louisiana is of immense importance to our future tranquility, inasmuch as it removes the intrigues of foreign nations to a distance from which they can no longer produce disturbance between the Indians & us. it will also open an asylum for these unhappy people, in a country which may suit their habits of life better than that they now occupy, which perhaps they will be willing to exchange with us: and to our posterity it opens a noble prospect of provision for ages. the world will here see such an extent of country under a free and moderate government as it has never yet seen. being in the hurry of departure for Washington I must here offer you my friendly salutations & assurances of great respect & esteem.

Th: Jefferson

Jefferson was the first President to deliver an inaugural address in the new Capitol. Above is a glimpse of the village of Washington about 1803, from a water color made by the city surveyor, Nicholas King. The President's house is in the rear center, and the Blodgett Hotel on the right.

this sacred principle, that though the will of the majority is in all cases to prevail, that will to be rightful must be reasonable; that the minority possess their equal rights, which equal law must protect, and to violate would be oppression.

Let us, then, fellow-citizens, unite with one heart and one mind. Let us restore to social intercourse that harmony and affection without which liberty and even life itself are but dreary things. And let us reflect that, having banished from our land that religious intolerance under which mankind so long bled and suffered, we have yet gained little if we countenance a political intolerance as despotic, as wicked, and capable of as bitter and bloody persecutions.

During the throes and convulsions of the ancient world, during the agonizing spasms of infuriated man, seeking through blood and slaughter his long-lost liberty, it was not wonderful that the agitation of the billows should reach even this distant and peaceful shore; that this should be more felt and feared by some and less by others, and should divide opinions as to measures of safety. But every difference of opinion is not a difference of principle. We have called by different names brethren of the same principle. We are all Republicans, we are all Federalists. If there be any among us who would wish to dissolve this Union or to change its republican form, let them stand undisturbed as monuments of the safety with which error of opinion may be tolerated where reason is left free to combat it. I know, indeed, that some honest men fear that a republican government can not be strong, that this Government is not strong enough; but would the honest patriot, in the full tide of successful experiment, abandon a government which has so far kept us free and firm on the theoretic and visionary fear that this Government, the world's best hope, may by possibility want energy to preserve itself? I trust not. I believe this, on the contrary, the strongest Government on earth. I believe it the only one where every man, at the call of the law, would fly to the standard of the law, and would meet invasions of the public order as his own personal concern. Sometimes it is said that man can not be trusted with the government of himself. Can he, then, be trusted with the government of others? Or have we found angels in the forms of kings to govern him? Let history answer this question . . .

as bitter & bloody persecutions. during the throes & convulsions of the antient world, during the
agonising spasms of infuriated man, seeking thro' blood & slaughter his long-lost liberty, it was
not wonderful that the agitation of the billows should reach even this distant & peaceful shore;
that this should be more felt & feared by some & less by others; & should divide opinions as to
measures of safety. but every difference of opinion, is not a difference of principle. we
have called by different names brethren of the same principle. we are all republicans: we
are all federalists. if there be any among us who would wish to dissolve this Union or
to change it's republican form, let them stand undisturbed as monuments of the safety
with which error of opinion may be tolerated, where reason is left free to combat it. I
know indeed that some honest men fear that a republican government cannot be
strong; that this government is not strong enough. but would the honest patriot
in the full tide of successful experiment abandon a government which has so far kept
us free and firm, on the theoretic & visionary fear, that this government, the world's
best hope, may, by possibility, want energy to preserve itself? I trust not. I believe
this, on the contrary the strongest government on earth. I believe it the only one,
where every man, at the call of the law, would fly to the standard of the law, and
would meet invasions of the public order as his own personal concern. some
-times it is said that man cannot be trusted with the government of himself. can he then
be trusted with the government of others? or have we found angels, in the form of kings, to
govern him? Let history answer this question.

Let us then, with courage & confidence, pursue our own federal & republican principles; our attachment
~~to union & representative government~~. kindly separated by nature & a wide ocean from the extermina
-ting havoc of one quarter of the globe; too high-minded to endure the degradations of the others,
possessing a chosen country, with room enough for our descendants to the thousandth & thou-
-sandth generation, ~~enjoying the most favourable temperatures of climate~~, entertaining a
due sense of our equal right to the use of our own faculties, to the acquisitions of our own indus
-try, to honour & confidence from our fellow citizens, resulting not from birth, but from our actions
& their sense of them, enlightened by a benign religion, professed indeed & practised in various forms,
yet all of them inculcating honesty, truth, temperance, gratitude & the love of man, acknowledging
and adoring an overruling providence, which by all it's dispensations proves that it delights in the
happiness of man here, & his greater happiness hereafter; with all these blessings, what more is

Near the top of this page from Jefferson's draft of his first inaugural address appear the famous lines: "If there be any among us who would wish to dissolve this Union or to change its republican form, let them stand undisturbed as monuments of the safety with which error of opinion may be tolerated where reason is left free to combat it."

A bust of Jefferson by the French sculptor, Jean-Antoine Houdon, whose portrait sculpture gallery included Washington and Franklin.

A law repugnant to the Constitution is void

In 1800 the Federalists lost not only the Presidency to Jefferson, but the Congress to the Republicans. Preparing to move out of office, John Adams sought to keep control of the judiciary, at least, in his party's hands. Sixteen new judgeships were created and several minor judicial offices. As the clock ticked to the last minute of his administration, President Adams signed the commissions of Federalists he wanted to fill those offices.

Jefferson refused to honor these "midnight" appointees. One of them, William Marbury, brought suit against Secretary of State Madison to compel him to deliver the commission. The case of Marbury v. Madison *reached the Supreme Court in Feburary, 1803. Chief Justice John Marshall, although a Federalist appointed by Adams as one of his last defiant acts in office, refused to grant the writ. He held the section of the Judiciary Act of 1789, to which Marbury appealed, was "repugnant" to the Constitution, and hence null and void.*

That decision was epoch-making, for it enshrined the doctrine of judicial review. It was the first time the Supreme Court declared a Congressional act unconstitutional. Marshall assumed this power for the Court—a power nowhere granted in the Constitution itself—and made the Court supreme over the rest of the federal government. Marshall himself, however, never again declared a Congressional act unconstitutional.

Three contemporary silhouettes of Chief Justice John Marshall.

John Marshall. He was a distant cousin of Jefferson's, but the two men deeply disliked each other. Marshall held the office of Chief Justice of the U.S. Supreme Court for over three decades (1801–1835). Through five administrations in the Jeffersonian and Jacksonian eras he laid down fundamental principles of American constitutional law. His decisions bolstered the Federal government against the States, and helped solidify the power of the growing nation.

IT IS EMPHATICALLY the province and duty of the judicial department to say what the law is. Those who apply the rule to particular cases, must of necessity expound and interpret that rule. If two laws conflict with each other, the courts must decide on the operation of each.

So if a law be in opposition to the constitution; if both the law and the constitution apply to a particular case, so that the court must either decide that case conformably to the law, disregarding the constitution; or conformably to the constitution, disregarding the law; the court must determine which of these conflicting rules governs the case. This is of the very essence of judicial duty.

If, then, the courts are to regard the constitution, and the constitution is superior to any ordinary act of the legislature, the constitution, and not such ordinary act, must govern the case to which they both apply.

Those, then, who controvert the principle that the constitution is to be considered, in court, as a paramount law, are reduced to the necessity of maintaining that courts must close their eyes on the constitution, and see only the law.

This doctrine would subvert the very foundation of all written constitutions. It would declare that an act which, according to the principles and theory of our government, is entirely void, is yet, in practice, completely obligatory. It would declare that if the legislature shall do what is expressly forbidden, such act, notwithstanding the express prohibition, is in reality effectual. It would be giving to the legislature a practical and real omnipotence, with the same breath which professes to restrict their powers within narrow limits. It is prescribing limits, and declaring that those limits may be passed at pleasure.

That it thus reduces to nothing what we have deemed the greatest improvement on political institutions, a written constitution, would of itself be sufficient, in America, where written constitutions have been viewed with so much reverence, for rejecting the construction. But the peculiar expressions of the constitution of the United States furnish additional arguments in favour of its rejection.

The judicial power of the United States is extended to all cases arising under the constitution.

Could it be the intention of those who gave this power, to say that in using it the constitution should not be looked into? That a case arising under the constitution should be decided without examining the instrument under which it arises?

This is too extravagant to be maintained.

In some cases, then, the constitution must be looked into by the judges. And if they can open it at all, what part of it are they forbidden to read or to obey?

There are many other parts of the constitution which serve to illustrate this subject.

It is declared that "no tax or duty shall be laid on articles exported from any state." Suppose a duty on the export of cotton, of tobacco, or of flour, and a suit instituted to recover it. Ought judgment to be rendered in such a case? ought the judges to close their eyes on the constitution, and only see the law?

The constitution declares "that no bill of attainder or *ex post facto* law shall be passed."

If, however, such a bill should be passed, and a person should be prosecuted under it; must the court condemn to death those victims whom the constitution endeavors to preserve?

"No person," says the constitution, "shall be convicted of treason unless on the testimony of two witnesses to the same overt act, or on confession in open court."

Here the language of the constitution is addressed especially to the courts. It prescribes, directly for them, a rule of evidence not to be departed from. If the legislature should change that rule, and declare one witness, or a confession out of court, sufficient for conviction, must the constitutional principle yield to the legislative act?

From these, and many other selections which might be made, it is apparent, that the framers of the constitution contemplated that instrument as a rule for the government of *courts,* as well as of the legislature.

Why otherwise does it direct the judges to take an oath to support it? This oath certainly applies in an especial manner, to their conduct in their official character. How immoral to impose it on them, if they were to be used as the instruments, and the knowing instruments, for violating what they swear to support!

The oath of office, too, imposed by the legislature, is completely demonstrative of the legislative opinion on this subject. It is in these words: "I do solemnly swear that I will administer justice without respect to persons, and do equal right to the poor and to the rich; and that I will faithfully and impartially discharge all the duties incumbent on me as———, according to the best of my abilities and understanding agreeably to *the constitution* and laws of the United States."

Why does a judge swear to discharge his duties agreeably to the constitution of the United States, if that constitution forms no rule for his government? if it is closed upon him, and cannot be inspected by him?

If such be the real state of things, this is worse than solemn mockery. To prescribe, or to take this oath, becomes equally a crime.

It is also not entirely unworthy of observation, that in declaring what shall be the *supreme* law of the land, the constitution itself is first mentioned; and not the laws of the United States generally, but those only which shall be made in *pursuance* of the constitution, have that rank.

Thus, the particular phraseology of the constitution of the United States confirms and strengthens the principle, supposed to be essential to all written constitutions, that a law repugnant to the constitution is void; and that courts, as well as other departments, are bound by that instrument.

James Monroe, Virginia, fifth President of the U.S. A veteran of the Revolutionary War, he studied law under Jefferson, served as U.S. Senator, governor of Virginia, Minister to France, and Secretary of State and of War. His two terms as President (1817–25) were characterized as an "Era of Good Feeling."

The American continents are not subjects for future colonization

As Napoleon's armies swept over Spain and Portugal in 1807–1808 the Latin American colonies of the two imperial powers revolted. The new flags of freedom were enthusiastically hailed by the people of the United States, their own revolutionary traditions still young and fresh. Public opinion warmly supported recognition of the republics which had thrown off the Old World's yoke. In March, 1822, upon completing negotiations with Spain for the purchase of Florida, President Monroe recognized the new governments of the nations to the south. By now Spain's empire in the West had shrunk to Cuba and Puerto Rico, and Brazil had declared herself independent of Portugal.

Later in the same year Europe's great powers, hostile to revolutionary democracy, agreed to attempt to restore Spanish authority. Rumors that French and Spanish naval power would try to crush the new republics alarmed American ears. England's government, Tory though it was, dissented from the view that revolution in any European state should be suppressed by the major powers, and insisted that all nations should "be left free to manage their own affairs, so long as they left other nations to manage theirs."

The United States feared that European intervention in Latin America might result in new empires at our borders, and especially desired to keep declining Spanish power from transferring Cuba to any other European country. Great Britain's interest lay in the promise of rich markets in South America, with the continent freed of Spanish control.

Britain's foreign secretary, George Canning, suggested joint Anglo-American action in warning other powers against intervention in the New World. Jefferson and Madison counseled President Monroe to cooperate with the British, but Secretary of State

Simón Bolívar, whose leadership in the struggle for independence of many South American countries won him the title of The Liberator. An aristocrat born in Venezuela, then under Spanish rule, he dedicated his life and fortune to the fight for freedom. In 1822 the U.S. recognized five of the new independent nations—Chile, Colombia, Mexico, Peru, and Argentina. Bolívar helped free Colombia, Venezuela, Ecuador, Peru, and Bolivia, which was named after him.

John Quincy Adams strongly advised against making the United States appear merely "as a cockboat bobbing in the wake of the British man-of-war." Monroe listened to Adams and with his help prepared a wholly independent statement of policy which he sent to Congress on December 2, 1823, as his seventh annual message.

In two widely separated passages he warned Russia against her advance down the Pacific Coast and told the allied European powers that any attempt to suppress the new Latin American republics would be considered unfriendly to the United States. The two hemispheres have essentially different political systems, he asserted; the New World is closed to the power politics of the Old.

The voicing of this policy of the right of self-determination and of noninterference in the internal affairs of other nations did not cause much stir at the time. The term it is now known by—the Monroe Doctrine—was not even applied for a quarter-century. But gradually in later years the bold commitment to leadership in world politics became recognized as one of the most significant statements of American policy in international affairs.

AT THE PROPOSAL of the Russian Imperial Government, made through the minister of the Emperor residing here, a full power and instructions have been transmitted to the minister of the United States at St. Petersburg to arrange by amicable negotiation the respective rights and interests of the two nations on the northwest coast of this continent. A similar proposal had been made by His Imperial Majesty to the Government of Great Britain, which has likewise been acceded to. . . . In the discussions to which this interest has given rise and in the arrangements by which they may terminate, the occasion has been judged proper for asserting, as a principle in which the rights and interests of the United States are involved, that the American continents, by the free and independent condition which they have assumed and maintain, are henceforth not to be considered as subjects for future colonization by any European powers. . . .

. . . Of events in that quarter of the globe, with which we have so much intercourse and from which we derive our origin, we have always been anxious and interested spectators. The citizens of the United States cherish sentiments the most friendly in favor of the liberty and happiness of their fellow-men on that side of the Atlantic. In the wars of the European powers in matters relating to themselves we have never taken any part, nor does it comport with our policy so to do. It is only when our rights are invaded or seriously menaced that we resent injuries or make preparation for our defense. With the movements in this hemisphere we are of necessity more immediately connected, and by causes which must be obvious to all enlightened and impartial observers. The political system of the allied powers is essentially different in this respect from that of America. This difference proceeds from that which exists in their respective Governments; and to the defense of our own, which has been achieved by the loss of so much blood and treasure, and matured by the wisdom of their most enlightened citizens, and under which we have enjoyed unexampled felicity, this whole nation is devoted. We owe it, therefore, to candor and to the amicable relations existing between the United States and those powers to declare that we should consider any attempt on their part to extend their system to any portion of this hemisphere as dangerous to our peace and safety. With the existing colonies or dependencies of any European power we have not interfered and shall not interfere. But with the Governments who have declared their independence and maintained it, and whose independence we have, on great consideration and on just principles, acknowledged, we could not view any interposition for the purpose of oppressing them, or controlling in any other manner their destiny, by any European power in any other light than as the manifestation of an unfriendly disposition toward the United States. . . .

The late events in Spain and Portugal shew that Europe is still unsettled. Of this important fact no stronger proof can be adduced than that the allied powers should have thought it proper, on any principle satisfactory to themselves, to have interposed by force in the internal concerns of Spain. To what extent such interposition may be carried, on the same principle, is a question in which all independent powers whose governments differ from theirs are interested, even those most remote, and surely none more so than the United States. Our policy in regard to Europe, which was adopted at an early stage of the wars which have so long agitated that quarter of the globe, nevertheless remains the same, which is, not to interfere in the internal concerns of any of its powers; to consider the government *de facto* as the legitimate government for us; to cultivate friendly relations with it, and to preserve those relations by a frank, firm, and manly policy, meeting in all instances the just claims of every power, submitting to injuries from none. But in regard to those continents circumstances are eminently and conspicuously different. It is impossible that the allied powers should extend their political system to any portion of either continent without endangering our peace and happiness; nor can anyone believe that our southern brethren, if left to themselves, would adopt it of their own accord. It is equally impossible, therefore, that we should behold such interposition in any form with indifference. . . .

The spirit of improvement is abroad upon the earth

To John Quincy Adams, man was a "sociable being" whose welfare and happiness must be the aim of all government. A free government must do more than police against external danger and internal violence. There were great national goals, he believed, which American government had the responsibility to realize. It was the duty of the federal legislature and executive to use the power of government to improve their country and mankind. Elected sixth president of the United States in 1824, Adams sounded this note briefly in his inaugural, and later, on December 6, 1825, in his first annual message to Congress, advocated several measures to direct knowledge and science in behalf of the common welfare.

His doctrine of internal improvement was considerably in advance of his time. His sweeping view of constitutional power to seek social improvement anticipated the twentieth century. None of his proposals was acted upon. Defeated overwhelmingly by Andrew Jackson when he stood for a second term, Adams left the White House believing "the sun of my political life sets in the deepest gloom." But not long after, he was elected to Congress where he served magnificently as "Old Man Eloquent" for seventeen years. In these excerpts from his First Annual Message to Congress, Adams called for establishment of a national university, an astronomical observatory, exploring expeditions, a system of uniform weights and measures, and public support of the arts and sciences.

THE CONSTITUTION under which you are assembled is a charter of limited powers . . . if these powers and others enumerated in the Constitution may be effectually brought into action by laws promoting the improvement of agriculture, commerce, and manufactures, the cultivation and encouragement of the mechanic and of the elegant arts, the advancement of literature, and the progress of the sciences, ornamental and profound, to refrain from exercising them for the benefit of the people themselves would be to hide in the earth the talent committed to our charge—would be treachery to the most sacred of trusts.

The spirit of improvement is abroad upon the earth. It stimulates the hearts and sharpens the faculties not of our fellow-citizens alone, but of the nations of Europe and of their rulers. While dwelling with pleasing satisfaction upon the superior excellence of our political institutions, let us not be unmindful that liberty is power; that the nation

John Quincy Adams, the sixth President, son of the second President, John Adams. The head in this portrait was painted by Gilbert Stuart; the body, by Thomas Sully, after Stuart's death.

blessed with the largest portion of liberty must in proportion to its numbers be the most powerful nation upon earth, and that the tenure of power by man is, in the moral purposes of his Creator, upon condition that it shall be exercised to ends of beneficence, to improve the condition of himself and his fellowmen.

While foreign nations less blessed with that freedom which is power than ourselves are advancing with gigantic strides in the career of public improvement, were we to slumber in indolence or fold up our arms and proclaim to the world that we are palsied by the will of our constituents, would it not be to cast away the bounties of Providence and doom ourselves to perpetual inferiority?

In the course of the year now drawing to its close we have beheld, under the auspices and at the expense of one State of this Union, a new university unfolding its portals to the sons of science and holding up the torch of human improvement to eyes that seek the light. We have seen under the persevering and enlightened enterprise of another State the

On the day the second session of the Twenty-Fifth Congress convened (December 4, 1837) Representative John Quincy Adams of Massachusetts wrote this poem. He must have been moved to offer up this private prayer by the savage pressures which had been invoked against him for his unrelenting support of the right of free petition in the House. During his eight successive terms, Adams was the chief channel through which antislavery petitions poured into Congress. At eighty, he died at his desk in the House.

Monday 4. December 1837
25 Congress 2. Session.

Almighty Father! look in Mercy down:
Oh! grant me Virtue, to perform my part—
The Patriot's fervour, and the Statesman's art
In thought, word, deed, preserve me from thy frown.

Direct me to the paths of bright Renown—
Guide my frail bark, by Truth's unerring chart.
Inspire my Soul; and purify my heart;
And with Success, my stedfast purpose crown.

My Country's weal—be that my Polar Star—
Justice—thou Rock of Ages' is thy Law—
And when thy Summons calls me to thy Bar
Be this my plea, thy gracious smile to draw—
That all my ways to Justice were inclin'd—
And all my aims—the blessing of mankind.

J. Q. Adams

This 1824 cartoon shows John Quincy Adams, William H. Crawford, and Andrew Jackson coming in nearly neck and neck in the Presidential foot race, with Henry Clay a poor fourth. The electoral college gave Jackson 99, Adams 84, Crawford 41, and Clay 37. With no one holding a majority, the House of Representatives chose Adams as President. Waving the cocked hat to cheer his son on is John Adams.

waters of our Western lakes mingle with those of the ocean. If undertakings like these have been accomplished in the compass of a few years by the authority of single members of our Confederation, can we, the representative authorities of the whole Union, fall behind our fellow-servants in the exercise of the trust committed to us for the benefit of our common sovereign by the accomplishment of works important to the whole and to which neither the authority nor the resources of any one State can be adequate?

The masthead of *The Liberator*. Garrison published it for 35 years, until the Civil War ended slavery.

1831 William Lloyd Garrison: "To the Public" Editorial

And I will be heard

In the same year he launched *The Liberator*, **William Lloyd Garrison (left) helped to** found the New England Antislavery Society. In 1835 the editor was dragged through the streets of Boston by a mob and almost lynched. But terror could not make him miss an issue. "I have a system to destroy," he said, "and I have no time to waste."

The antislavery societies made special appeals to every section of the public. The Juvenile Department of *The Liberator* recorded the miseries of slave children, illustrated by the auction block; and the Ladies' Department, rephrasing the 18th century slogan—"Am I not a Man and a Brother?"—carried a cut of a slave in chains.

America knew dozens of movements to right the world's wrongs in the early nineteenth century, but the one which heated the public mind most was abolitionism. The antislavery crusade was piloted by many captains. Some advocated voluntary and compensated emancipation, some a back-to-Africa colonization plan, and others a compensated manumission by state law.

William Lloyd Garrison, a Massachusetts journalist, early in his career dropped gradual emancipation for the uncompromising position of immediate emancipation. With the relentless passion of an Old Testament prophet he challenged the conscience of a nation to live up to the doctrine of human brotherhood. On New Year's Day, 1831, he published the first issue of his newspaper, The Liberator. *Assenting to the "self-evident truth" that "all men are created equal," he pledged himself to "strenuously contend for the immediate enfranchisement of our slave population." His dedicated words in that fearless editorial were heard far beyond the handful of readers with whom* The Liberator *began its long history.*

DURING my recent tour for the purpose of exciting the minds of the people by a series of discourses on the subject of slavery, every place that I visited gave fresh evidence of the fact, that a greater revolution in public sentiment was to be effected in the free states—*and particularly in New England*—than at the South. I found contempt more bitter, opposition more active, detraction more relentless, prejudice more stubborn, and apathy more frozen, than among slave owners themselves. . . . I determined, at every hazard, to lift up the standard of emancipation in the eyes of the nation, *within sight of Bunker Hill and in the birth place of liberty. . . .*

I am aware, that many object to the severity of my language; but is there not cause for severity? I *will be* as harsh as truth, and as uncompromising as justice. On this subject, I do not wish to think, or speak, or write, with moderation. No! No! Tell a man whose house is on fire, to give a moderate alarm; tell him to moderately rescue his wife from the hands of the ravisher; tell the mother to gradually extricate her babe from the fire into which it has fallen;—but urge me not to use moderation in a cause like the present. I am in earnest—I will not equivocate—I will not excuse—I will not retreat a single inch—AND I WILL BE HEARD. . . .

Masters were vigilant in protecting their investment in slaves. Some developed elaborate and painful devices (left) to punish wrongdoers or hinder a fugitive's escape. The Underground Railroad helped some 75,000 slaves run away to freedom in the decade preceding the Civil War. In 1861, slaves were still being bought and sold in the public marketplace, as this New Orleans print (above) shows. Although a Congressional law of 1807 forbade importation of African slaves, as late as 1859 slave ships were still landing Negroes at Southern ports.

We take a stand against the advancement of the few at the expense of the many

"Emperor Biddle's Monster" was what Andrew Jackson called the second Bank of the United States. Granted a twenty-year charter by Congress in 1816, the bank was a private corporation with great powers amounting to monopoly. It used public funds, derived from taxes, to make profits for the wealthy who could buy its shares. And use of the same funds to extend loans and credit to businessmen it preferred made the bank as corrupt as it was undemocratic, Jackson believed. Jackson's war on government-backed monopoly reached its peak in his struggle against Nicholas Biddle, the bank's president. At the ambitious Henry Clay's urging, Biddle pushed a bill through Congress to recharter the bank in 1832. Clay, his eye on the presidency, believed that if Jackson vetoed the bill, the issue would cost the President his re-election.

On July 10, 1832, Jackson returned the bill to Congress with a veto which the Senate failed to override. The veto message contained a classic expression of Jackson's belief in economic as well as political democracy.

Backwoods lawyer, land speculator, trader, Indian fighter, and hero of the Battle of New Orleans—President Andrew Jackson. In his two terms as the spokesman of the small farmer, the working man and the middle-class businessman, he used the full power of his office to check economic privilege.

"The Downfall of Mother Bank" was drawn in 1833 to celebrate Jackson's defeat of Biddle. The Bank's pillars crash about the ears of Biddle and his Whig politicians and editors. The government's removal of its deposits from the Bank crippled its business. When its charter expired in 1836 it became a state bank but did not survive the economic crisis that began in 1837.

IT IS TO BE REGRETTED that the rich and powerful too often bend the acts of government to their selfish purposes. Distinctions in society will always exist under every just government. Equality of talents, of education, or of wealth can not be produced by human institutions. In the full enjoyment of the gifts of Heaven and the fruits of superior industry, economy, and virtue, every man is equally entitled to protection by law; but when the laws undertake to add to these natural and just advantages artificial distinctions, to grant titles, gratuities, and exclusive privileges, to make the rich richer and the potent more powerful, the humble members of society—the farmers, mechanics, and laborers—who have neither the time nor the means of securing like favors to themselves, have a right to complain of the injustice of their Government. There are no necessary evils in government. Its evils exist only in its abuses. If it would confine itself to equal protection, and, as Heaven does its rains, shower its favors alike on the high and the low, the rich and the poor, it would be an unqualified blessing. In the act before me there seems to be a wide and unnecessary departure from these just principles.

Nor is our Government to be maintained or our Union preserved by invasions of the rights and powers of the several States. In thus attempting to make our General Government strong we make it weak. Its true strength consists in leaving individuals and States as much as possible to themselves—in making itself felt, not in its power, but in its beneficence; not in its control, but in its protection; not in binding the States more closely to the center, but leaving each to move unobstructed in its proper orbit.

Experience should teach us wisdom. Most of the difficulties our Government now encounters and most of the dangers which impend over our Union have sprung from an abandonment of the legitimate objects of Government by our national legislation, and the adoption of such principles as are embodied in this act. Many of our rich men have not been content with equal protection and equal benefits, but have besought us to make them richer by act of Congress. By attempting to gratify their desires we have in the results of our legislation arrayed section against section, interest against interest, and man against man, in a fearful commotion which threatens to shake the foundations of our Union. It is time to pause in our career to review our principles, and if possible revive that devoted patriotism and spirit of compromise which distinguished the sages of the Revolution and the fathers of our Union. If we can not at once, in justice to interests vested under improvident legislation, make our Government what it ought to be, we can at least take a stand against all new grants of monopolies and exclusive privileges, against any prostitution of our Government to the advancement of the few at the expense of the many, and in favor of compromise and gradual reform in our code of laws and system of political economy . . .

General Jackson was a self-made frontiersman who acquired a 640-acre cotton plantation and an aristocratic mansion, The Hermitage. He was the first to reach the White House as a "man of the people" candidate. This is an election poster of 1828, his first campaign.

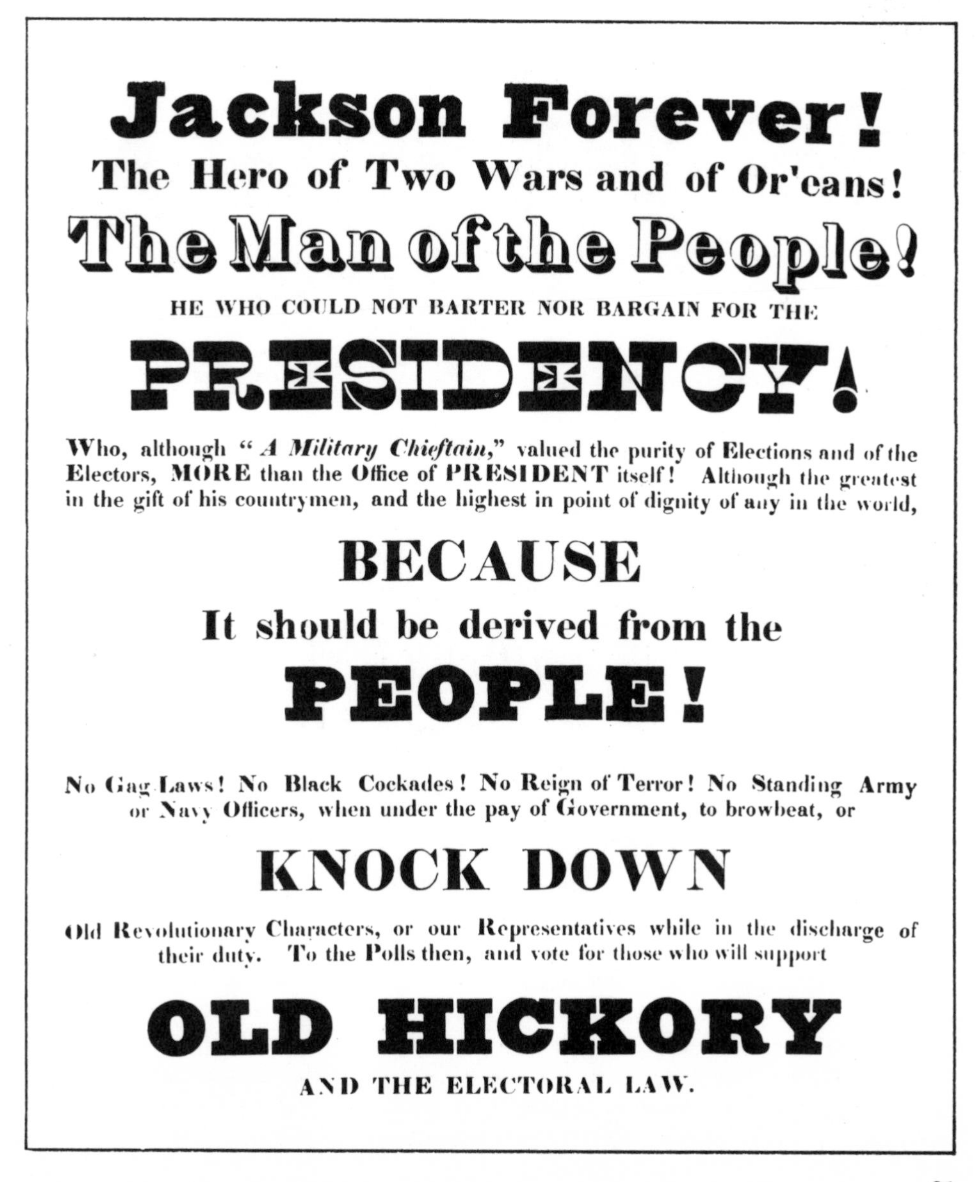

A drawing by George Catlin of Cherokees, made in the eighteen-thirties. Some of the tribe evaded Jackson's troops and hid out in the North Carolina mountains, where they still occupy a reservation.

1836 Memorial and Protest of the Cherokee Nation

We are all children of the same Great Parent

By the time of Andrew Jackson's administration, there were only five Indian nations still retaining large lands in the Southeast. The Cherokees were in Georgia, the Creeks in western Georgia and Alabama, the Choctaws and Chickasaws in Alabama and Mississippi, and the Seminoles in Florida. These were the nations that later won fame as the "Five Civilized Tribes." Each farmed on a large scale in its own territory, and lived in solidly built houses grouped in towns. When the whites of the new American nation began pushing westward, taking more and more land, some of the five tribes resisted. In 1814, the Creeks were crushed in battle by General Jackson, and lost much of their land to the United States. A few years later Jackson marched against the Seminoles and brought East Florida under military control. But the Seminoles resisted extermination, and thousands of troops and millions of dollars never succeeded in forcing complete surrender.

The Cherokees, feeling war was futile against the powerful whites, tried to assimilate. One of their brilliant leaders, Sequoyah, invented a Cherokee alphabet. His nation rapidly became literate, used printing presses, issued newspapers, developed farms, mills, and schools, intermarried with whites and Negroes, and adopted a formal constitution with a legislature. They announced they would stay permanently where they were. Georgia promptly annulled the redmen's laws and sought to evict them. President John Quincy Adams tried to protect the Indians but the state defied him and Congress ignored the problem.

When a slave discovered gold on Cherokee land, greed put an end to Cherokee hopes. Squatters stormed in as race hatred erupted. Georgia invoked martial law and jailed missionaries for helping the Indians. The tribesmen carried their case to the Supreme Court, asserting they were a separate nation under federal protection. Chief Justice Marshall ruled in the Cherokees' favor but President Jackson refused to enforce the decision. "John Marshall has made his opinion," he was supposed to have said, "now let him enforce it."

Bribery, fraud, and force drove fifteen thousand of the Indians out of their homeland by 1839. On the "trail of tears" to a reservation in Oklahoma territory, thousands died. As the mass evictions were taking place, tribal leaders on March 11, 1836, laid the "Memorial and Protest of the Cherokee Nation" before the Senate in Washington. The cry for justice went unheard.

IT CANNOT be concealed that the situation of the Cherokees is peculiarly distressing. In adverting to that situation it is not done to arouse, at this late day, a useless sympathy, but only as matter of history, and from necessity in giving a fair and impartial illustration of their difficulties. It is well known to those who have paid any attention to their history for the last five years, that they have been contending for the faithful execution of treaties between their nation and the United States, and that their distresses have not been mitigated; their efforts seem to have increased their difficulties. It remains for them to seek an adjustment by treaty, and an equitable acknowledgement of their rights and claims, so far as circumstances will permit.

For this purpose, this delegation has been deputed, as the proper organ of the Cherokee people, to settle, by treaty, their difficulties; and they wish, in sincerity, to have them settled, for the good, peace, and harmony of the whole nation. This desired end can only be attained by a contract with the constituted and acknowledged authorities of the Cherokee nation. If the difficulties are attempted to be arranged in any other way, it will not meet the wishes of the Cherokees, and their situation will be miserable beyond description, and their distresses augmented, for they will never agree to a treaty made with unauthorized individuals. Deal with them as friends, and suffer them to be relieved from their sorrows and difficulties by their own act, and whatever may be their situation in time to come, they will console themselves by the reflection, it is the dispensation of an all-wise Providence.

The delegation are sure it cannot be the wish of the Senate of the United States to ratify and have enforced upon the unoffending Cherokee people, a treaty made without their authority, false upon its face, and against the known wishes of the nation. Such is the instrument submitted to your honorable body. For the truth of this statement, should the Senate require further proof, it can be obtained from numerous persons of unimpeachable integrity and veracity. But if it be the fate of the Cherokee people, and the decree has gone forth, that they must leave their homes and native land, and seek

Sequoyah, son of a Cherokee mother and a white man. He was an artist, writer, and silversmith. in 1821 he invented the Cherokee alphabet, working from an English primer. When his people were forced out of their homes, he moved west, dying in old age in northern Mexico. The redwoods of the Pacific Coast bear his name.

ᏣᎳᎩ ᏧᎴᎯᏌᏅᎯ.

PROTECTION

CHEROKEE PHŒNIX.

VOL. I. NEW ECHOTA, WEDNESDAY JULY 9, 1828. NO. 20.

EDITED BY ELIAS BOUDINOTT.
PRINTED WEEKLY BY
ISAAC H. HARRIS,
FOR THE CHEROKEE NATION.

At $2 50 if paid in advance, $3 in six months, or $3 50 if paid at the end of the year.

To subscribers who can read only the Cherokee language the price will be $2.00 in advance, or $2,50 to be paid within the year.

Every subscription will be considered as continued unless subscribers give notice to the contrary before the commencement of a new year.

Any person procuring six subscribers, and becoming responsible for the payment, shall receive a seventh gratis.

Advertisements will be inserted at seventy-five cents per square for the first insertion, and thirty-seven and a half cents for each continuance; longer ones in proportion.

☞ All letters addressed to the Editor, post paid, will receive due attention.

Resolved by the National Committee and Council, That no person shall be allowed to erect or establish a billiard table in the Cherokee Nation, without first obtaining a license from the Treasurer of the Nation, and paying into the Treasury the sum of two hundred dollars as a tax pr. annum, and such license shall not be given for a longer period than one year at a time; and any person or persons, who shall erect or establish a billiard table without first obtaining a license as herein required shall, upon conviction pay a fine of four hundred dollars, for the benefit of the Cherokee Nation.

New Echota, Nov. 16, 1826.

JNO. ROSS, Prest N. Com.
MAJOR RIDGE, Speaker.
his
Approved—PATH ✕ KILLER.
mark.
CHARLES HICKS.
A. McCOY, Clerk of the N. Com.
E. BOUDINOTT, Clk. N. Coun.

With the help of New England missionaries, Sequoyah and his nation made his alphabet the basis of a newspaper, the *Cherokee Phoenix*. It was printed in both English and Cherokee.

a new residence in the wilds of the far west, without their consent, let them be expelled and removed by an act of Congress, when they or their posterity, in after times, may have some claims upon the magnanimity of the American people.

The delegation do solemnly declare, they would consider such an act preferable and more humane than the ratification and enforcement of a fraudulent treaty, false upon its face, and made without the consent of one of the professed contracting parties. The past history of the United States furnishes admonitions against the ratification of treaties made with unauthorized individuals. Resting upon the sacred rights of the Cherokee nation, so often recognized and solemnly guarantied on the faith of treaties, the delegation now appeal to the sympathies, the honor, good faith, and magnanimity of the United States, to preserve and protect their nation from fraud, rapine, plunder, and destruction. They have now discharged their duty to themselves and to their unfortunate people, with that frankness that becomes the occasion. Their case is fairly before your honorable body, and the destiny of the Cherokee people in the hands of the American Senate.

We are all children of the same Great Parent, and bound to be kind to each other, without regard to the situation in which we may be placed. If an earthly parent have a child unfortunately weak and poor, how would he feel to see the brothers of that child abusing it for its misfortunes, insulting its feelings, exulting in their own superiority, curling the lip of scorn, with a significant cant of the head, at its earnest supplication for justice? Let every man's own heart give him the answer. You have before you that unfortunate child in the weak and dependent Cherokees. With hands elevated towards the throne of grace and mercy, we all supplicate, saying: Our brothers, is it true you will drive us from the land of our nativity, and from the tombs of our fathers and our mothers? We know you possess the power, but, by the tie that unites us yonder, we implore you to forbear. Our case is with you.

Ralph Waldo Emerson, a crayon portrait by Samuel Worcester Rowse. Emerson was born in Boston in 1803. He settled in nearby Concord in 1835, forming friendships there with Thoreau, Alcott, and Hawthorne.

The free and brave scholar

America's "intellectual Declaration of Independence" was what Oliver Wendell Holmes called the Phi Beta Kappa address Ralph Waldo Emerson delivered at Harvard in 1837. "We have listened too long to the courtly muses of Europe," said the Concord philosopher. "We will walk on our own feet; we will work with our own hands; we will speak our own minds."

Emerson had left the Unitarian pulpit five years earlier to preach the intuitive doctrine of transcendentalism with its belief that divinity was latent in every man. "Whoso would be a man must be a nonconformist," he said. "Nothing is at last sacred but the integrity of your own mind."

Emerson's ideas tugged the scholar into the tide of reform. "Only so much do I know as I have lived. . . . The true scholar grudges every opportunity of action past by, as a loss of power. . . . Experience is converted into thought." Let the scholar turn from his narrow specialty to the broad world of ideas and action, he pointed out, and "the huge world will come round to him."

At noon that August day, 215 members of Phi Beta Kappa and their guests heard Emerson's lecture. It was soon printed: Emerson was pleased when all five hundred copies sold in a month.

Mr. President and Gentlemen:

I GREET YOU on the recommencement of our literary year. Our anniversary is one of hope, and, perhaps, not enough of labor. . . . Our day of dependence, our long apprenticeship to the learning of other lands, draws to a close. The millions that around us are rushing into life, cannot always be fed on the sere remains of foreign harvests. Events, actions arise, that must be sung, that will sing themselves. . . .

In this hope I accept the topic which not only usage but the nature of our association seem to prescribe to this day,—the AMERICAN SCHOLAR. Year by year we come up hither to read one more chapter of his biography. Let us inquire what light new days and events have thrown on his character and his hopes.

It is one of those fables which out of an unknown antiquity convey an unlooked-for wisdom, that the gods, in the beginning divided Man into men, that he might be more helpful to himself; just as the hand was divided into fingers, the better to answer its end.

The old fable covers a doctrine ever new and sublime; that there is One Man,—present to all particular men only partially, or through one faculty;

The caricatures on this and the next pages were drawn by Christopher P. Cranch in amusing illustration of Emerson's "American Scholar" oration. This one is labelled "A popgun is a popgun."

and that you must take the whole society to find the whole man. Man is not a farmer, or a professor, or an engineer, but he is all. Man is priest, and scholar, and statesman, and producer, and soldier. In the *divided* or social state these functions are parcelled out to individuals, each of whom aims to do his stint of the joint work, whilst each other performs his. . . .

Man is thus metamorphosed into a thing, into many things. The planter, who is Man sent out into the field to gather food, is seldom cheered by any idea of the true dignity of his ministry. He sees his bushel and his cart, and nothing beyond, and sinks into the farmer, instead of Man on the farm. The tradesman scarcely ever gives an ideal worth to his work, but is ridden by the routine of his craft, and the soul is subject to dollars. The priest becomes a form; the attorney a statute-book; the mechanic a machine; the sailor a rope of the ship.

In this distribution of functions the scholar is the delegated intellect. In the right state he is *Man Thinking*. In the degenerate state, when the victim of society, he tends to become a mere thinker, or still worse, the parrot of other men's thinking.

In this view of him, as Man Thinking, the theory of his office is contained. Him Nature solicits with all her placid, all her monitory pictures; him the past instructs; him the future invites. Is not indeed every man a student, and do not all things exist for the student's behoof? And, finally, is not the true scholar the only true master? But the old oracle said, "All things have two handles: beware of the wrong one." In life, too often, the scholar errs with mankind and forfeits his privilege. Let us see him in his school, and consider him in reference to the main influences he receives.

I. The first in time and the first in importance of the influences upon the mind is that of nature. Every day, the sun; and, after sunset, Night and her stars. Ever the winds blow; ever the grass grows. Every day, men and women, conversing—beholding and beholden. The scholar is he of all men whom this spectacle most engages. He must settle its value in his mind. What is nature to him? There is never a beginning, there is never an end, to the inexplicable continuity of this web of God, but always circular power returning into itself. Therein it resembles his own spirit, whose beginning, whose ending, he never can find,—so entire, so boundless. Far too as her splendors shine, system on system shooting like rays, upward, downward, without centre, without circumference,—in the mass and in the particle, Nature hastens to render account of herself to the mind. Classification begins. To the young mind every thing is individual, stands by itself. By and by, it finds how to join two things and see in them one nature; then three, then three thousand; and so, tyrannized over by its own unifying instinct, it goes on tying things together, diminishing anomalies, discovering roots running under ground whereby contrary and remote things cohere and flower out from one stem. It presently learns that since the dawn of history there has been a constant accumulation and classifying of facts. But what is classification but the perceiving that these objects are not chaotic, and are not foreign, but have a law which is also a law of the human mind? The astronomer discovers that geometry, a pure abstraction of the human mind, is the measure of planetary motion. The chemist finds proportions and intelligible method throughout matter; and science is nothing but the finding of analogy, identity, in the most remote parts. The ambitious soul sits down before each refractory fact; one after another reduces all strange constitutions, all new powers, to their class and the law, and goes on forever to animate the last fibre of organization, the outskirts of nature, by insight.

. . . He shall see that nature is the opposite of the soul, answering to it part for part. One is seal and one is print. Its beauty is the beauty of his own mind. Its laws are the laws of his own mind. Nature then becomes to him the measure of his attainments. So much of nature as he is ignorant of, so much of his own mind does he not yet possess. And, in fine, the ancient precept, "Know thyself," and the modern precept, "Study nature," become at last one maxim.

II. The next great influence into the spirit of the scholar is the mind of the Past,—in whatever form, whether of literature, of art, of institutions, that mind is inscribed. Books are the best type of the influence of the past, and perhaps we shall get at the truth,—learn the amount of this influence more conveniently,—by considering their value alone.

The theory of books is noble. The scholar of the first age received into him the world around; brooded thereon; gave it the new arrangement of his own mind, and uttered it again. It came into him life; it went out from him truth. It came to him short-lived actions; it went out from him immortal thoughts. It came to him business; it went from him poetry. It was dead fact; now, it is quick thought. It can stand, and it can go. It now endures, it now flies, it now inspires. Precisely in proportion to the depth of mind from which it issued, so high does it soar, so long does it sing. . . .

Yet hence arises a grave mischief. The sacredness which attaches to the act of creation, the act of thought, is transferred to the record. The poet chanting was felt to be a divine man: henceforth the chant is divine also. The writer was a just and wise spirit: henceforward it is settled the book is perfect; as love of the hero corrupts into worship of his statue. Instantly the book becomes noxious: the guide is a tyrant. The sluggish and perverted mind of the multitude, slow to open to the incursions of Reason, having once so opened, having once received this book, stands upon it, and makes an outcry if it is disparaged. Colleges are built on it. Books are written on it by thinkers, not by Man Thinking; by men of talent, that is, who start wrong, who set out from accepted dogmas, not from their own sight of principles. Meek young men grow up in libraries, believing it their duty to accept the views which Cicero, which Locke, which Bacon, have given; forgetful that Cicero, Locke, and Bacon were only young men in libraries when they wrote these books. . . .

III. There goes in the world a notion that the

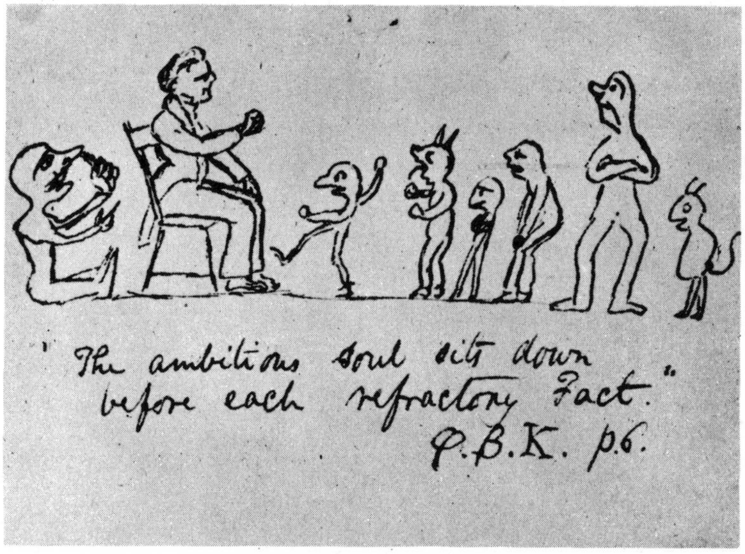

"Before each refractory fact."

scholar should be a recluse, a valetudinarian,—as unfit for any handwork or public labor as a penknife for an axe. The so-called "practical men" sneer at speculative men, as if, because they speculate or *see*, they could do nothing. I have heard it said that the clergy,—who are always, more universally than any other class, the scholars of their day,—are addressed as women; that the rough, spontaneous conversation of men they do not hear, but only a mincing and diluted speech. They are often virtually disfranchised; and indeed there are advocates for their celibacy. As far as this is true of the studious classes, it is not just and wise. Action is with the scholar subordinate, but it is essential. Without it he is not yet man. Without it thought can never ripen into truth. Whilst the world hangs before the eye as a cloud of beauty, we cannot even see its beauty. Inaction is cowardice, but there can be no scholar without the heroic mind. The preamble of thought, the transition through which it passes from the unconscious to the conscious, is action. Only so much do I know, as I have lived. Instantly we know whose words are loaded with life, and whose **not.** . . .

If it were only for a vocabulary, the scholar would be covetous of action. Life is our dictionary. Years are well spent in country labors; in town; in the insight into trades and manufactures; in frank intercourse with many men and women; in science; in art; to the one end of mastering in all their facts a language by which to illustrate and embody our perceptions. I learn immediately from any speaker how much he has already lived, through the poverty or the splendor of his speech. Life lies behind us as the quarry from whence we get tiles and copestones for the masonry of to-day. This is the way to learn grammar. Colleges and books only copy the language which the field and the work-yard made.

But the final value of action, like that of books, and better than books, is that it is a resource. That great principle of Undulation in nature, that shows itself in the inspiring and expiring of the breath; in desire and satiety; in the ebb and flow of the sea; in day and night; in heat and cold; and, as yet more deeply ingrained in every atom and every fluid, is known to us under the name of Polarity,—these "fits of easy transmission and reflection," as Newton called them, are the law of nature because they are the law of spirit.

The mind now thinks, now acts, and each fit reproduces the other. When the artist has exhausted his materials, when the fancy no longer paints, when thoughts are no longer apprehended and books are a weariness,—he has always the resource *to live*. Character is higher than intellect. Thinking is the function. Living is the functionary. The stream retreats to its source. A great soul will be strong to live, as well as strong to think. Does he lack organ or medium to impart his truths? He can still fall

"This is my music."

"They pin me down."

back on this elemental force of living them. This is a total act. Thinking is a partial act. Let the grandeur of justice shine in his affairs. Let the beauty of affection cheer his lowly roof. Those "far from fame," who dwell and act with him, will feel the force of his constitution in the doings and passages of the day better than it can be measured by any public and designed display. Time shall teach him that the scholar loses no hour which the man lives. Herein he unfolds the sacred germ of his instinct, screened from influence. What is lost in seemliness is gained in strength. Not out of those on whom systems of education have exhausted their culture, comes the helpful giant to destroy the old or to build the new, but out of unhandselled savage nature; out of terrible Druids and Berserkers come at last Alfred and Shakspeare. . . .

I have now spoken of the education of the scholar by nature, by books, and by action. It remains to say somewhat of his duties.

They are such as become Man Thinking. They may all be comprised in self-trust. . . .

. . . it becomes him to feel all confidence in himself, and to defer never to the popular cry. He and he only knows the world. The world of any moment is the merest appearance. Some great decorum, some fetish of a government, some ephemeral trade, or war, or man, is cried up by half mankind and cried down by the other half, as if all depended on this particular up or down. The odds are that the whole question is not worth the poorest thought which the scholar has lost in listening to the controversy. Let him not quit his belief that a popgun is a popgun, though the ancient and honorable of the earth affirm it to be the crack of doom. In silence, in steadiness, in severe abstraction, let him hold by himself; add observation to observation, patient of neglect, patient of reproach, and bide his own time,—happy enough if he can satisfy himself alone that this day he has seen something truly. . . .

In self-trust all the virtues are comprehended. Free should the scholar be,—free and brave. Free even to the definition of freedom, "without any hindrance that does not arise out of his own constitution." Brave; for fear is a thing which a scholar by his very function puts behind him. Fear always springs from ignorance. . . . The world is his who can see through its pretension. What deafness, what stone-blind custom, what overgrown error you behold is there only by sufferance,—by your sufferance. See it to be a lie, and you have already dealt it its mortal blow.

Yes, we are the cowed,—we the trustless. It is a mischievous notion that we are come late into nature; that the world was finished a long time ago. As the world was plastic and fluid in the hands of God, so it is ever to so much of his attributes as we bring to it. To ignorance and sin, it is flint. They adapt themselves to it as they may; but in proportion as a man has any thing in him divine, the firmament flows before him and takes his signet and form. . . .

Another sign of our times, also marked by an analogous political movement, is the new importance given to the single person. Every thing that tends to insulate the individual,—to surround him with barriers of natural respect, so that each man shall feel the world is his, and man shall treat with man as a sovereign state with a sovereign state,—tends to true union as well as greatness. . . . The scholar is that man who must take up into himself all the ability of the time, all the contributions of the past, all the hopes of the future. He must be an university of knowledges. If there be one lesson more than another which should pierce his ear, it is, The world is nothing, the man is all; in yourself is the law of all nature, and you know not yet how a globule of sap ascends; in yourself slumbers the whole of Reason; it is for you to know all; it is for you to dare all. Mr. President and Gentlemen, this confidence in the unsearched might of man belongs, by all motives, by all prophecy, by all preparation, to the American Scholar. We have listened too long to the courtly muses of Europe. The spirit of the American freeman is already suspected to be timid, imitative, tame. Public and private avarice make the air we breathe thick and fat. The scholar is decent, indolent, complaisant. See already the tragic consequence. The mind of this country, taught to aim at low objects, eats upon itself. There is no work for any but the decorous and the complaisant. Young men of the fairest promise, who begin life upon our shores, inflated by the mountain winds, shined upon by all the stars of God, find the earth below not in unison with these, but are hindered from action by the disgust which the principles on which business is managed inspire, and turn drudges, or die of disgust, some of them suicides. What is the remedy? They did not yet see, and thousands of young men as hopeful now crowding to the barriers for the career do not yet see, that if the single man plant himself indomitably on his instincts, and there abide, the huge world will come round to him. Patience,—patience; with the shades of all the good and great for company; and for solace the perspective of your own infinite life; and for work the study and the communication of principles, the making those instincts prevalent, the conversion of the world. Is it not the chief disgrace in the world, not to be an unit;—not to be reckoned one character;—not to yield that peculiar fruit which each man was created to bear, but to be reckoned in the gross, in the hundred, or the thousand, of the party, the section, to which we belong; and our opinion predicted geographically, as the north, or the south? Not so, brothers and friends—please God, ours shall not be so. We will walk on our own feet; we will work with our own hands; we will speak our own minds. The study of letters shall be no longer a name for pity, for doubt, and for sensual indulgence. The dread of man and the love of man shall be a wall of defence and a wreath of joy around all. A nation of men will for the first time exist, because each believes himself inspired by the Divine Soul which also inspires all men.

The true dignity of labor

Theodore Parker died of tuberculosis in Italy, where this cameo was made of him in 1859. At forty-nine, Parker had worn himself out in a prodigious life of action devoted to reform movements, especially abolitionism. He was a leader of the Boston Vigilance Committee and minister-at-large to the slaves seeking refuge in his city.

The problem of property and wealth and their influence upon the social order loomed large by the time Andrew Jackson came to power. "See the unnatural disparity in man's condition," the young Rev. Theodore Parker told his Boston congregation. "Bloated opulence and starving penury in the same street. See the pauperism, want, licentiousness, intemperance, and crime in the midst of us; see the havoc made of woman; see the poor deserted by their elder brother, while it is their sweat which enriches your ground, builds your railroads, and piles up your costly houses."

To make democracy work in an industrial age, the inequalities between wealth and poverty must be diminished. Simultaneously social reform moved in two directions: the organization of workers into trade unions to win better wages and the intercession of government in behalf of the poor.

Theodore Parker, himself the son of a poor farmer and mechanic, groaned when he looked into the evils of the new industrial society. Christianity, the minister believed, must be not simply a belief, but a life. It must be taken out of old books and into the world. In the New England mills he saw women and children work thirteen-hour shifts, from daylight to dark, at pitiful wages and under scandalous conditions. Again and again he preached and wrote against this economic injustice. In 1841, his "Thoughts on Labor" appeared in the April issue of the new transcendentalist magazine, the Dial.

Children worked alongside adults in the mills of New England during Parker's day. Laboring often at tasks beyond their strength, they pocketed hardly more than $1 a week. Public protest brought some states to legislate against hiring children under twelve, but major reform was slow and hard in coming.

THERE ARE SOME who count labor a curse and a punishment. They regard the necessity of work as the greatest evil brought on us by the "Fall"; as a curse that will cling to our last sand. Many submit to this yoke, and toil, and save, in hope to leave their posterity out of the reach of this primitive curse!

Others, still more foolish, regard it as a disgrace. Young men,—the children of honest parents, who living by their manly and toil-hardened hands, bear up the burthen of the world on their shoulders, and eat with thankful hearts their daily bread, won in the sweat of their face,—are ashamed of their fathers' occupation, and forsaking the plough, the chisel, or the forge, seek a livelihood in what is sometimes named a more respectable and genteel vocation; that is, in a calling which demands less of the hands than their fathers' hardy craft, and quite often less of the head likewise; for that imbecility which drives men to those callings has its seat mostly in a higher region than the hands. Affianced damsels beg their lovers to discover (or invent) some ancestor in buckram who did not work. The Sophomore in a small college is ashamed of his father who wears a blue frock, and his dusty brother who toils with the saw and the axe. These men, after they have wiped off the dirt and the soot of their early life, sometimes become arrant coxcombs, and standing like the head of Hermes without hands, having only a mouth, make faces at such as continue to serve the state by plain handiwork. . . .

It were to be wished that this notion of labor being disgraceful was confined to vain young men, and giddy maidens of idle habits and weak heads, for then it would be looked upon as one of the diseases of early life, which we know must come, and rejoice when our young friends have happily passed through it, knowing it is one of "the ills that flesh is heir to," but is not very grievous, and comes but once in the lifetime. This aversion to labor, this notion that it is a curse and a disgrace, this selfish desire to escape from the general and natural lot of man is the sacramental sin of "the better class" in our great cities. The children of the poor pray to be rid of work; and what son of a rich man learns a trade or tills the soil with his own hands? Many men look on the ability to be idle as the most desirable and honorable ability. They glory in being the mouth that consumes, not the hand that works. Yet one would suppose a man of useless hands and idle head, in the midst of God's world, where each thing works for all, in the midst of the toil and sweat of the human race, must needs make an apology for his sloth, and would ask pardon for violating the common law, and withdrawing his neck from the general yoke of humanity. Still more does he need an apology if he is active only in getting into his hands the result of others' work. But is not so. The man who is rich enough to be idle, values himself on his leisure; and what is worse, others value him for it. Active men must make a shamefaced excuse for being busy, and working men for their toil, as if business and toil were not the duty of all, and the support of the world. In certain countries men are divided horizontally into two classes, the men who work and the men who rule, and the latter despise the employment of the former as mean and degrading. It is the slave's duty to plough, said a heathen poet, and a freeman's business to enjoy at leisure the fruit of that ploughing. This same foolish notion finds favor with many here. It is a remnant of those barbarous times when all labor was performed by serfs and bondsmen, and exemption from toil was the exclusive sign of the free-born. But this notion, that labor is disgraceful, conflicts as sharply with our political institutions as it does with common sense, and the law God has writ on man. An old author, centuries before Christ, was so far enlightened on this point as to see the true dignity of manual work, and to say, "God is well pleased with honest works; he suffers the laboring man, who ploughs the earth by night and day, to call his life most noble. If he is good and true, he offers continual sacrifice to God, and is not so lustrous in his dress as in his heart."

Manual labor is a blessing and a dignity. But to state the case on its least favorable issue, admit it were both a disgrace and a curse, would a true man desire to escape it for himself, and leave the curse to fall on other men? Certainly not. The generous

A sketch of Parker preaching in New York, made by Eyre Crow who accompanied William Thackeray during the British novelist's 1852 tour of America.

soldier fronts death, and charges in the cannon's mouth; it is the coward who lingers behind. If labor were hateful, as the proud would have us believe, then they who bear its burthens, and feed and clothe the human race, and fetch and carry for them, should be honored as those have always been who defend society in war. If it be glorious, as the world fancies, to repel a human foe, how much more is he to be honored who stands up when Want comes upon us, like an armed man, and puts him to rout! One would fancy the world was mad when it bowed in reverence to those who by superior cunning possessed themselves of the earnings of others, while it made wide the mouth and drew out the tongue at such as do the world's work. "Without these," said an ancient, "cannot a city be inhabited, but they shall not be sought for in public council, nor sit high in the congregation"; and those few men and women who are misnamed the World, in their wisdom have confirmed the saying. Thus they honor those who sit in idleness and ease; they extol such as defend a state with arms, or those who collect in their hands the result of Asiatic or American industry; but pass by with contempt the men who rear corn and cattle, and weave and spin, and fish and build for the whole human race. Yet if the state of labor were so hard and disgraceful as some fancy, the sluggard in fine raiment, and that trim figure which, like the lilies in the Scripture, neither toils nor spins, and is yet clothed in more glory than Solomon, would both bow down before colliers and farmers, and bless them as the benefactors of the race. Christianity has gone still further, and makes a man's greatness consist in the amount of service he renders to the world. Certainly he is the most honorable who, by his head or his hand, does the greatest and best work for his race. The noblest soul the world ever saw appeared not in the ranks of the indolent; but "took on him the form of a servant," and when he washed his disciples' feet, meant something not very generally understood, perhaps, in the nineteenth century.

"Theodore Parker in Heaven—a German bookstore" was the wry title Christopher Cranch gave his cartoon of the friend he often met when both visited Brook Farm in West Roxbury. Parker had an unlimited thirst for knowledge, mastered many languages, and collected a huge library.

Now, manual labor, though an unavoidable duty, though designed as a blessing, and naturally both a pleasure and a dignity, is often abused till, by its terrible excess, it becomes really a punishment and a curse. It is only a proper amount of work that is a blessing. Too much of it wears out the body before its time; cripples the mind, debases the soul, blunts the senses, and chills the affections. It makes a man a spinning-jenny, or a ploughing-machine, and not "a being of a large discourse, that looks before and after." He ceases to be a man, and becomes a thing.

In a rational and natural state of society,—that is, one in which every man went forward towards the true end he was designed to reach; towards perfection in the use of all his senses; towards perfection in wisdom, virtue, affection, and religion,—labor would never interfere with the culture of what is best in each man. His daily business would be a school to aid in developing the whole man, body and soul, because he would then do what nature fitted him to do. Then his business would be really his calling. The diversity of gifts is quite equal to the diversity of work to be done. There is some one thing which each man can do with pleasure, and better than any other man; because he was born to do it. Then all men would labor, each at his proper vocation, and an excellent farmer would not be spoiled to make a poor lawyer, a blundering physician, or a preacher who puts the world asleep. Then a small body of men would not be pampered in indolence, to grow up into gouty worthlessness, and die of inertia; nor would the large part of men be worn down as now be excessive toil before half their life is spent. They would not be so severely tasked as to have no time to read, think, and converse. When he walked abroad, the laboring man would not be forced to catch mere transient glimpses of the flowers by the way-side, or the stars over his head, as the dogs, it is said, drink the waters of the Nile, running while they drink, afraid the crocodiles should seize them if they stop. When he looked from his window at the landscape, distress need not stare at him from every bush. He would then have leisure to cultivate his mind and heart no less than to do the world's work.

George Ripley, as he looked in 1882. Inspired by William Ellery Channing's denunciation of the "evils of competition," Ripley, with his wife and sister, and a handful of converts, planted their utopia on a few acres in West Roxbury, near Boston.

A life of wisdom, justice, and love

The goal of a more just distribution of wealth through labor organization was hard to achieve in early nineteenth-century America. A trade union was a "conspiracy" in the eyes of the law. To strike for higher wages or better working conditions often meant arrest and imprisonment. It was 1842 before the first state, Massachusetts, proclaimed it was not criminal for workers to organize in their own interests. Progress toward economic democracy was so slow that many humanitarians developed plans for utopian communities that would dignify labor and restore it to equality. Experiments in cooperative living sprang up from Maine to Wisconsin. One of the first, and the best known, was founded in Massachusetts in April, 1841, by a small band under the leadership of George Ripley, a former Unitarian minister. It hoped to be a self-supporting community, uniting labor and culture. Many among the group were to become quite distinguished—Nathaniel Hawthorne, the editors Charles A. Dana and George William Curtis, the music critic John S. Dwight, Isaac Hecker, founder of the Paulist Fathers—but like all the other utopias of that day, Brook Farm was a failure. It neither solved problems nor reformed institutions. But its idealism, recorded in the Brook Farm constitution, was a measure of what the humanitarians thought was wrong with their society.

IN ORDER more effectually to promote the great purposes of human culture; to establish the external relations of life on a basis of wisdom and purity; to apply the principles of justice and love to our social organization in accordance with the laws of Divine Providence; to substitute a system of brotherly cooperation for one of selfish competition; to secure to our children and those who may be entrusted to our care, the benefits of the highest physical, intellectual, and moral education in the present state of human knowledge, the resources at our command will permit; to institute an attractive, efficient, and productive system of industry; to prevent the exercise of worldly anxiety by the competent supply of our necessary wants; to diminish the desire of excessive accumulation by making the acquisition of individual property subservient to upright and disinterested uses; to guarantee to each other the means

Brook Farm buildings, sketched as they looked in the eighteen-forties. On the right is the main building, called The Hive.

of physical support, and of spiritual progress, and this to impart a greater freedom, simplicity, truthfulness, refinement, and moral dignity, to our mode of life,—

We, the undersigned, do unite in a Voluntary Association, to wit:

Article 1. The name and style of the Association shall be "(The Brook Farm) Institute of Agriculture and Education." All persons who shall hold one or more shares in the stock of the Association, and shall sign the articles of agreement, or who shall hereafter be admitted by the pleasure of the Association, shall be members thereof.

Art. 2. No religious test shall ever be required of any member of the Association; no authority assumed over individual freedom of opinion by the Association, nor by any member over another; nor shall anyone be held accountable to the Association except for such acts as violate rights of the members, and the essential principles on which the Association is founded; and in such cases the relation of any member may be suspended, or discontinued, at the pleasure of the Association.

Art. 3. The members of this Association shall own and manage such real and personal estate, in joint-stock proprietorship, as may, from time to time, be agreed on, and establish branches of industry as may be deemed expedient and desirable.

Art. 4. The Association shall provide such employment for all of its members as shall be adapted

Young Nathaniel Hawthorne, painted by Charles Osgood in 1840, while he was a weigher and gauger in the Boston Custom House. The next year he put his $1000 savings into Brook Farm, hoping that in return for his labor he would have security and leisure to write. Disappointed, he later sued Ripley for half his investment, a blow which added to the community's misfortunes.

to their capacities, habits, and tastes, and each member shall select and perform such operation of labor, whether corporal or mental, as he shall deem best suited to his own endowments, and the benefit of the Association.

Art. 5. The members of this Association shall be paid for all labor performed under its direction and for its advantage, at a fixed and equal rate, both for men and women. This rate shall not exceed one dollar per day, nor shall more than ten hours in the day be paid for as a day's labor.

Art. 6. The Association shall furnish to all its members, their children and family dependents, house-rent, fuel, food and clothing, and all other comforts and advantages possible, at the actual cost, as nearly as the same can be ascertained; but no charge shall be made for education, medical or nursing attendance, or the use of the library, public rooms or baths to the members; nor shall any charge be paid for food, rent, or fuel by those deprived of labor by sickness, nor for food of children under ten years of age, unless at the special request of the individual by whom the charges are paid, or unless the credits in his favor exceed, or equal, the amount of such charges.

Art. 7. All labor performed for the Association shall be duly credited, and all articles furnished shall be charged, and a full settlement made with every member once every year.

Art. 8. Every child over ten years of age shall be charged for food, clothing, and articles furnished at cost, and shall be credited for his labor, not exceeding fifty cents per day, and on the completion of his education in the Association at the age of twenty, shall be entitled to a certificate of stock, to the amount of credits in his favor, and may be admitted a member of the Association.

Art. 9. Every share-holder in the joint-stock proprietorship of the Association, shall be paid on such stock, at the rate of five per cent, annually.

Art. 10. The net profits of the Association remaining in the treasury after the payments of all demands for interest on stock, labor performed, and necessary repairs, and improvements, shall be divided into a number of shares corresponding with the number of day's labor, and every member shall be entitled to one share for every day's labor performed by him.

Art. 11. All payments may be made in certificates of stock at the option of the Association; but in any case of need, to be decided by himself, every member may be permitted to draw on the funds of the treasury to an amount not exceeding the credits in his favor.

Charles S. Dana, at Brook Farm for his health, worked as captain of the waiters' crew. Later he became the famous editor of the New York *Sun*.

Another editor-to-be who made the trip to Arcadia with Ripley was George W. Curtis of *Harper's Weekly*.

THE HARBINGER,

DEVOTED TO SOCIAL AND POLITICAL PROGRESS.

ALL THINGS, AT THE PRESENT DAY, STAND PROVIDED AND PREPARED, AND AWAIT THE LIGHT.

BURGESS, STRINGER, AND COMPANY, No. 222 BROADWAY, NEW YORK. | PUBLISHED BY THE BROOK FARM PHALANX. | REDDING AND COMPANY, No. 8 STATE STREET, BOSTON

VOLUME I. | SATURDAY, JULY 26, 1845. | NUMBER 7.

CORRESPONDENCE.

centuries since, He did materially ; — and, not to recognise the Divinity of the

ity shall be endowed with " power from on high," and nerved with Omnipotence.

The mastead of *The Harbinger*, published by the Brook Farmers. The paper survived the community's collapse, continuing until February, 1849, under George Ripley's editorship. Eight years later, Ripley and Dana launched the first American encyclopedia, the *New American Encyclopedia.*

Horace Greeley, who founded his New York *Tribune* the year Brook Farm was born. The noted reformer took up Charles Fourier's theory that a society should be organized to permit congenial and varied work for all and in 1844 convinced Ripley to remodel Brook Farm along these lines. It became a notable example of the Fourier phalanx, but it lost the interest of the transcendentalists.

Margaret Fuller, who with Emerson and Alcott often visited Brook Farm to lead evenings of conversation. She helped edit the *Dial*, one of the first journals to carry comment on the experiment, and wrote the pioneering feminist work, *Woman in the Nineteenth Century*.

Margaret Fuller

Art. 12. The Association shall hold an annual meeting for the choice of officers, and such other necessary business as shall come before them.

Art. 13. The officers of the Association shall be twelve directors, divided into four departments, as follows: first, General Direction; second, Direction of Agriculture; third, Direction of Education; fourth, Direction of Finance; consisting of three persons each, provided that the same persons may be a member of each Direction at the pleasure of the Association.

Art. 14. The Chairman of the General Direction shall be presiding officer in the Association, and together with the Direction of Finance, shall constitute a Board of Trustees, by whom the property of the Association shall be managed.

Art. 15. The General Direction shall oversee and manage the affairs of the Association so that every department shall be carried on in an orderly and efficient manner. Each department shall be under the general supervision of its own Direction, which shall select, and, in accordance with the General Direction, shall appoint, all such overseers, directors and agents, as shall be necessary to the complete and systematic organization of the department, and shall have full authority to appoint such persons to these stations as they shall judge best qualified for the same.

Art. 16. No Directors shall be deemed to possess any rank superior to the other members of the Association, nor shall be chosen in reference to any other consideration than their capacity to serve the Association; nor shall they be paid for their official service except at the rate of one dollar for ten hours in a day, actually employed in official duties.

Art. 17. The Association may, from time to time, adopt such rules and regulations, not inconsistent with the spirit and purpose of the Articles of Agreement, as shall be found expedient and necessary.

1843 Dorothea Dix: Memorial to the Massachusetts Legislature

I come to present the strong claims of suffering humanity

Dorothea Lynde Dix was born in Maine in 1802. To her credit is the enlargement or establishment of state hospitals for the insane in fifteen states and in Canada and England. Appointed superintendent of women nurses in the Civil War, she was of great value to the Union forces. She died in 1887.

One of the most dedicated leaders of the many reform movements America knew in the eighteen-thirties and forties was Dorothea Dix. At nineteen, she was running a school for girls in Boston. At thirty-six, she began investigating the barbarities practiced by society upon the poor, the insane, and the imprisoned. The inhuman treatment of the dependent, permitted to continue by public indifference, aroused her pity and anger. By 1841 she was speaking in public against man's inhumanity to man and demanding reforms which had earlier been advocated by the Quakers and European philanthropists. Her appeals were vivid and factual, based upon the closest observation of reality. In three years she visited eighteen state penitentiaries, three hundred county jails and over five hundred almshouses, as well as hospitals and other institutions.

In January, 1843, she presented her Memorial to the Legislature of Massachusetts, the first of many exposés by which she won support for improving the conditions and treatment of the insane.

I COME to present the strong claims of suffering humanity. I come to place before the Legislature of Massachusetts the condition of the miserable, the desolate, the outcast. I come as the advocate of helpless, forgotten, insane, and idiotic men and women; of beings sunk to a condition from which the most unconcerned would start with real horror; of beings wretched in our prisons, and more wretched in our almshouses. . . .

If my pictures are displeasing, coarse, and severe, my subjects, it must be recollected, offer no tranquil, refined, or composing features. The condition of human beings, reduced to the extremest states of degradation and misery cannot be exhibited in softened language, or adorn a polished page.

I proceed, gentlemen, briefly to call your attention to the *present* state of insane persons confined within this Commonwealth, in *cages, closets, cellars, stalls, pens! Chained, naked, beaten with rods,* and *lashed* into obedience. . . .

. . . In illustration of my subject, I offer the following extracts from my Note-book and Journal:—

Springfield. In the jail, one lunatic woman, furiously mad, a State pauper, improperly situated, both in regard to the prisoners, the keepers, and herself. It is a case of extreme self-forgetfulness and oblivion to all the decencies of life, to describe which would be to repeat only the grossest scenes. She is much worse since leaving Worcester. In the almshouse of the same town is a woman apparently only needing judicious care, and some well-chosen employment, to make it unnecessary to confine her in solitude, in a dreary unfurnished room. Her appeals for employment and companionship are most touching, but the mistress replied "she had no time to attend to her." . . .

Lincoln. A woman in a cage. *Medford.* One idiotic subject chained, and one in a close stall for seventeen years. *Pepperell.* One often doubly chained, hand and foot; another violent; several peaceable now. *Brookfield.* One man caged, comfortable. *Granville.* One often closely confined; now losing the use of his limbs from want of exercise. *Charlemont.* One man caged. *Savoy.* One man caged. *Lenox.* Two in the jail, against whose unfit condition there the jailer protests.

Dedham. The insane disadvantageously placed in the jail. In the almshouse, two females in stalls, situated in the main building; lie in wooden bunks filled with straw; always shut up. One of these subjects is supposed curable. The overseers of the poor have declined giving her a trial at the hospital, as I was informed, on account of expense. . . .

Besides the above, I have seen many who, part of the year, are chained or caged. The use of cages all but universal. Hardly a town but can refer to some not distant period of using them; chains are less common; negligences frequent; wilful abuse less frequent than sufferings proceeding from ignorance, or want of consideration. . . . I give a few illustrations; but description fades before reality.

Danvers. November. Visited the almshouse. A large building, much out of repair. Understand a new one is in contemplation. Here are from fifty-six to sixty inmates, one idiotic, three insane; one of the latter in close confinement at all times.

. . . Found the mistress, and was conducted to the place which was called "the home" of the *forlorn* maniac, a young woman, exhibiting a condition of neglect and misery blotting out the faintest idea of comfort, and outraging every sentiment of decency. She had been, I learnt, "a respectable person, industrious and worthy. Disappointments and trials shook her mind, and, finally, laid prostrate reason and self-control. She became a maniac for life. She had been at Worcester Hospital for a considerable time, and had been returned as incurable." The mistress told

Prison reformers opposed such legal cruelties as the whipping post (above), suspension from pulleys (below), and the crown (bottom), portrayed in prints of Miss Dix's time. The disciplinary ideal was to "be pitiless and just."

The New Jersey State Hospital at Trenton was the first such institution to be established directly as a result of Dorothea Dix's efforts. "My first-born child" was how she recalled it.

me she understood that, "while there, she was comfortable and decent." Alas, what a change was here exhibited! She had passed from one degree of violence to another, in swift progress. There she stood, clinging to or beating upon the bars of her caged apartment, the contracted size of which afforded space only for increasing accumulations of filth, a *foul* spectacle. There she stood with naked arms and dishevelled hair, the unwashed frame invested with fragments of unclean garments, the air so extremely offensive, though ventilation was afforded on all sides save one, that it was not possible to remain beyond a few moments without retreating for recovery to the outward air. Irritation of body, produced by utter filth and exposure, incited her to the horrid process of tearing off her skin by inches. Her face, neck, and person were thus disfigured to hideousness. She held up a fragment just rent off. To my exclamation of horror, the mistress replied: "Oh, we can't help it. Half the skin is off sometimes. We can do nothing with her; and it makes no difference what she eats, for she consumes her own filth as readily as the food which is brought her." . . .

Men of Massachusetts, I beg, I implore, I demand pity and protection for these of my suffering, outraged sex. Fathers, husbands, brothers, I would supplicate you for this boon; but what do I say? I dishonor you, divest you at once of Christianity and humanity, does this appeal imply distrust. If it comes burdened with a doubt of your righteousness in this legislation, then blot it out; while I declare confidence in your honor, not less than your humanity. Here you will put away the cold, calculating spirit of selfishness and self-seeking; lay off the armor of local strife and political opposition; here and now, for once, forgetful of the earthly and perishable, come up to these halls and consecrate them with one heart and one mind to works of righteousness and just judgment. . . .

Injustice is also done to the *convicts:* it is certainly very wrong that they should be doomed day after day and night after night to listen to the ravings of madmen and madwomen. This is a kind of punishment that is not recognized by our statutes, and is what the criminal ought not to be called upon to undergo. The confinement of the criminal and of the insane in the same building is subversive of that good order and discipline which should be observed in every well-regulated prison. . . .

Gentlemen, I commit to you this sacred cause. Your action upon this subject will affect the present and future condition of hundreds and of thousands. In this legislation, as in all things, may you exercise that "wisdom which is the breath of the power of God." . . .

Resolved, That woman is man's equal

As Jacksonian democracy took the reins of government, dedicated social reformers began an exuberant drive to improve human welfare. "What is man born for," Emerson asked, "but to be a reformer, a remaker of what man has made, a renouncer of lies, a restorer of truth and good?"

Feminism stood strong in the ranks of isms. With the growth of reform movements, a host of women took their not unchallenged place in public life. Rapidly they found that it was not enough to fight against slavery; a woman had also to fight many of her fellow-abolitionists for the right to join in the crusade. The refusal of the 1840 World Antislavery Convention in London to seat women delegates from the United States sent Elizabeth Cady Stanton and Lucretia Mott home determined to launch a modern feminist movement. By 1848 they were able to hold the first national convention at Seneca Falls, New York. The declaration of independence proclaimed from that meeting rallied women to a militant crusade that even now, more than a hundred years later, has not won all its goals. What follows is the convention's Declaration of Sentiments.

THE HISTORY of mankind is a history of repeated injuries and usurpations on the part of man toward woman, having in direct object the establishment of an absolute tyranny over her. To prove this, let facts be submitted to a candid world.

He has never permitted her to exercise her inalienable right to the elective franchise.

He has compelled her to submit to laws, in the formation of which she had no voice.

He has withheld from her rights which are given to the most ignorant and degraded men—both natives and foreigners.

Having deprived her of this first right of a citizen, the elective franchise, thereby leaving her without representation in the halls of legislation, he has oppressed her on all sides.

He has made her, if married, in the eye of the law, civilly dead.

He has taken from her all right in property, even to the wages she earns.

Amelia Jenks Bloomer, whose "Bloomer" costume, designed for freedom of movement, became a symbol of woman's emancipation. Public derision forced a retreat from this dress reform.

Cartoonists soon piled a mountain of clichés on top of the campaign for woman's rights. This drawing, satirizing a woman's candidacy for President, appeared in 1849.

He has made her, morally, an irresponsible being, as she can commit many crimes with impunity, provided they be done in the presence of her husband. In the covenant of marriage, she is compelled to promise obedience to her husband, he becoming, to all intents and purposes, her master—the law giving him power to deprive her of her liberty, and to administer chastisement.

He has so framed the laws of divorce, as to what shall be the proper causes, and in case of separation, to whom the guardianship of the children shall be given, as to be wholly regardless of the happiness of women—the law, in all cases, going upon a false supposition of the supremacy of man, and giving all power into his hands.

After depriving her of all rights as a married woman, if single, and the owner of property, he has taxed her to support a government which recognizes her only when her property can be made profitable to it.

He has monopolized nearly all the profitable employments, and from those she is permitted to follow, she receives but a scanty remuneration. He closes against her all the avenues to wealth and distinction which he considers most honorable to himself. As a teacher of theology, medicine, or law, she is not known.

He has denied her the facilities for obtaining a thorough education, all colleges being closed against her.

He allows her in Church, as well as State, but a subordinate position, claiming Apostolic authority for her exclusion from the ministry, and, with some exceptions, from any public participations in the affairs of the Church.

He has created a false public sentiment by giv-

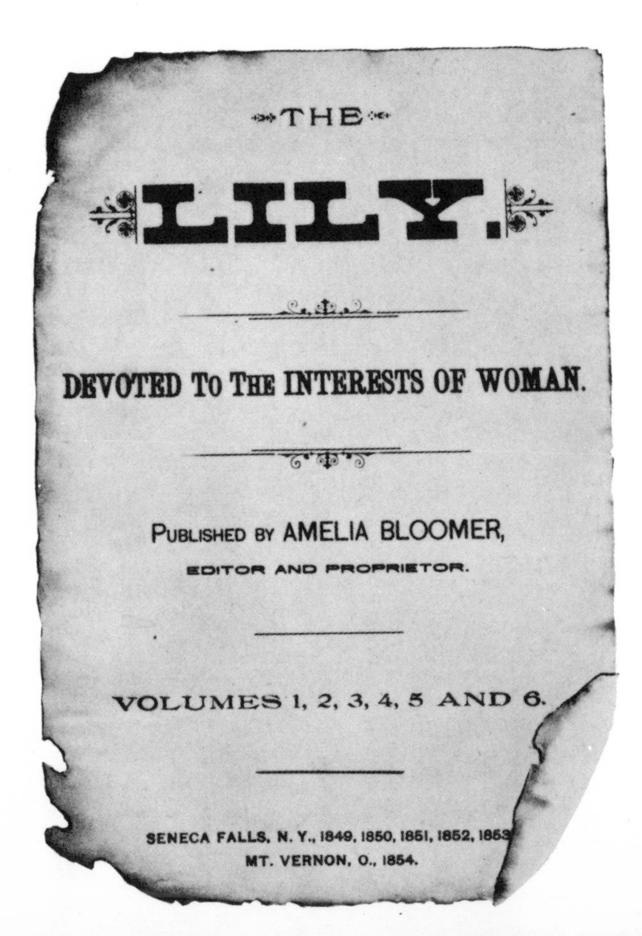

THE

LILY.

DEVOTED TO THE INTERESTS OF WOMAN.

PUBLISHED BY AMELIA BLOOMER,
EDITOR AND PROPRIETOR.

VOLUMES 1, 2, 3, 4, 5 AND 6.

SENECA FALLS, N. Y., 1849, 1850, 1851, 1852, 1853
MT. VERNON, O., 1854.

The Lily, edited by Amelia Bloomer, was published at Seneca Falls after the Woman's Rights Convention.

A Senate Committee in Washington hears testimony from Elizabeth Cady Stanton. Mrs. Stanton was active not only in the feminist but in the temperance and abolitionist movements, too.

A Currier & Ives print of 1869 on "The Age of Brass, or the triumphs of woman's rights."

Victoria Woodhull, asserts her right to vote, as reported by *Harper's Weekly* in 1871. A beautiful and ardent feminist who also ran a Wall Street brokerage house, she began publishing *Woodhull & Claflin's Weekly* in 1870. It campaigned for many causes, including Victoria for President. She and her sister, Tennessee Claflin, were among the most colorful and controversial feminists of that day.

ing to the world a different code of morals for men and women, by which moral delinquencies which exclude women from society, are not only tolerated, but deemed of little account in man.

He has usurped the prerogative of Jehovah himself, claiming it as his right to assign for her a sphere of action, when that belongs to her conscience and to her God.

He has endeavored, in every way that he could, to destroy her confidence in her own powers, to lessen her self-respect and to make her willing to lead a dependent and abject life.

Now, in view of this entire disfranchisement of one-half the people of this country, their social and religious degradation—in view of the unjust laws above mentioned, and because women do feel themselves aggrieved, oppressed, and fraudulently deprived of their most sacred rights, we insist that they have immediate admission to all the rights and privileges which belong to them as citizens of the United States.

In entering upon the great work before us, we anticipate no small amount of misconception, misrepresentation, and ridicule; but we shall use every instrumentality within our power to effect our object. We shall employ agents, circulate tracts, petition the State and National legislatures, and endeavor to enlist the pulpit and the press in our behalf. We hope this Convention will be followed by a series of Conventions embracing every part of the country.

"Hugging a Delusion" was *Life's* title for this 1915 cartoon. Five years later, however, the 19th Amendment, providing for woman suffrage, was ratified.

Not a few, but the many; not a part, but all

A farmer's son whose childhood was spent in work and churchgoing became the architect of the American free public school system. "I never had more than ten weeks of schooling in a year until I was sixteen," Horace Mann remembered. At twenty he was able to enter Brown, a one-building "university" in that day. He became a lawyer, then a legislator. As President of the Massachusetts Senate, in 1837 he signed a bill creating a State Board of Education. Elected the board's first Secretary, he devoted himself "to the supremest welfare of mankind on earth" for an annual salary of $1500. To win support for his new methods and materials he lectured widely, held teachers' institutes, launched a semimonthly magazine, organized the first three state normal schools in the country. His twelve annual Reports *surveyed conditions and proposed improvements with an eloquent conviction that changed the course of public education nationally. He believed in a free, nonsectarian education for all, designed to make better citizens. "Be ashamed to die," he told his students, "until you have won some victory for humanity." Here, taken from his* Common School Journal, *is his credo.*

School districts ran their own affairs and, as this 1837 cartoon indicates, made teaching a poorly paid profession. Men earned $155 annually and women a third of that. 'The little red schoolhouse" was a dingy, dilapidated institution the reformers were determined to better.

Horace Mann. A portrait engraved from a pencil sketch made by Sophia Peabody Hawthorne, sister of Mann's wife, Mary. In his dozen years as Secretary of the Massachusetts Board of Education, Mann doubled teacher's salaries, lengthened the minimum school year to six months, and opened fifty new high schools.

WHAT SPHERE of patriotic exertion is left open for the lover of his country, but the sphere of improving the rising generation through the instrumentality of a more perfect and efficient system for their education? We call our fathers patriots, because they loved their country and made sacrifices for its welfare. But what was their country? A vast tract of wilderness territory did not constitute it. It was not unconscious, insentient plains, or rivers, or mountains, however beautifully and majestically they might spread, or flow, or shine, beneath the canopy of heaven. Their country was chiefly their descendants, the human beings who were to throng these vast domains, the sentient, conscious natures which were to live here,—and living, to enjoy or suffer.

The question with them was, whether this should be a land of liberty or bondage, of light or darkness, of religion or superstition. It was to redeem and elevate the millions who, in the providence of God, should people these wide-spreading realms, that they engaged in a cause where those who suffered death seemed to suffer least, where the survivors most challenge our sympathy.

But we have not battles to fight by land or sea, against a foreign foe. We have no fathers, or broth-

The battle for free public schools was fought in many states. This passage from an 1835 speech of Thaddeus Stevens, then in the Pennsylvania House, reflects his powerful influence upon the common schools.

If an elective Republic is to endure for any great length of time, *every* elector must have sufficient information, not only to accumulate wealth and take care of his pecuniary concerns, but to direct wisely the Legislature, the ambassadors, and the Executive of the Nation—for *some* part of all these things, *some* agency in approving or disapproving of them, falls to every freeman. If, then, the permanency of our Government depends upon such knowledge, it is the duty of Government to see that the means of information be diffused to every citizen. This is a sufficient answer to those who deem education a private and not a public duty—who argue that they are willing to educate their *own* childreb, but not their *neighbors* children.

ers, or sons, in the camp, suffering cold, and hunger, and nakedness. We have no edifice of government to rear, with exhausting study and anxiety. These labors are done and ended, and we have entered into the rich inheritance. What, then, shall we do that we may be patriotic? How shall our love of country, if any we have, be made manifest? How, but by laboring for our descendants,—not in the same way, but with the same fidelity, as our fathers labored for us? Otherwise, there is no moral consanguinity between ourselves and them. Otherwise, we are not of their blood, but gentiles and heathens, boasting a lineage which our acts and lives belie. It is mockery to say, "We have Abraham to our father," while we perform the deeds of pagans.

The only sphere, then, left open for our patriotism, is the improvement of our children,—not the few, but the many; not a part of them, but all. This is but one field of exertion, but it opens an infinite career; for the capacities of mankind can go on developing, improving, perfecting, as long as the cycles of eternity revolve. For this improvement of the race, a high, a generous, an expansive education is the true and efficient means. There is not a good work which the hand of man has ever undertaken, which his heart has ever conceived, which does not require a good education for its helper. There is not an evil afflicting the earth, which can be extirpated until the auxiliary of education shall lend its mighty aid.

If an angel were to descend from heaven to earth, on an errand of mercy and love, he would hasten to accomplish his mission by illuminating the minds and purifying the hearts of children. The Savior took little children in his arms and blessed them; he did not by any miraculous exertion of power, bar up all passages to sin and error, and at once make mankind the passive recipients of perfection. He left it for us to be agents and co-workers with him in their redemption. He gave to us, not so much the boon of being blessed, as the more precious, the heavenly boon of blessing others. For this end, an instrument has been put into our hands, fully adequate to the accomplishment of so divine a purpose. We have the power to train up children in accordance with those wise and benign laws which the Creator has stamped upon their physical, their intellectual, and their moral nature; and of this stewardship we must assuredly give account. May it be rendered with joy, and not with sorrow!

The first American Normal School, opened at Lexington, Mass., in 1839. Only for girls, it taught such new pedagogical subjects as child physiology and psychology, and the principles and practice of teaching. The first principal served as janitor, too. Only a few of the original thirty students completed their course, but the school was a great step forward in better training for teachers.

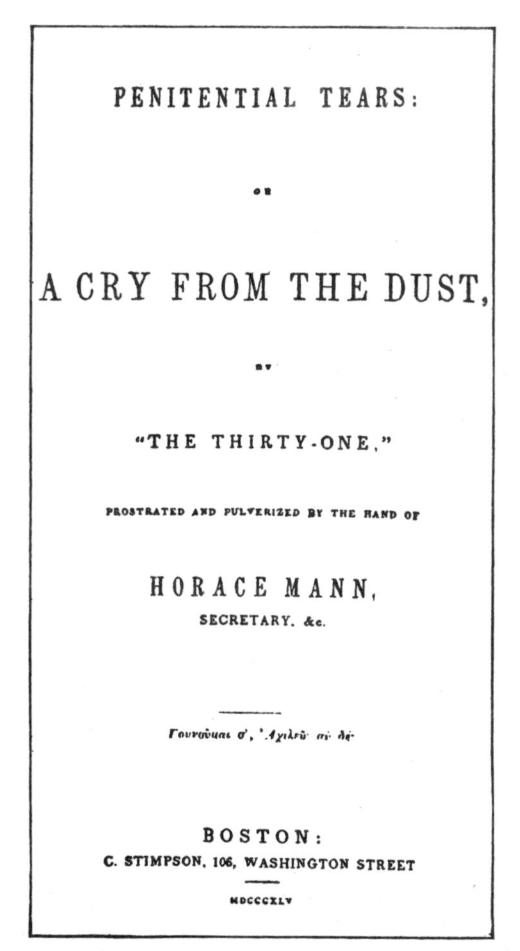

PENITENTIAL TEARS:

OR

A CRY FROM THE DUST,

BY

"THE THIRTY-ONE,"

PROSTRATED AND PULVERIZED BY THE HAND OF

HORACE MANN,

SECRETARY, &c.

Γουνοῦμαι σ', Ἀχιλεῦ· σὺ δέ·

BOSTON:

C. STIMPSON, 106, WASHINGTON STREET

MDCCCXLV

Pamphlets such as this were frequently fired at his critics by Horace Mann. "The Thirty-One" were Boston schoolmasters bitterly opposed to Mann's modern methods and determined to discredit him. Mann's caustic wit defeated them.

Concord, the quiet Massachusetts town where Thoreau was born in 1817. A Harvard graduate, he taught school briefly, studied nature, made pencils for a living, lectured, and kept a massive journal out of which he quarried some of America's best writing.

1849 Henry David Thoreau: Civil Disobedience

A majority of one

Early one evening toward the end of July, 1846, Henry David Thoreau walked from his hut at Walden Pond in to Concord to pick up a mended shoe from the cobbler. He was seized and put into jail for nonpayment of his poll tax. That night someone paid the tax and the next morning Thoreau was released. What began as a casual errand concluded with an essay of profound significance in spreading the doctrine of civil disobedience around the world.

Thoreau had not paid his poll tax since 1842, probably as a protest against a government which permitted the buying and selling of men, women, and children. In May, 1846, seeking new territory in the southwest for the expansion of slavery, the United States had declared war on Mexico. When a nation which had undertaken to be the refuge of liberty unjustly overruns and conquers a whole country with a foreign army, "it is not too soon for honest men to rebel and revolutionize." Thoreau felt. He refused to give the state a dollar to buy "a man or a musket to shoot one with."

It is likely that Thoreau had meant to make a test case of the poll-tax law, but the unknown donor's payment at least did not prevent him from taking his idea to the people, first as a lecture, then as a magazine piece in 1849. Now, under the title of "Civil Disobedience," it has become his most famous essay.

THE practical reason why, when the power is once in the hands of the people, a majority are permitted, and for a long period continue, to rule is not because they are most likely to be in the right, nor because this seems fairest to the minority, but because they are physically the strongest. But a government in which the majority rule in all cases cannot be based on justice, even as far as men understand it. Can there not be a government in which majorities do not virtually decide right and wrong, but conscience?—in which majorities decide only those questions to which the rule of expediency is applicable? Must the citizen ever for a moment, or in the least degree, resign his conscience to the legislator? Why has every man a conscience, then? *I think that we should be men first, and subjects afterward. It is not desirable to cultivate a respect for the law, so much as for the right.* The only obligation which I have a right to assume is to do at any time what I think right. It is truly enough said, that a corporation has no conscience; but a corporation of conscientious men is a corporation *with* a conscience. Law never made men a whit more just; and, by means of their respect for it, even the well-disposed are daily made the agents of injustice. . . .

The mass of men serve the state thus, not as men mainly, but as machines, with their bodies. They are the standing army, and the militia, jailors, constables, posse comitatus, etc. In most cases there is no free exercise whatever of the judgment or of the moral sense; but they put themselves on a level with wood and earth and stones; and wooden men can perhaps be manufactured that will serve the purpose as well. Such command no more respect than men of straw or a lump of dirt. They have the same sort of worth only as horses and dogs. Yet such as these even are commonly esteemed good citizens. Others—as most legislators, politicians, lawyers, ministers, and office-holders—serve the state chiefly with their heads; and, as they rarely make any moral distinctions, they are as likely to serve the Devil, without *intending* it, as God. A very few, as heroes, patriots, martyrs, reformers in the great sense, and *men*, serve the state with their consciences also, and so necessarily resist it for the most part; and they are commonly treated as enemies by it.

A scene in that "glorious little war" of 1846-48 in which the United States conquered more than half of Mexico. Among those opposing the Mexican War were an obscure Whig Congressman named Abraham Lincoln and an unknown moral philosopher named Henry Thoreau.

How does it become a man to behave toward this American government to-day? I answer, that he cannot without disgrace be associated with it. I cannot for an instant recognize that political organization as *my* government which is the *slave's* government also.

All men recognize the right of revolution; that is, the right to refuse allegiance to, and to resist, the government, when its tyranny or its inefficiency are great and unendurable. But almost all say that such is not the case now. But such was the case, they think, in the Revolution of '75. If one were to tell me that this was a bad government because it taxed certain foreign commodities brought to its ports, it is most probable that I should not make an ado about it, for I can do without them. All machines have their friction; . . . But when the friction comes to have its machine, and oppression and robbery are organized, I say, let us not have such a machine any longer. In other words, when a sixth of the population of a nation which has undertaken to be the refuge of liberty are slaves, and a whole country is unjustly overrun and conquered by a foreign army, and subjected to military law, I think that it is not too soon for honest men to rebel and revolutionize. What makes this duty the more urgent is the fact that the country so overrun is not our own, but ours is the invading army. . . .

Practically speaking, the opponents to a reform in Massachusetts are not a hundred thousand politicians at the South, but a hundred thousand merchants and farmers here, who are more interested in commerce and agriculture than they are in humanity, and are not prepared to do justice to the slave and to Mexico, *cost what it may.* I quarrel not with far-off foes, but with those who, near at home, coöperate with, and do the bidding of, those far away, and without whom the latter would be harmless. We are accustomed to say, that the mass of men are unprepared; but improvement is slow, because the few are not materially wiser or better than the many. It is not so important that many should be as good as you, as that there be some absolute goodness somewhere; for that will leaven the whole lump. There are thousands who are *in opinion* opposed to slavery and to the war, who yet in effect do nothing to put an end to them; who, esteeming themselves children of Washington and Franklin, sit down with their hands in their pockets, and say that they know not what to do, and do nothing; who even postpone the question of freedom to the question of free-trade, and quietly read the prices-current along with the latest advices from Mexico, after dinner, and, it may be, fall asleep over them both. What is the price-current of an honest man and patriot to-day? They hesitate, and they regret, and sometimes they petition; but they do nothing in earnest and with effect. They will wait, well disposed, for others to remedy the evil, that they may no longer have it to regret. At most, they give only a cheap vote, and a feeble countenance and God-speed, to the right, as it goes

Gandhi's guide for his civil disobedience campaign in India was Thoreau's essay, which he reprinted in pamphlet form to distribute among his followers. He always carried a copy with him to jail. The British Labour Party, in its early years, published 'Civil Disobedience" as a manual of political action. During the Nazi occupation of Europe it became a handbook for the resistance movement.

by them. There are nine hundred and ninety-nine patrons of virtue to one virtuous man. But it is easier to deal with the real possessor of a thing than with the temporary guardian of it. . . .

Unjust laws exist: shall we be content to obey them, or shall we endeavor to amend them, and obey them until we have succeeded, or shall we transgress them at once? Men generally, under such a government as this, think that they ought to wait until they have persuaded the majority to alter them. They think that, if they should resist, the remedy would be worse than the evil. But it is the fault of the government itself that the remedy *is* worse than the evil. *It* makes it worse. Why is it not more apt to anticipate and provide for reform? Why does it not cherish its wise minority? Why does it cry and resist before it is hurt? Why does it not encourage its citizens to be on the alert to point out its faults, and *do* better than it would have them? Why does it always crucify Christ, and excommunicate Copernicus and Luther, and pronounce Washington and Franklin rebels? . . .

I do not hesitate to say, that those who call themselves Abolitionists should at once effectually withdraw their support, both in person and property, from the government of Massachusetts and not wait till they constitute a majority of one, before they suffer the right to prevail through them. I think that it is enough if they have God on their side, without waiting for that other one. Moreover, any man more right than his neighbors constitutes a majority of one already.

I meet this American government, or its representative, the state government, directly, and face to face, once a year—no more—in the person of its tax-gatherer; this is the only mode in which a man situated as I am necessarily meets it; and it then says distinctly, Recognize me; and the simplest, most effectual, and, in the present posture of affairs, the indispensablest mode of treating with it on this head, of expressing your little satisfaction with and love for it, is to deny it then. My civil neighbor, the tax-gatherer, is the very man I have to deal with,—for it is, after all, with men and not with parchment that I quarrel,—and he has voluntarily chosen to be an agent of the government. How shall he ever know well what he is and does as an officer of the government, or as a man, until he is obliged to consider whether he shall treat me, his neighbor, for whom he has respect, as a neighbor and well-disposed man, or as a maniac and disturber of the peace, and see if he can get over this obstruction to his neighborliness without a ruder and more impetuous thought or speech corresponding with his action. I know this well, and if one thousand, if one hundred, if ten men whom I could name,—if ten *honest* men only,—ay if *one* HONEST man, in this State of Massachusetts, *ceasing to hold slaves,* were actually to withdraw from this copartnership, and be locked up in the county jail therefor, it would be the abolition of slavery in America. For it matters not how small the beginning may seem to be: what is once well done is done forever. . . .

Thoreau died in 1862, his reputation still to come. His *Week on the Concord and Merrimack Rivers* was published at his own expense in 1849. *Walden,* his best-known work, appeared in 1854.

Under a government which imprisons any unjustly, the true place for a just man is also a prison. The proper place to-day, the only place which Massachusetts has provided for her freer and less desponding spirits, is in her prisons, to be put out and locked out of the State by her own act, as they have already put themselves out by their principles. It is there that the fugitive slave, and the Mexican prisoner on parole, and the Indian come to plead the wrongs of his race should find them; on that separate, but more free and honorable ground, where the State places those who are not *with* her, but *against* her,—the only house in a slave State in which a free man can abide with honor. If any think that their influence would be lost there, and their voices no longer afflict the ear of the State, that they would not be as an enemy within its walls, they do not know by how much truth is stronger than error, nor how much more eloquently and effectively he can combat injustice who has experienced a little in his own person. Cast your whole vote, not a strip of paper merely, but your whole influence. A minority is powerless while it conforms to the majority; it is not even a minority then; but it is irresistible when it clogs by its whole weight. If the alternative is to keep all just men in prison, or give up war and slavery, the State will not hesitate which to choose. If a thousand men were not to pay their tax-bills this year, that would not be a violent and bloody measure, as it would be to pay them, and enable the State to commit violence and shed innocent blood. This is, in fact, the definition of a peaceable revolution, if any such is possible. If the tax-gatherer, or any other public officer, asks me, as one has done, "But what shall I do?" my answer is, "If you really wish to do anything, resign your office." When the subject has refused allegiance, and the officer has resigned his office, then the revolution is accomplished. But even suppose blood should flow. Is there not a sort of blood shed when the conscience is wounded? Through this wound a man's real manhood and immortality flow out, and he bleeds to an everlasting death. I see this blood flowing now. . . .

The authority of government, even such as I am willing to submit to,—for I will cheerfully obey those who know and can do better than I, and in many things even those who neither know nor can do so well,—is still an impure one: to be strictly just, it must have the sanction and consent of the governed. It can have no pure right over my person and property but what I concede to it. The progress from an absolute to a limited monarchy, from a limited monarchy to a democracy, is a progress toward a true respect for the individual. Even the Chinese philosopher was wise enough to regard the individual as the basis of the empire. Is a democracy, such as we know it, the last improvement possible in government? Is it not possible to take a step further towards recognizing and organizing the rights of man? There will never be a really free and enlightened State until the State comes to recognize the individual as a higher and independent power, from which all its own power and authority are derived, and treats him accordingly. I please myself with imagining a State at last which can afford to be just to all men, and to treat the individual with respect as a neighbor; which even would not think it inconsistent with its own repose if a few were to live aloof from it, not meddling with it, nor embraced by it, who fulfilled all the duties of neighbors and fellow-men. A State which bore this kind of fruit, and suffered it to drop off as fast as it ripened, would prepare the way for a still more perfect and glorious State, which also I have imagined, but not yet anywhere seen.

The Russian novelist and philosopher Leo Tolstoy said that Thoreau, along with Emerson, Garrison, and Theodore Parker, was one of the American writers who "specially influenced" him in his concern for suffering and his hope that man would learn to live what he believed in.

Peace has its heroism

A blacksmith who earned twenty-five cents a day in a foundry became the nineteenth century's foremost advocate of world peace. Elihu Burritt, the son of a soldier in the Revolution, was born in a Connecticut village in 1810. Although his schooling was skimpy, his hunger for learning was so intense that he soon taught himself a score of languages while working at the forge. Offered the chance to study at Harvard, he said he preferred "to stand in the ranks of the workingmen of New England and beckon them onward and upward . . . to the full stature of intellectual men." In his early twenties he became widely known as "the learned blacksmith" and began lecturing and writing in behalf of temperance, abolitionism, and the peace movement.

How wars could be avoided was by this time the concern of thousands of Americans organized in a peace crusade that had been born out of the Napoleonic Wars and the War of 1812. By 1828 the American Peace Society was formed from several local groups. Periodicals and tracts poured from their presses condemning war as contrary to Christianity and progress. Cooperation was developed with peace societies in European capitals. The movement had its two wings—the nonresisters who would not fight under any conditions, and those who opposed offensive wars but supported defensive or "just" wars.

William Lloyd Garrison led the nonresisters and cooperated with William Ladd of Maine, a former sea captain and farmer, in advocating a congress of nations and a world court of arbitration. Upon Ladd's death, Elihu Burritt dedicated his great energies to his program and carried it to the international stage. He initiated the first world peace congress at Brussels in 1848 and followed it with other conferences in Europe. Among his many writings on international pacifism is Thoughts and Things at Home and Abroad, *issued in 1854, in which he made this moving plea for peace.*

WE HAVE CONSIDERED the power and dignity of passive resistance, when opposed to assaults from without, or oppression from within. We have tried to show that necessity does not make it a virtue in any case; but that its inherent virtue always makes it a necessity. We now proceed to demonstrate its patriotism. We deem it due to the principles and advocates of peace, to rebut the charge that is often brought against them, that they are "the complacent allies of depotism—that they would stand by and see, without concern or remonstrance, communities, peoples, and nations manacled hand and foot, by tyrants; their rights, liberties, hopes, and aspirations, trodden out of existence by the iron heel of oppression." The imputation of cowardice, unmanly imbecility, a crouching, abject spirit, is involved in this charge. "What! would you have us lie down in the dust, and be trampled upon by these despotic powers and governments! Would you have us permit them to enslave us, and hold out our arms and feet to the fettering without a struggle or a murmur?" And then, having filled their bosoms to bursting with patriotic indignation at the course and disposition described interrogatively by these triumphant questions, they exclaim, "No! we would spill the last drop of our blood;—we would see our cities burned with fire;—we would perish with arms in our hands on the battle-field, or pine in exile in Siberia or Botany Bay, before we would tamely submit to be slaves! Liberty or death!"

Elihu Burritt, the self-taught "Learned Blacksmith." He organized the League for Universal Brotherhood in 1846. The international members pledged themselves "never to yield any voluntary support or sanction to the preparation for or prosecution of any war." When war with England over the Oregon dispute was threatened in 1846, Burritt helped avert it by his "friendly address" appeals in the press of both countries. The arbitration principle his peace movement pioneered won its first success in the Alabama Claims dispute of 1871. A generation after Burritt's death, the institutional means he helped fashion were working tools in the hands of the peacemakers.

These are the most striking and usual terms of comparison in the vocabulary of martial patriotism. Frequently the sentiments they express take a figurative form more fearful still. We recollect one employed by the editor of an American journal, pending the Oregon controversy, to this effect: "Sooner than relinquish our just rights to the disputed territory, we would shed every drop of blood in the heart of the nation!" Mr. Borrow, agent of the Bible Society, records "a broken prayer for my native land, which, after my usual thanksgiving, I breathed forth to the Almighty, ere retiring to rest that Sunday night at Gibraltar"; a prayer *for* his native country which contains this passage—"May'st thou sink, if thou dost sink, amidst blood and flame, with a mighty noise, causing more than one nation to participate in thy downfall!"

And these are regarded as the outbursts of a patriotic feeling—of a love of country so intense that they would see it engulfed in fire and blood, and even the last vein of the nation's heart pierced, and its existence extinguished, rather than endure insult, injury, or oppression! They measure their attachment and devotion to their country and its institutions by the awful calamities which they would bring upon it, in defending its honor and rights. What a fearful antithesis of alternatives! How many peoples and nations have "sunk, amidst blood and flame, and with a mighty noise," in the abyss which yawns between these alternative conditions! How many patriots of this order have seen their country a smoking sea of ruin, without finding a bulrush ark in which to float "the immediate jewel of its soul"—the charter of its existence as a nation!

We wish no one to accept or share the responsibility of our convictions, or of the views we wish to express in reference to this aspect of the subject. If peace has its victories no less than war, it has its heroism and its patriotism. The men of peace can find no attribute, in the great Gospel principles of their faith, that can side with despotism, or wink with indifference at oppression. They are not cowards. They counsel no tame, unmanly submission to wrong; but to oppose to wrong a courage of the human will that shall never faint or waver at any extremity of endurance;—aye, to "resist unto blood," if it be unavoidable,—to give their own necks to the axe or to the halter, on the block or the scaffold, but never to shed themselves a single drop, or perpetrate a single act of malevolent injury on any human being, under the severest pressure of despotic rule. Peace has its heroism, serene and dauntless, that neither trembles nor pales before the guillotine, the halter, or the knout. Peace has its patriotism; deep, earnest, unselfish, self-sacrificing, and sensitive,—a love of country that would bleed to the last vein, but never wound, for its rights, honor, and prosperity. Peace has its battle-fields; bloodless, but brave to a degree of heroic endurance of wrong and outrage to which martial courage could never attain.

This is true Americanism

In 1830 there were under a half-million foreign-born in the United States. By 1860 economic hardship, religious and political persecution, and the belief that America was the door to a fuller life, had brought another five million Europeans here. Among them was Carl Schurz, who reached these shores in 1852, a 23-year-old veteran of the German Revolution of '48. Young Schurz helped organize the Republican Party, and became a lawyer and an ardent Lincoln man.

One of the most distinguished immigrants of the nineteenth century, Schurz made many contributions to the strengthening of democracy and the growth of intellectual life. When the anti-immigrant and anti-Catholic movement swelled dangerously in the eighteen-fifties, Schurz, a superb orator, spoke out against efforts to restrict the rights of the foreign-born. His "True Americanism" speech, delivered in Boston on April 18, 1859, helped defeat a Massachusetts bill to prevent foreigners from voting until two years after they had become citizens. Inscribed on the American banner, he said, is "Liberty and equal rights—common to all as the air of Heaven—Liberty and equal rights, one and inseparable!"

After serving as Lincoln's Minister to Spain, Carl Schurz had a distinguished career in the army. The war over, he turned to journalism. In 1869 he served Missouri in the U.S. Senate for one term, and then became President Hayes's Secretary of the Interior. He pilloried business corruption of politics and campaigned for civil service reform. *Leslie's* illustrated weekly shows him addressing a reform meeting in New York in 1876.

The first Chinese arrived in America to seek their lucky strike in the gold fields. Later they were brought in as cheap labor for the mines and railroads, under a treaty authorizing their wholesale immigration. White laborers and farmers were inflamed by demagogues to riot against the Chinese, as this print of the eighteenth-seventies shows, and by 1882 a Chinese Exclusion Law was adopted by Congress.

Immigration continued after the Civil War. In this 1868 print labor agents meet new arrivals at Castle Garden, New York. From 1870 to 1900 over ten million new Americans entered the country.

THE TIME of a new migration was at hand, and that migration rolled its waves towards America. The old process repeated itself under new forms, milder and more congenial to the humane ideas it represented. It is now not a barbarous multitude pouncing upon old and decrepit empires; not a violent concussion of tribes accompanied by all the horrors of general destruction; but we see the vigorous elements of all nations, we see the Anglo-Saxon, the leader in the practical movement, with his spirit of independence, of daring enterprise and of indomitable perseverance; the German, the original leader in the movement of ideas, with his spirit of inquiry and his quiet and thoughtful application; the Celt, with the impulsive vivacity of his race; the Frenchman, the Scandinavian, the Scot, the Hollander, the Spaniard and the Italian—all these peaceably congregating and mingling together on virgin soil, where the backwoodsman's hatchet is the only battle-axe of civilization; led together by the irresistible attraction of free and broad principles; undertaking to commence a new era in the history of the world, without first destroying the results of the progress of past periods; undertaking to found a new cosmopolitan nation without marching over the dead bodies of slain millions. Thus was founded the great colony of free humanity, which has not old England alone, but the world, for its mother-country . . .

It is an old dodge of the advocates of despotism throughout the world, that the people who are not experienced in self-government are not fit for the exercise of self-government, and must first be educated under the rule of a superior authority. But at the same time the advocates of despotism will never offer them an opportunity to acquire experience in self-government, lest they suddenly become fit for its independent exercise. To this treacherous sophistry the fathers of this republic opposed the noble doctrine, that liberty is the best school for liberty, and that self-government cannot be learned but by practicing it. This, sir, is a truly American idea; this is true Americanism, and to this I pay the tribute of my devotion.

You object that some people do not understand their own interests? There is nothing that, in the course of time, will make a man better understand his interests than the independent management of

The Irish, among the earliest settlers in the New World, were greatly multiplied by a migration that began around 1820. Famines in the eighteen-forties lifted the tide to a flood. Above, an Irish migrant of 1854 studies the schedules of packets bound for the United States. The starving Irish were crammed into stinking holds and from the American docks were herded into factory, railroad, and domestic jobs at low wages.

Thomas Nast, the great cartoonist, pointed up this irony of the late eighteen-seventies. The freed Negroes of the South moved westward to escape post-Reconstruction terror as the Chinese of the West Coast moved east to seek refuge from hoodlums.

Carl Schurz as a brigadier general. He commanded a division at 2nd Bull Run and, promoted to major-general, took part in the battles of Chancellorsville and Gettysburg.

his own affairs on his own responsibility. You object that people are ignorant? There is no better schoolmaster in the world than self-government, independently exercised. You object that people have no just idea of their duties as citizens? There is no other source from which they can derive a just notion of their duties, than the enjoyment of the rights from which they arise. You object that people are misled by their religious prejudices, and by the intrigues of the Roman hierarchy? Since when have the enlightened citizens of this Republic lost their faith in the final invincibility of truth? Since when have they forgotten that if the Roman or any other church plants the seed of superstition, liberty sows broadcast the seed of enlightenment? . . .

Liberty, sir, is like a spirited housewife; she will have her whims, she will be somewhat unruly sometimes, and, like so many husbands, you cannot always have it all your own way. She may spoil your favorite dish sometimes; but will you, therefore, at once smash her china, break her kettles and shut her out from the kitchen? Let her practice, let her try again and again, and even when she makes a mistake, encourage her with a benignant smile, and your broth will be right after a while. But meddle with her concerns, tease her, bore her, and your little squabbles, spirited as she is, will ultimately result in a divorce. What then? It is one of Jefferson's wisest words that "he would much rather be exposed to the inconveniences arising from too much liberty, than to those arising from too small a degree of it." It is a matter of historical experience, that nothing that is wrong in principle can be right in practice. People are apt to delude themselves on that point; but the ultimate result will always prove the truth of the maxim. A violation of equal rights can never serve to maintain institutions which are founded upon equal rights. A contrary policy is not only pusillanimous and small, but it is senseless. It reminds me of the soldier who, for fear of being shot in battle, committed suicide on the march; or of the man who would cut off his foot because he had a corn on his toe. It is that ridiculous policy of premature despair, which commences to throw the freight overboard when there is a suspicious cloud in the sky . . .

An artist lampoons the Know-Nothing gangs of Baltimore. Opposed to foreigners and Catholics, the young thugs roamed the streets, armed for trouble. Their secret lodges were organized as the American Party, which at its peak in the eighteen-fifties carried many local elections in Northern states.

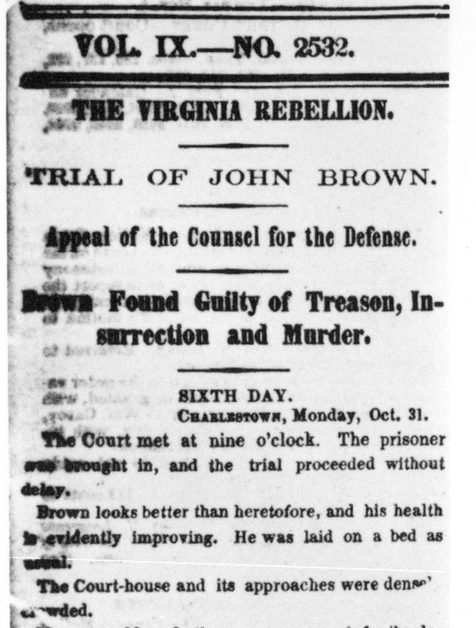

VOL. IX.—NO. 2532.

THE VIRGINIA REBELLION.

TRIAL OF JOHN BROWN.

Appeal of the Counsel for the Defense.

Brown Found Guilty of Treason, Insurrection and Murder.

SIXTH DAY.

CHARLESTOWN, Monday, Oct. 31.

The Court met at nine o'clock. The prisoner was brought in, and the trial proceeded without delay.

Brown looks better than heretofore, and his health is evidently improving. He was laid on a bed as usual.

The Court-house and its approaches were dense[illegible] crowded.

Mr. [illegible] speech for the defense, taking up the several charges in the indictment, and replying to the points made in the opening

VOL. IX.—NO. 2534.

VIRGINIA REBELLION.

John Brown Sentenced to Death.

His Address to the Court and Jury.

EDWARD COPPIE FOUND GUILTY.

CHARLESTOWN, Wednesday, Nov. 2.

Messrs. RUSSELL and SENNETT, from Boston, reached here to-day.

COOK was brought before the Magistrate's Court, and waived an examination.

COPPIE'S trial was resumed. No witnesses were called for the defence.

Mr. HARDING opened for the Commonwealth; Messrs. HOYT and GRISWOLD followed for the defendant, and Mr. HUNTER closed for the prosecution. The speeches were of marked ability.

Mr. GRISWOLD asked for several instructions to the ju[illegible] which were all granted by the Court, and [illegible]

1859 John Brown: Last Speech

In behalf of God's despised poor

Marines under Col. Robert E. Lee stormed the engine house in which Brown and a few raiders had taken final refuge. Two of Brown's sons died by his side in the last hours of the fighting.

At eight o'clock on Sunday evening, October 16, 1859, John Brown rose to his feet and said, "Men, get on your arms; we will proceed to the Ferry." It was cold and dark as the men stepped through the door of the Kennedy farmhouse. A horse and wagon stood outside, in the rain, and some pikes, a sledge hammer, and a crowbar were put aboard. Brown set his old Kansas cap on his head and mounted the wagon. Two by two the eighteen men followed him on foot down the main road. They walked some distance apart, quiet, displaying no arms. No one was met on the road. Down through the woods they came, on to the bridge across the Potomac. Under the bridge's cover they belted on their cartridge boxes and rounds of ammunition, and now their rifles were plainly to be seen. Nearing the Virginia side the watchman patrolling the bridge met them and was taken prisoner. Now it was half past ten, and Brown and his men were breaking open the federal armory gate with the crowbar. Rushing inside they captured a watchman, and Brown and two men mounted guard at the gate. The others dispersed through the village, occupying the bridge over the Shenandoah, the rifleworks, the arsenal. Not a gun was fired, and by midnight Harper's Ferry was completely in the hands of the raiders.

Not until Tuesday morning's newspapers appeared did the country know the "fearful and exciting intelligence" . . .

The federal arsenal at the Ferry was Brown's goal. The abolitionist, steeled in the recent battle to make Kansas a free state, may have hoped to capture the arms, spread panic among the slaveholders, gather up the slave recruits who would rally to him, and

A photo of John Brown made in Boston in May, 1859, some five months before the Harper's Ferry attack. Later, prints were sold to raise funds for the relief of Brown's large family. Mary, Brown's second wife, bore him thirteen children in twenty-one years. Seven died in childhood, one was killed in Kansas and two at Harper's Ferry. To her and his children Brown wrote from prison: "You have given full proof of your fidelity to the great family of man. Be faithful unto death."

As Brown was taken from jail on the morning of his execution, he gave this prophetic sentence, written in his own hand, to one of the guards.

Charlestown, Va, 2d December, 1859.
I John Brown am now quite certain that the crimes of this guilty, land: will never be purged away; but with Blood. I had as I now think: vainly flattered myself that without very much bloodshed; it might be done.

ADDRESS OF JOHN BROWN

To the Virginia Court, when about to receive the

SENTENCE OF DEATH,

For his heroic attempt at Harper's Ferry, to

Give deliverance to the captives, and to let the oppressed go free.

[MR. BROWN, upon inquiry whether he had anything to say why sentence should not be pronounced upon him, in a clear, distinct voice, replied :]

I have, may it please the Court, a few words to say.

In the first place, I deny every thing but what I have already admitted, of a design on my part to *free Slaves*. I intended, certainly, to have made a clean thing of that matter, as I did last winter, when I went into Missouri, and there took Slaves, without the snapping of a gun on either side, moving them through the country, and finally leaving them in Canada. I desired to have done the same thing again, on a much larger scale. *That was all I intended.* I never did intend murder, or treason, or the destruction of property, or to excite or incite Slaves to rebellion, or to make insurrection.

I have another objection, and that is, that it is *unjust* that I should suffer such a penalty. Had I interfered in the manner, and which I admit has been fairly proved,—for I admire the truthfulness and candor of the greater portion of the witnesses who have testified in this case,— had I so interfered in behalf of the Rich, the Powerful, the Intelligent, the so-called Great, or in behalf of any of their friends, either father, mother, brother, sister, wife, or children, or any of *that class*, and suffered and sacrificed what I have in this interference, *it would have been all right.* Every man in this Court would have deemed it an act worthy a reward, rather than a punishment.

This Court acknowledges too, as I suppose, the validity of the LAW OF GOD. I saw a book kissed, which I suppose to be the BIBLE, or at least the NEW TESTAMENT, which teaches me that, "All things whatsoever I would that men should do to me, I should do even so to them." It teaches me further, to "Remember them that are in bonds, as bound with them." I endeavored to act up to that instruction. I say I am yet too young to understand that GOD is any *respecter of persons*. I believe that to have interfered as I have done, as I have always freely admitted I have done, in behalf of his *despised poor*, I have done no wrong, but RIGHT.

Now, if it is deemed necessary that I should forfeit my life, for the furtherance of the ends of justice, and MINGLE MY BLOOD FURTHER WITH THE BLOOD OF MY CHILDREN, and with the blood of millions in this Slave country, whose rights are disregarded by wicked, cruel, and unjust enactments,—I say, LET IT BE DONE.

Let me say one word further: I feel entirely satisfied with the treatment I have received on my trial. Considering all the circumstances, it has been more generous than I expected; but I feel no consciousness of guilt. I have stated from the first what was my *intention*, and what was not. I never had any design against the liberty of any person, nor any disposition to commit treason, or excite Slaves to rebel, or make any general insurrection. I never encouraged any man to do so, but always discouraged any idea of that kind.

Let me say something, also, in regard to the statements made by some of those who were connected with me. I hear that it has been stated by some of them, that I have induced them to join me; but the contrary is true. I do not say this to injure them, but as regarding their weakness. Not one but joined me of his own accord, and the greater part at their own expense. A number of them I never saw and never had a word of conversation with, till the day they came to me, and that was for the purpose I have stated. Now I have done.

John Brown

The speech Brown made in court was swiftly telegraphed around the country. *The New York Times* printed it on page one. Here is the text, published as a broadside, and sold at *The Liberator*'s office in Boston.

The wounded Brown lay on his cot during the trial. When sentence of death by hanging was pronounced, he walked back across the street to his cell. He had thirty days to live.

In the month before execution, Brown's letters and interviews found their way into print and had a tremendous influence upon public opinion. December 2, 1859, was clear and warm. "This is a beautiful country," Brown said as the death wagon drew up and his eyes lifted to the Blue Ridge mountains. Around the scaffold were massed fifteen hundred soldiers. A blow of the sheriff's hatchet, and the body dropped through the trap door. John Brown's soul was marching on.

disappear into the mountains. Harper's Ferry was the gateway to the swamps and mountains of the South, where the slaves he expected to liberate might find refuge.

The plan failed, and Brown was captured. As he lay in Charlestown jail awaiting trial, the press across the country blazed with editorials for and against his act. Republican papers first called him crazy, but soon saw in the little band of men "martyrs of a cause in itself noble." Anger, horror, and terror were the South's response, mingled with respect for Brown's courage and daring.

The army of liberators was small indeed, noted Henry Thoreau, "because few could be found worthy to pass muster . . . When were the good and the brave ever in a majority? These alone were ready to step between the oppressor and the oppressed. Surely they were the very best men you could select to be hung . . ."

During the days in jail Brown became "fully persuaded that I am worth inconceivably more to hang than for any other purpose." His jury took forty-five minutes to bring in a verdict of guilty. Asked if he had anything to say about why sentence should not be pronounced upon him, the old Puritan rose from his cot to voice an ideal of equality and democracy for which millions were soon to give their lives.

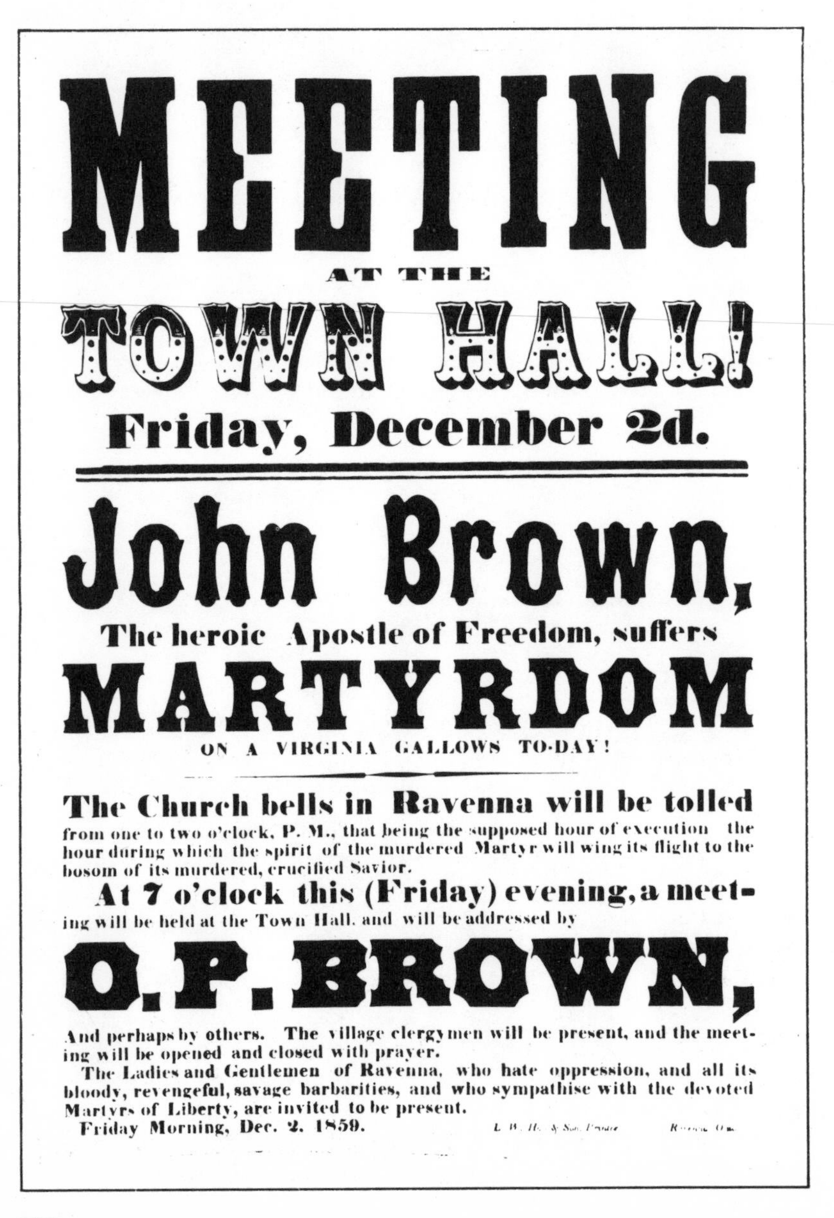

No sooner was Brown dead—the man had become a legend in his own lifetime—than his martyrdom began to win new adherents to the cause of emancipation.

An 1860 campaign poster for Lincoln and his running mate, Hannibal Hamlin, Senator from Maine.

1861 Abraham Lincoln: First Inaugural Address

This country, with its institutions, belongs to the people who inhabit it

On November 6, 1860, Abraham Lincoln was elected President of the United States. Running against three candidates, he won 40 per cent of the popular vote, but a clear majority of the Electoral College. In the four months that he sat quietly at home in Springfield, waiting to take office, seven states of the Lower South seceded, seized federal forts and arsenals, and called a constitutional convention. President James Buchanan announced to Congress that in his opinion the federal government had no power to stop secession. North and South, the great majority of Americans dreaded war and hoped for a compromise to preserve peace. But as the months passed it became clear that the issue of slavery could not be bargained away. Slavery must be protected in all the U.S. territories, the secessionists insisted, while Lincoln replied "I am inflexible" on the question of extending slavery under the national auspices.

What would Lincoln do to meet the crisis? On March 4, 1861, in his inaugural address, the new president answered. With all his superb skill in analyzing complex issues and putting them into moving words he pointed out that there was only one course to be followed: the secessionists had no right to use force to change a decision made by the majority in a democratic election. If they chose civil war to destroy the government, the President, bound by oath to "preserve, protect, and defend" the Union, would meet force with force.

"Wretched Condition of the Old Party at the White House" is how this cartoon in the New York *Illustrated News* was headed. While the Southerner threatens force, President Buchanan is reminded by the Northerner of the Constitution he had sworn to uphold.

When Buchanan remained passive in the face of South Carolina's secession, *Vanity Fair* printed this sarcastic tribute to a President who stood in sharp contrast to Jackson's vigorous action which halted the same State's move toward nullification in 1832.

Fellow-Citizens of the United States:

A DISRUPTION of the Federal Union, heretofor only menaced, is now formidably attempted.

I hold that, in contemplation of universal law and of the Constitution, the Union of these States is perpetual. Perpetuity is implied, if not expressed, in the fundamental law of all national governments. It is safe to assert that no government proper ever had a provision in its organic law for its own termination. Continue to execute all the express provisions of our national Constitution, and the Union will endure forever, it being impossible to destroy it except by some action not provided for in the instrument itself.

Again: If the United States be not a government proper, but an association of States in the nature of contract merely, can it as a contract be peaceably unmade by less than all the parties who made it? One party to a contract may violate it—break it, so to speak—but does it not require all to lawfully rescind it?

Descending from these general principles, we find the proposition that in legal contemplation the Union is perpetual confirmed by the history of the Union itself. The Union is much older than the Constitution. It was formed, in fact, by the Articles of Association in 1774. It was matured and continued by the Declaration of Independence in 1776. It was further matured, and the faith of all the then thirteen States expressly plighted and engaged that it should be perpetual, by the Articles of Confederation in 1778. And, finally, in 1787 one of the declared objects for ordaining and establishing the Constitution was *"to form a more perfect Union."* . . .

It follows from these views that no State upon its own mere motion can lawfully get out of the Union; that *resolves* and *ordinances* to that effect are legally void, and that acts of violence, within any State or States against the authority of the United States, are insurrectionary or revolutionary, according to circumstances.

I therefore consider that, in view of the Constitution and the laws the Union is unbroken and to the extent of my ability I shall take care, as the Constitution itself expressly enjoins upon me, that the laws of the Union be faithfully executed in all the States. Doing this I deem to be only a simple duty on my part, and I shall perform it so far as practicable unless my rightful masters, the American people, shall withhold the requisite means, or in some authoritative manner direct the contrary. I trust this will not be regarded as a menace, but only as the declared purpose of the Union that it *will* constitutionally defend and maintain itself. . . .

Plainly the central idea of secession is the essence of anarchy. A majority held in restraint by constitutional checks and limitations, and always changing easily with deliberate changes of popular opinions and sentiments, is the only true sovereign of a free people. Whoever rejects it does, of necessity, fly to anarchy or to despotism. Unanimity is impossible. The rule of a minority, as a permanent arrangement, is wholly inadmissible; so that, rejecting the majority principle, anarchy or despotism in some form is all that is left. . . .

One section of our country believes slavery is *right* and ought to be extended, while the other believes it is *wrong* and ought not to be extended. This is the only substantial dispute. . . .

Physically speaking, we cannot separate. We cannot remove our respective sections from each other nor build an impassable wall between them. A husband and wife may be divorced and go out of the presence and beyond the reach of each other, but the different parts of our country can not do this. They can not but remain face to face, and intercourse either amicable or hostile, must continue between them. Is it possible, then, to make that intercourse more advantageous or more satisfactory *after* separation than *before*? Can aliens make treaties easier than friends can make laws? Can treaties be more faithfully enforced between aliens than laws can among friends? Suppose you go to war, you can not fight always; and when, after much loss on both sides and no gain on either, you cease fighting, the identical old questions, as to terms of intercourse, are again upon you.

This country, with its institutions, belongs to the people who inhabit it. Whenever they shall grow weary of the existing Government, they can exer-

A Currier & Ives cartoon that appeared late in 1860, after Lincoln's victory at the polls. Using the "good bat" of Equal Rights and Free Territory, Lincoln has scored a home run. His defeated opponents, drawn very accurately, are John Bell, Stephen A. Douglas, and John C. Breckinridge. Baseball had just come into its own as a popular pastime and was used by the artist in place of the tired symbols of the horse race, the prize fight, and the cockpit.

This is Lincoln on the day he arrived in Washington to prepare for his inaugural. It was February 23, 1861. He sat for his portrait in Mathew B. Brady's Photographic Parlor. Brady had taken his picture once before, in New York, the day of Lincoln's Cooper Union speech.

The Chief Magistrate derives all his authority from the people, and they have conferred none upon him to fix terms for the separation of the States. The people themselves can do this also if they choose; but the executive, as such, has nothing to do with it. His duty is to administer the present government, as it came to his hands, and to transmit it, unimpaired by him, to his successor.

Why should there not be a patient confidence in the ultimate justice of the people? Is there any better or equal hope, in the world? In our present differences, is either party without faith of being in the right? If the Almighty Ruler of nations, with his eternal truth and justice, be on your side of the North, or on yours of the South, that truth, and that justice, will surely prevail, by the judgment of this great tribunal, the American people.

By the frame of the government under which we live, this same people have wisely given their public servants but little power for mischief; and have, with equal wisdom, provided for the return of that little to their own hands at very short intervals.

While the people retain their virtue, and vigilance, no administration, by any extreme of wickedness or folly, can very seriously injure the government, in the short space of four years.

☞ My countrymen, one and all, think calmly and *well*, upon this whole subject. Nothing valuable can be lost by taking time. If there be an object to *hurry* any of you, in hot haste, to a step which you would never take *deliberately*, that object will be frustrated by taking time; but no good object can be frustrated by it. Such of you as are now dissatisfied, still have the old Constitution unimpaired, and, on the sensitive point, the laws of your own framing under it; while the new administration will have no immediate power, if it would, to change either. If it were admitted that you who are dissatisfied, hold the right side in the dispute, there still is no single good reason for precipitate action. Intelligence, patriotism, Christianity, and a firm reliance on Him, who has never yet forsaken this favored land, are still competent to adjust, in the best way, all our present difficulty.

In *your* hands, my dissatisfied fellow countrymen, and not in *mine*, is the momentous issue of civil war. The government will not assail *you*. You can have no conflict, without being yourselves the aggressors. *You* have no oath registered in Heaven to destroy the government, while *I* shall have the most solemn one to "preserve, protect and defend" it.

7744

☞ I am loth to close. We are not enemies, but friends— We must not be enemies. Though passion may have strained, it must not break our bonds of affection. The mystic chords of memory, streching from every battlefield, and patriot grave, to every living heart and hearthstone, all over this broad land, will yet swell the chorus of the Union, when again touched, as surely they will be, by the better angels of our nature.

After his draft had been set in type at home in Springfield, Lincoln edited it and made some additions. The last page, shown here, contains the famous closing lines on a theme suggested by William Seward, but phrased in Lincoln's own words.

Chief Justice Roger B. Taney administers the oath of office to Lincoln. At left is the retiring President, James Buchanan. The drawing is by Thomas Nast.

cise their *constitutional* right of amending it, or their *revolutionary* right to dismember or overthrow it. I can not be ignorant of the fact that many worthy and patriotic citizens are desirous of having the National Constitution amended. While I make no recommendation of amendments, I fully recognize the rightful authority of the people over the whole subject, to be exercised in either of the modes prescribed in the instrument itself; and I should, under existing circumstances, favor rather than oppose a fair opportunity being afforded the people to act upon it. . . .

The Chief Magistrate derives all his authority from the people, and they have conferred none upon him to fix terms for the separation of the States. . . . His duty is to administer the present Government as it came to his hands and to transmit it unimpaired by him to his successor.

Why should there not be a patient confidence in the ultimate justice of the people? Is there any bet-

As an artist from *Harper's Weekly* saw Lincoln's inaugural on March 4, 1861.

ter or equal hope in the world? In our present differences is either party without faith of being in the right? If the Almighty Ruler of Nations, with His eternal truth and justice, be on your side of the North, or on yours of the South, that truth and that justice will surely prevail by the judgment of this great tribunal of the American people.

By the frame of the Government under which we live, this same people have wisely given their public servants but little power for mischief, and have with equal wisdom provided for the return of that little to their own hands at very short intervals. While the people retain their virtue and vigilance no Administration by any extreme of wickedness or folly can very seriously injure the Government in the short space of four years.

My countrymen, one and all, think calmly and *well* upon this whole subject. Nothing valuable can be lost by taking time. If there be an object to *hurry* any of you in hot haste to a step which you would never take *deliberately*, that object will be frustrated by taking time; but no good object can be frustrated by it. Such of you as are now dissatisfied still have the old Constitution unimpaired, and, on the sensitive point, the laws of your own framing under it; while the new Administration will have no immediate power, if it would, to change either. If it were admitted that you who are dissatisfied hold the right side in the dispute, there still is no single good reason for precipitate action. Intelligence, patriotism, Christianity, and a firm reliance on Him who has never yet forsaken this favored land, are still competent to adjust in the best way all our present difficulty.

In *your* hands, my dissatisfied fellow-countrymen, and not in *Mine*, is the momentous issue of civil war. The government will not assail *you*. You can have no conflict without being yourselves the aggressors. *You* have no oath registered in heaven to destroy the government, while *I* shall have the most solemn one to "preserve, protect, and defend it."

I am loath to close. We are not enemies, but friends. We must not be enemies. Though passion may have strained it must not break our bonds of affection. The mystic chords of memory, stretching from every battlefield and patriot grave to every living heart and hearthstone all over this broad land, will yet swell the chorus of the Union when again touched, as surely they will be, by the better angels of our nature.

Forever free

Although Lincoln was an enemy of slavery, he was never an abolitionist. "My paramount object in this struggle," he wrote Horace Greeley in 1862, "is to save the Union, and is not either to save or destroy slavery. If I could save the Union without freeing any slave, I would do it; if I could save it by freeing all the slaves, I would do it; and if I could save it by freeing some and leaving others alone, I would also do that."

Under the pressure of military and political necessity, the question of emancipation became ever more urgent. With every bloody battle more people came to hold the abolitionist belief that the war's sacrifices would be meaningless unless their fruit was the death of slavery. The slaves themselves, abandoned by their masters as the Union lines moved South, flocked to the army of liberators. Confederate agents seeking aid and recognition from England

This lithograph depicts Lincoln at the task of drafting the Emancipation Proclamation.

Early in June, 1862, Lincoln began work on the draft of the document concerning slavery. On July 22, he read it to a meeting of his Cabinet, who approved it but recommended that it not be made public until a major Union victory had been won. Five days after the battle of Antietam the preliminary proclamation was issued. This mezzotint is from Francis B. Carpenter's famous painting of the first reading to the Cabinet. From the left are Edwin Stanton, Secretary of War; Salmon P. Chase, Secretary of the Treasury; Lincoln; Gideon Welles, Secretary of the Navy; William H. Seward, Secretary of State; Caleb B. Smith, Secretary of the Interior; Montgomery Blair, Postmaster General; Edward Bates, Attorney General.

and France were showing an alarming success in their efforts. As the summer of 1862 came on, the President began to realize different tactics were needed. If the war was to be won and the Union preserved, the slaves must be emancipated. Secretly, Lincoln prepared a draft of an emancipation proclamation and then went over it with his Cabinet.

On September 22, 1862, he issued a preliminary proclamation declaring that on January 1, 1863, the slaves of any state then in rebellion would become "then, thenceforward, and forever free."

On New Year's Day, 1863, as "an act of justice, warranted by the Constitution upon military necessity," Lincoln issued the Emancipation Proclamation. Since the regions which it covered were those still controlled by the Confederacy, the act did not free a single slave. But it signaled the doom of the "peculiar institution." Public opinion in the North and in England swung more strongly behind the Union cause. Negro troops joined the ranks in swelling numbers. Slavery itself was ended legally in all parts of the nation with the ratification of the Thirteenth Amendment on December 18, 1865.

A Union soldier reads the Emancipation Proclamation to a Negro family.

BY THE PRESIDENT OF THE UNITED STATES OF AMERICA:

A Proclamation

WHEREAS on the 22d day of September, A.D. 1862, a proclamation was issued by the President of the United States, containing, among other things, the following, to wit:

> That on the 1st day of January, A.D. 1863, all persons held as slaves within any State or designated part of a State the people whereof shall then be in rebellion against the United States shall be then, thenceforward, and forever free; and the executive government of the United States, including the military and naval authority thereof, will recognize and maintain the freedom of such persons and will do no act or acts to repress such persons, or any of them, in any efforts they may make for their actual freedom. . . .

Now, therefore, I, Abraham Lincoln, President of the United States, by virtue of the power in me vested as Commander in Chief of the Army and Navy of the United States in time of actual armed rebellion against the authority and government of the United States, and as a fit and necessary war measure for suppressing said rebellion, do, on this 1st day of January, A.D., 1863, and in accordance with my purpose so to do, publicly proclaimed for the full period of one hundred days from the first day above mentioned, order and designate as the States and parts of States wherein the people thereof, respectively, are this day in rebellion against the United States the following, to wit:

[The Confederate states, excepting designated Louisiana parishes, Virginia counties, and the state of Tennessee.]

And by virtue of the power and for the purpose aforesaid, I do order and declare that all persons held as slaves within said designated States and parts of States are, and henceforward shall be, free; and that the Executive Government of the United States, including the military and naval authorities thereof, will recognize and maintain the freedom of said persons.

And I hereby enjoin upon the people so declared to be free to abstain from all violence, unless in necessary self-defense; and I recommend to them that, in all cases when allowed, they labor faithfully for reasonable wages.

And I further declare and make known that such persons of suitable condition will be received into the armed service of the United States to garrison forts, positions, stations, and other places, and to man vessels of all sorts in said service.

And upon this act, sincerely believed to be an act of justice, warranted by the Constitution upon military necessity, I invoke the considerate judgment of mankind and the gracious favor of Almighty God.

PROCLAMATION OF EMANCIPATION

BY THE PRESIDENT OF THE UNITED STATES OF AMERICA.

Whereas, On the Twenty-Second day of September, in the year of our Lord One Thousand Eight Hundred and Sixty-Two, a Proclamation was issued by the President of the United States, containing, among other things, the following, to wit:

"That on the First day of January, in the year of our Lord One Thousand Eight Hundred and Sixty-Three, all persons held as Slaves within any State, or designated part of a State, the people whereof shall then be in rebellion against the United States, shall be then, thenceforth, and **FOREVER FREE,** and the *Executive Government of the United States*, including the Military and Naval Authorities thereof, *will recognise and maintain the freedom of such persons*, and will do no act or acts to repress such persons, or any of them, in any efforts they may make for their actual freedom.

"That the Executive will, on the First day of January aforesaid, by proclamation, designate the States and parts of States, if any, in which the people thereof respectively shall then be in rebellion against the United States, and the fact that any State, or the people thereof, shall on that day be in good faith represented in the Congress of the United States by members chosen thereto at elections wherein a majority of the qualified voters of such State shall have participated, shall, in the absence of strong countervailing testimony, be deemed conclusive evidence that such State and the people thereof are not then in rebellion against the United States."

Now, therefore, I, ABRAHAM LINCOLN, PRESIDENT OF THE UNITED STATES, by virtue of the power in me vested as **Commander-in-Chief of the Army and Navy of the United States** in time of actual armed rebellion against the authority and government of the United States, and as a fit and necessary war measure for suppressing said rebellion, do, on this First day of January, in the year of our Lord One Thousand Eight Hundred and Sixty-Three, and in accordance with my purpose so to do, publicly proclaim for the full period of one hundred days from the day of the first above-mentioned order, and designate, as the States and parts of States wherein the people thereof respectively are this day in rebellion against the United States, the following, to wit:— **Arkansas, Texas, Louisiana,** (except the Parishes of St. Bernard, Plaquemines, Jefferson, St. John, St. Charles, St. James, Ascension, Assumption, Terre Bonne, La Fourche, St. Mary, St. Martin, and Orleans, including the City of Orleans,) **Mississippi, Alabama, Florida, Georgia, South Carolina, North Carolina, and Virginia,** (except the forty-eight counties designated as West Virginia, and also the counties of Berkeley, Accomac, Northampton, Elizabeth City, York, Princess Ann, and Norfolk, including the cities of Norfolk and Portsmouth,) and which excepted parts are for the present left precisely as if this Proclamation were not issued.

And by virtue of the power and for the purpose aforesaid, I do order and declare that **ALL PERSONS HELD AS SLAVES** within said designated States and parts of States ARE, AND HENCEFORWARD **SHALL BE FREE!** and that the Executive Government of the United States, including the Military and Naval Authorities thereof, will recognize and maintain the freedom of said persons.

And I hereby enjoin upon the people so declared to be free to abstain from all violence, UNLESS IN NECESSARY SELF-DEFENCE; and I recommend to them that in all cases, when allowed, they LABOR FAITHFULLY FOR REASONABLE WAGES.

And I further declare and make known that such persons of suitable condition will be received into the armed service of the United States, to garrison forts, positions, stations, and other places, and to man vessels of all sorts in said service.

And upon this act, sincerely believed to be AN ACT OF JUSTICE, warranted by the Constitution, upon military necessity, I invoke the considerate judgment of mankind and the gracious favor of ALMIGHTY GOD!

In Testimony Whereof, *I have hereunto set my name, and caused the seal of the United States to be affixed.*

[L. S.] *Done at the* CITY OF WASHINGTON, *this First day of January, in the Year of our Lord One Thousand Eight Hundred and Sixty-Three, and of the Independence of the United States the Eighty Seventh.*

By the President,

William H. Seward

Secretary of State.

A. Lincoln

J. MAYER & CO. LITH. 4 STATE ST. BOSTON.

A lithograph with the text of the Proclamation. Scenes of slavery are contrasted with those of freedom in many such broadsides distributed widely after the event.

The Thirteenth Amendment, with Lincoln's signature of approval on February 1, 1865, and the signatures below of those who voted for it in the Senate and House.

Thirty-Eighth Congress of the United States.

A Resolution: Submitting to the Legislatures of the several States a proposition to amend the Constitution of the United States.

Resolved by the Senate and House of Representatives of the United States of America in Congress assembled, (two-thirds of both Houses concurring) That the following article be proposed to the Legislatures of the several States as an amendment to the Constitution of the United States, which, when ratified by three-fourths of said Legislatures, shall be valid, to all intents and purposes as a part of the said Constitution, namely:

ARTICLE XIII.

Section 1. Neither slavery nor involuntary servitude, except as a punishment for crime, whereof the party shall have been duly convicted, shall exist within the United States, or any place subject to their jurisdiction.

Section 2. Congress shall have power to enforce this article by appropriate legislation.

Attest: Schuyler Colfax, Speaker of the House of Representatives

Secretary of the Senate — H. Hamlin, Vice President of the United States and President of the Senate

Clerk of the House of Representatives

Approved, February 1. 1865. Abraham Lincoln

In the Senate, April 8. 1864.

In the House of Representatives, January 31, 1865

The New-York Times.

VOL. XIII—NO. 3794. NEW-YORK, FRIDAY, NOVEMBER 20, 1863. PRICE THREE CENTS.

IMPORTANT FROM EAST TENNESSEE

The Rebels Advancing upon Knoxville.

THE PLACE COMPLETELY INVESTED.

HEAVY SKIRMISHING YESTERDAY.

The Position Very Strongly Fortified.

THE REBEL FORCES UNDER LONGSTREET.

THE HEROES OF JULY.

A Solemn and Imposing Event.

Dedication of the National Cemetery at Gettysburgh.

IMMENSE NUMBERS OF VISITORS.

Oration by Hon. Edward Everett—Speeches of President Lincoln, Mr. Seward and Governor Seymour.

THE PROGRAMME SUCCESSFULLY CARRIED OUT

surrounded the position taken by the immense multitude of people.

The Marshal took up a position on the left of the stand. Numerous flags and banners, suitably draped, were exhibited on the stand among the audience. The entire scene was one of grandeur due to the importance of the occasion. So quiet were the people that every word uttered by the orator of the day must have been heard by them all, notwithstanding the immensity of the concourse.

Among the distinguished persons on the platform were the following: Governors Bradford, of Maryland; Curtin, of Pennsylvania; Morton, of Indiana; Seymour, of New-York; Parker, of New-Jersey, and Tod, of Ohio; Ex-Gov. Dennison, of Ohio; John Brough, Governor Elect, of Ohio; Charles Anderson, [illegible] Ohio; Major-Generals Schenck, Stahel, Doubleday, and [illegible] Brigadier-General Gibbon; and Provost-Marshal-General Fry.

PRESIDENT LINCOLN'S ADDRESS.

The President then delivered the following dedicatory speech:

Fourscore and seven years ago our Fathers brought forth upon this Continent a new nation, conceived in liberty and dedicated to the proposition that all men are created equal. [Applause.] Now we are engaged in a great civil war, testing whether that nation, or any nation so conceived and so dedicated, can long endure. We are met on a great battle-field of that war. We are met to dedicate a portion of it as the final resting-place of those who here gave their lives that that nation might live. It is altogether fitting and proper that we should do this. But in a larger sense we cannot dedicate. We cannot consecrate, we cannot hallow this ground. The brave men, living and dead, who struggled here have consecrated it far above our power to add or detract. [Applause.] The world will little note nor long remember, what we say here, but it can never forget what they did here. [Applause.] It is for us, the living, rather to be dedicated here to the refinished work that they have thus so far nobly carried on. [Applause.] It is rather for us to be here dedicated to the great task remaining before us, that from these honored dead we take increased devotion to that cause for which they here gave the last full measure of devotion; that we here highly resolve that the dead shall not have died in vain; [applause] that the Nation shall under God have a new birth of freedom, and that Governments of the people, by the people and for the people, shall not perish from the earth. [Long continued applause.]

Three cheers were then given for the President and the Governors of the States.

After the delivery of the addresses, the dirge and [illegible] the immense assemblage separated at about 4 o'clock.

About 3 o'clock in the afternoon, the Fifth New York regiment of heavy artillery, Col. MURRAY, was marched to the temporary residence of Gov. SEYMOUR, where they passed in review before the Governor, presenting a handsome spectacle. Upon the conclusion of this ceremony, which attracted quite a crowd of sight-seers. Gov. SEYMOUR presented a handsome silk regimental standard to the regiment, accompanying the gift with the following speech:

GREAT BRITAIN AND AMERICA.

Welcome to Rev. Henry Ward Beecher.

Demonstration at the Brooklyn Academy of Music.

A GREAT SPEECH:

Impressions of British Feeling Toward America.

Hardly more than two minutes was needed for Lincoln to read his address at Gettysburg on November 19, 1863. The next morning, *The New York Times* reported the ceremonies on page one, including Lincoln's remarks (encircled) toward the end of the story. The New York *Herald* saw even less significance in the President's words. Its report mentioned in passing that the President had also made some "dedicatory remarks."

1863 Abraham Lincoln: Gettysburg Address

That government of the people, by the people, for the people, shall not perish from the earth

General Lee's second attempt to invade the North ended disastrously at Gettysburg in the first week of July, 1863. The battle marked the turning point of the Civil War. The Unionists lost 23,000 killed, wounded, or captured, and the Confederates 20,400, a loss Lee could not sustain. Headed by Pennsylvania, eighteen states banded together to convert the battlefield site into a national cemetery. The committee asked the celebrated orator Edward Everett to make an address at the dedication ceremonies. Among the many invited to attend was President Lincoln. It was only some two weeks before the event that it occurred to the committee that protocol required Mr. Lincoln be asked to say a few words, too. Busy with the prosecution of the war, the President found time to draft a few sentences which he revised the morning of November 19, as he waited in Gettysburg for the ceremonies to begin. When Mr. Everett concluded his two-hour oration, Lincoln rose to make the brief speech which has become treasured as one of the most poetic expressions of the meaning of liberty.

Four score and seven years ago our fathers
brought forth, upon this continent, a new nation, conceived in Liberty, and dedicated to the proposition
that all men are created equal.

Now we are engaged in a great civil war, testing whether that nation, or any nation, so conceived,
and so dedicated, can long endure. We are met
here on a great battle-field of that war. We ~~are~~ have
~~meet~~ come to dedicate a portion of it as ~~the~~ a final resting place ~~of~~ for those who here gave their lives that
that nation might live. It is altogether fitting
and proper that we should do this.

But in a larger sense we can not dedicate—
we can not consecrate— we can not hallow this
ground. The brave men, living and dead, who struggled here, have consecrated it far above our poor power
to add or detract. The world will little note,
nor long remember, what we say here, but
can never forget what they did here. It is
for us, the living, rather to be dedicated
here to the unfinished work which they have,
thus far, so nobly carried on. It is rather

for us to be here dedicated to the great
task remaining before us— that from these
honored dead we take increased devotion
to ~~the~~ that cause for which they here gave ~~gave~~
the last full measure of devotion— that
we here highly resolve that these dead
shall not have died in vain; that the
nation shall have a new birth of freedom,
and that this government of the people, by
the people, for the people, shall not perish
from the earth.

After breakfast on the morning of the day at Gettysburg, President Lincoln made a new draft, in ink, of his speech. Above and opposite are the two pages in his hand from which he spoke early in the afternoon. Coming after Senator Everett's long-distance run Lincoln's dash was over before the audience could appreciate it. It was a "flat failure," he told his friend Ward Hill Lamon. "I am distressed about it. I ought to have prepared it with more care."

FOUR SCORE and seven years ago our fathers brought forth on this continent, a new nation, conceived in Liberty, and dedicated to the proposition that all men are created equal.

Now we are engaged in a great civil war, testing whether that nation or any nation so conceived and so dedicated, can long endure. We are met on a great battle-field of that war. We have come to dedicate a portion of that field, as a final resting place for those who here gave their lives that that nation might live. It is altogether fitting and proper that we should do this.

But, in a larger sense, we can not dedicate—we can not consecrate—we can not hallow—this ground. The brave men, living and dead, who struggled here, have consecrated it, far above our poor power to add or detract. The world will little note, nor long remember what we say here, but it can never forget what they did here. It is for us the living, rather, to be dedicated here to the unfinished work which they who fought here have thus far so nobly advanced. It is rather for us to be here dedicated to the great task remaining before us—that from these honored dead we take increased devotion to that cause for which they gave the last full measure of devotion—that we here highly resolve that these dead shall not have died in vain—that this nation, under God, shall have a new birth of freedom—and that government of the people, by the people, for the people, shall not perish from the earth.

The greatest good to the greatest number

Jefferson's dream of a farmers' paradise was exploded in the shellfire of the Civil War. By Appomattox the industrial machine dominated the nation's economy and men and women were moving out of the farms and villages to people the new factories. Millions of immigrants swelled the tide of cheap labor pouring into the industrial centers. Most of the new Americans came penniless and in the fierce competition of expanding industrialism were at the mercy of low wages and miserable living conditions. Adding to their woes was the contempt in which the new arrivals were held by the "native" Ameri-

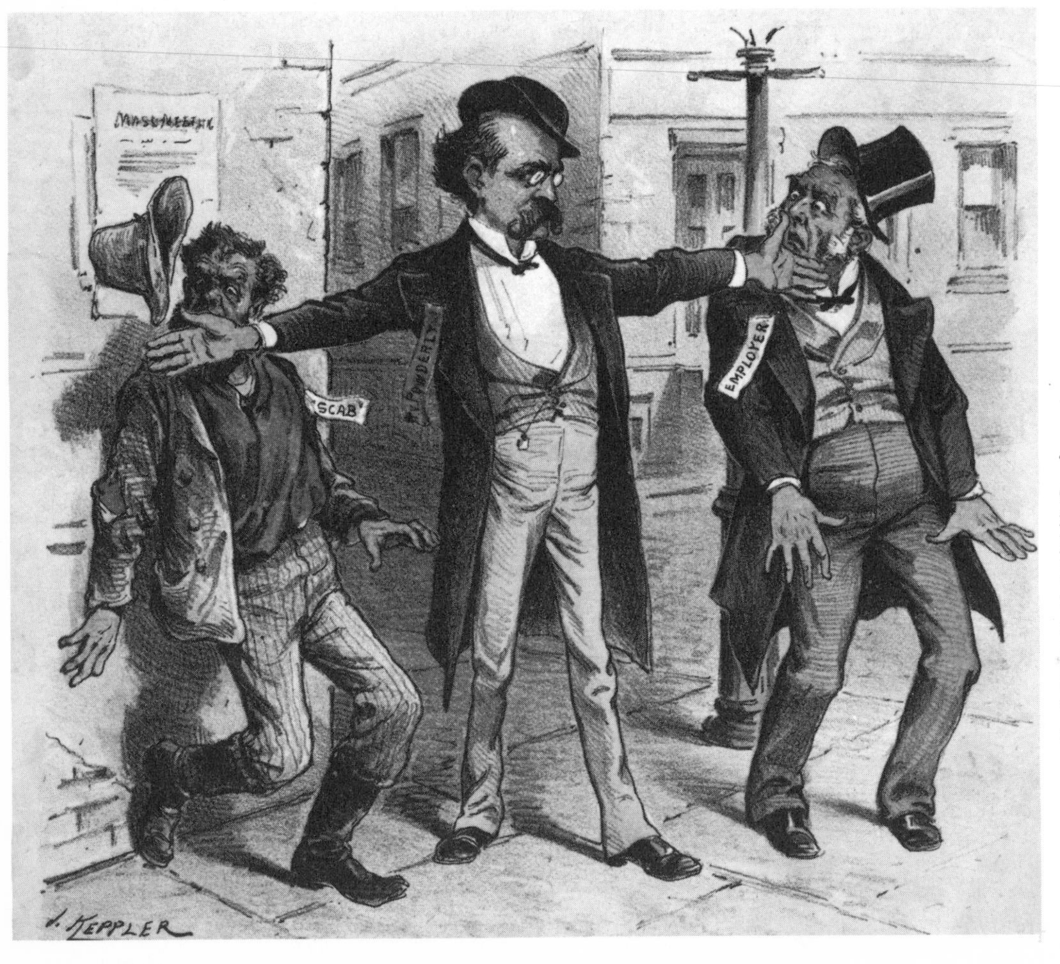

"The Gospel of the Knights of Labor"—an 1886 cartoon from *Puck*. Terence V. Powderly was the Grand Master of the national union, elected in 1879. He served as Mayor of Scranton in 1878–1882; in 1897 he was appointed U.S. Commissioner of Immigration.

The summer of 1877 saw a national strike wave, set rolling by a wage cut on the railroads. The railwaymen in this contemporary drawing were fired upon by militia called out by the governor of Maryland. A dozen in the crowd were killed, and eighteen wounded. As the strike spread, President Hayes sent troops to several states. The strike was broken, but unrest continued and found wider expression on the political stage.

cans, an antagonism which carried over to labor as a class in society.

Massed together in the factories, the workers soon found strength in uniting for better wages and working conditions. Little help came from government, for Congress was hostile to regulation of business interests and the courts unfriendly to restrictive legislation adopted by the states. What gains had been made before the war were seriously weakened by the long depression that began in 1873. The sturdy prewar doctrine of self-reliance and the dream of the self-made millionaire helped make unionism somehow suspect, and the employers' use of lockouts, blacklists, and legal prosecutions crippled attempts to extend organization.

But just as business found increased power in combination through trusts, so labor moved towards broader forms of organization. In 1869 the Noble and Holy Order of the Knights of Labor was founded at a garment cutters' meeting in Philadelphia. The Knights were an industrial union open to all workingmen, skilled or unskilled, regardless of race, creed, color, or sex. Only gamblers, saloonkeepers, lawyers, bankers, and stockbrokers were shut out. Unlike most of the earlier unions, which were limited to one trade or industry, the Knights reached out to combine all the nation's workers in one union. For almost a decade it grew only slowly and sporadically. In 1878, the year it adopted a constitution, it had fifty thousand members. In 1886, it had grown to seven hundred thousand. The Preamble to the Constitution of the Knights of Labor expressed the workingmen's ideals and charted the course they hoped would fulfill them.

Striking workmen in their Sunday best parade through the streets with placards and posters.

THE RECENT alarming development and aggression of aggregated wealth, which, unless checked, will invariably lead to the pauperization and hopeless degradation of the toiling masses, render it imperative, if we desire to enjoy the blessings of life, that a check should be placed upon its power and upon unjust accumulation, and a system adopted which will secure to the laborer the fruits of his toil; and as this much-desired object can only be accomplished by the thorough unification of labor, and the united efforts of those who obey the divine injunction that 'In the sweat of thy brow shalt thou eat bread,' we have formed the Knights of Labor with a view of securing the organization and direction, by co-operative effort, of the power of the industrial classes; and we submit to the world the object sought to be accomplished by our organization, calling upon all who believe in securing 'the greatest good to the greatest number' to aid and assist us:—

I. To bring within the folds of organization every department of productive industry, making knowledge a standpoint for action, and industrial and moral worth, not wealth, the true standard of individual and national good greatness.

II. To secure to the toilers a proper share of the

wealth that they create; more of the leisure that rightfully belongs to them; more societary advantages; more of the benefits, privileges, and emoluments of the world; in a word, all those rights and privileges necessary to make them capable of enjoying, appreciating, defending, and perpetuating the blessings of good government.

III. To arrive at the true condition of the producing masses in their educational, moral, and financial condition, by demanding from the various governments the establishment of bureaus of Labor Statistics.

IV. The establishment of co-operative institutions, productive and distributive.

V. The reserving of the public lands—the heritage of the people—for the actual settler; not another acre for railroads or speculators.

VI. The abrogation of all laws that do not bear equally upon capital and labor, the removal of unjust technicalities, delays, and discriminations in the administration of justice, and the adopting of measures providing for the health and safety of those engaged in mining, manufacturing, or building pursuits.

VII. The enactment of laws to compel chartered corporations to pay their employes weekly, in full, for labor performed during the preceding week, in the lawful money of the country.

VIII. The enactment of laws giving mechanics and laborers a first lien on their work for their full wages.

IX. The abolishment of the contract system on national, State, and municipal work.

X. The substitution of arbitration for strikes, whenever and wherever employers and employes are willing to meet on equitable grounds.

XI. The prohibition of the employment of children in workshops, mines, and factories before attaining their fourteenth year.

XII. To abolish the system of letting out by contract the labor of convicts in our prisons and reformatory institutions.

XIII. To secure for both sexes equal pay for equal work.

XIV. The reduction of the hours of labor to eight per day, so that the laborers may have more time for social enjoyment and intellectual improvement, and be enabled to reap the advantages conferred by the labor-saving machinery which their brains have created.

XV. To prevail upon governments to establish a purely national circulating medium, based upon the faith and resources of the nation, and issued directly to the people, without intervention of any system of banking corporations, which money shall be a legal tender in payment of all debts, public or private.

Henry George, father of the single-tax program. George proposed to replace the existing tax system with a single tax on all increments in the value of land. He believed that the single tax would prevent land speculation and depressions, and restore the small-businessman, the farmer, and the worker to a decent standard of living.

1879 Henry George: Progress and Poverty

Trust liberty and follow her

"For four years past," wrote Peter Cooper to President Hayes in 1877, "millions of men and women, in this hitherto rich and prosperous country, have been thrown out of employment, or living on precarious and inadequate wages, have felt embittered with a lot in which neither economy nor industry, nor a cheerful willingness to work hard, can bring an alleviation."

Speaking for the men "who hopelessly and cheerlessly make the wealth that enriches the idler and impoverishes the producers," novelist William Dean Howells said, "they feel that something is wrong, and they know that the wrong is not theirs."

Beneath the widely voiced grievances in the decades that followed the Civil War lay the strong American conviction that the individual has a natural right to his humanity. To be human is to live an existence worthy of a human being, and to order society so that its institutions are means to the fulfillment of man's humanity.

One of the many voices heard in protest against the growing inequalities of the Gilded Age came from an obscure printer, Henry George. Born in Philadelphia in 1839, he went briefly to sea as a boy, became a typesetter, then moved to the west coast where he lived precariously as a prospector and newspaperman. In 1869 he visited New York and saw the violent paradox of the greatest wealth and the deepest poverty existing side by side. Two years later he published a pamphlet sketching the basic elements of his single-tax theory—a system of land taxation calculated to eliminate large fortunes and provide decent security for all. His analysis developed into a book, Progress and Poverty, *which no one seemed to want to publish. In 1879 it finally appeared, in an edition of 500 copies. In two years it had sold 100,000 and by 1906 more than a hundred editions in a score of languages had been read by some six million people.*

Henry George's remedy for the economy's ills never won general acceptance, but his passionate portrait of the hard times millions of Americans were experiencing and his indignant contrast between "The House of Have" and "The House of Want" commanded the country's attention. In this excerpt from the last chapter of Progress and Poverty *he underscored liberty's relationship to economic conditions.*

WE SPEAK of Liberty as one thing, and of virtue, wealth, knowledge, invention, national strength and national independence as other things. But, of all these, Liberty is the source, the mother, the necessary condition. She is to virtue what light is to color; to wealth what sunshine is to grain; to knowledge what eyes are to sight. She is the genius of invention, the brawn of national strength, the spirit of national independence. Where Liberty rises, there virtue grows, wealth increases, knowledge expands, invention multiplies human powers, and in strength and spirit the freer nation rises among her neighbors as Saul amid his brethren—taller and fairer. Where Liberty sinks, there virtue fades, wealth diminishes, knowledge is forgotten, invention ceases, and empires once mighty in arms and arts become a helpless prey to freer barbarians! . . .

In our time, as in times before, creep on the insidious forces that, producing inequality, destroy

Liberty. On the horizon the clouds begin to lower. Liberty calls to us again. We must follow her further; we must trust her fully. Either we must wholly accept her or she will not stay. It is not enough that men should vote; it is not enough that they should be theoretically equal before the law. They must have liberty to avail themselves of the opportunities and means of life; they must stand on equal terms with reference to the bounty of nature. Either this, or Liberty withdraws her light! Either this, or darkness comes on, and the very forces that progress has evolved turn to powers that work destruction. This is the universal law. This is the lesson of the centuries. Unless its foundations be laid in justice the social structure cannot stand.

Our primary social adjustment is a denial of justice. In allowing one man to own the land on which and from which other men must live, we have made them his bondsmen in a degree which increases as material progress goes on. This is the subtile alchemy that in ways they do not realize is extracting from the masses in every civilized country the fruits of their weary toil; that is instituting a harder and more hopeless slavery in place of that which has been destroyed; that is bringing political despotism out of political freedom, and must soon transmute democratic institutions into anarchy.

It is this that turns the blessings of material progress into a curse. It is this that crowds human beings into noisome cellars and squalid tenement houses; that fills prisons and brothels; that goads men with want and consumes them with greed; that robs women of the grace and beauty of perfect womanhood; that takes from little children the joy and innocence of life's morning. . . .

But if, while there is yet time, we turn to Justice and obey her, if we trust Liberty and follow her, the dangers that now threaten must disappear, the forces that now menace will turn to agencies of elevation. Think of the powers now wasted; of the infinite fields of knowledge yet to be explored; of the possibilities of which the wondrous inventions of this century give us but a hint. With want destroyed; with greed changed to noble passions; with the fraternity that is born of equality taking the place of the jealousy and fear that now array men against each other; with mental power loosed by conditions that give to the humblest comfort and leisure; and who shall measure the heights to which our civilization may soar? Words fail the thought! It is the Golden Age of which poets have sung and high-raised seers have told in metaphor! It is the glorious vision which has always haunted man with gleams of fitful splendor. It is what he saw whose eyes at Patmos were closed in a trance. It is the culmination of Christianity—the City of God on earth, with its walls of jasper and its gates of pearl! It is the reign of the Prince of Peace!

In 1886 Henry George was the liberal and labor candidate for mayor of New York, running against Theodore Roosevelt and Abram S. Hewitt. When Hewitt won, Thomas Nast cartooned the results (above) with the caption: "That was a close shave. Old Knickerbocker's throat was endangered, 'by George!'" The single-taxer was the independent Democratic candidate for mayor again in 1897, but died while campaigning.

Edward Bellamy, whose utopian socialist novel, *Looking Backward,* published in 1888, was, like Henry George's *Progress and Poverty*, a philosophical challenge to the rugged individualists of their day.

I remember all the good words and all

The long struggle of the red man to defend his lands against the white man's invasion came to an end near the close of the nineteenth century. The vast homeland of the Great Plains and the prairies, an Indian domain until after the Civil War, was torn away by the building of the Union Pacific Railroad and the slaughter of the buffalo. His food and hunting grounds gone, the Indian was shunted from reservation to reservation, at the mercy of the frontiersman, the miner, the trader who seized what they wanted in the face of a corrupt and confused government. The warrior tribes fought back bitterly for a time, but by the eighteen-eighties they recognized their resistance was hopeless.

Among the last to attempt a final stand were the Nez Percés. Placed on a reservation, the tribe had accepted it quietly, and under pressure had even given up another part of their land. But when the white man asked for more, they refused to leave their home valley in Oregon. They fought bravely against the federal troops sent to evict them but finally decided to move to Canada, where, it was said, treaties were respected. With their women and children they retreated, marching over two thousand miles of mountains, conducting running battles with the soldiers, until at last, exhausted and near starvation, they were forced to surrender at the Canadian border.

The Nez Percés were led by Chief Joseph, whom Major General O. O. Howard called one of the greatest chiefs of Indian history. In 1879, three years after his surrender, Chief Joseph published An Indian's View of Indian Affairs, *recording his dealings with President Rutherford B. Hayes. A cry for justice, it is a tragic summary of the relations between Indian and white.*

Chief Joseph of the Nez Perces. The son of a chief, he was born in Oregon about 1841. The terms of the surrender he accepted were soon ignored, and his tribe removed to Oklahoma, where the climate proved devastating to their health.

the broken promises

MY FRIENDS, I have been asked to show you my heart. I am glad to have a chance to do so. I want the white people to understand my people. Some of you think an Indian is like a wild animal. This is a mistake. I will tell you all about our people, and then you can judge whether an Indian is a man or not. I believe much trouble and blood would be saved if we opened our hearts more. I will tell you in my way how the Indian sees things. The white man has more words to tell you how they look to him, but it does not require many words to speak the truth. What I have to say will come from my heart, and I will speak with a straight tongue. Ah-cum-kin-i-ma-me-hut (the Great Spirit) is looking at me, and will hear me.

My name is In-mut-too-yah-lat-lat (Thunder traveling over the Mountains). I am chief of the Wal-lam-wat-kin band of Chute-pa-lu, or Nez Percés

This 1876 cartoon points up the corrupt operation of government agents who collaborated with commercial interests to exploit the conquered Indians. Worthless blankets and rotten rations were bought with federal funds, and doled out to the helpless tribes confined to the reservations.

Chief Joseph and his warriors, pictured in a contemporary illustrated weekly, surrendering at General Nelson Miles's headquarters in October, 1876. With an army of 300, Chief Joseph had fought 11 engagements against a total of more than 2,000 soldiers. He lost 151 killed and 89 wounded; the U.S. Army lost 176 killed and 140 wounded. On the last day of the fighting General Miles brought up howitzers and Gatling guns to shell the Indian camp.

(nose-pierced Indians). I was born in eastern Oregon, thirty-eight winters ago. My father was chief before me. When a young man, he was called Joseph by Mr. Spaulding, a missionary. He died a few years ago. There was no stain on his hands of the blood of a white man. He left a good name on the earth. He advised me well for my people.

Our fathers gave us many laws, which they had learned from their fathers. These laws were good. They told us to treat all men as they treated us; that we should never be the first to break a bargain; that it was a disgrace to tell a lie; that we should speak only the truth; that it was a shame for one man to take from another his wife, or his property without paying for it. We were taught to believe that the Great Spirit sees and hears everything, and that he never forgets; that hereafter he will give every man a spirit-home according to his deserts: if he has been a good man, he will have a good home; if he has been a bad man, he will have a bad home. This I believe, and all my people believe the same . . .

At last I was granted permission to come to Washington and bring my friend Yellow Bull and our interpreter with me. I am glad I came. I have shaken hands with a good many friends, but there are some things I want to know which no one seems able to explain. I cannot understand how the Government sends a man out to fight us, as it did General Miles, and then breaks his word. Such a government has something wrong about it. I cannot understand why so many chiefs are allowed to talk so many different ways, and promise so many different things. I have seen the Great Father Chief (President Hayes); the Next Great Chief (Secretary of the Interior); the Commissioner Chief (Hoyt); the Law Chief (General Butler); and many other law chiefs (Congressmen) and they all say they are my friends, and that I shall have justice, but while all their mouths talk right I do not understand why nothing is done for my people. I have heard talk and talk but nothing is done. Good words do not last long unless they amount to something. Words do not pay for my dead people. They do not pay for my country now overrun by white men. They do not protect my father's grave. They do not pay for my horses and cattle. Good words do not give me back my children. Good words will not make good the promise of your war chief, General Miles. Good words will not give my people good health and stop them from dying. Good words will not get my people a home where they can live in peace and take care of themselves. I am tired of talk that comes to nothing. It makes my heart sick when I remember all the good words and all the broken promises. There has been too much talking by men who had no right to talk. Too many misinterpretations have been made; too many misunderstandings have come up between the white men and the Indians. If the white man wants to live in peace with the Indian he can live in peace. There need be no trouble. Treat all men alike. Give them the same laws. Give them all an even chance to live and grow. All men were made by the same Great Spirit Chief. They are all brothers. The earth is the mother of all people, and all people should have equal rights upon it. You might as well expect all rivers to run backward as that any man who was born a free man should be contented penned up and denied liberty to go where he pleases. If you tie a horse to a stake, do you expect he will grow fat? If you pen an Indian upon a small spot of earth and compel him to stay there, he will not be contented nor will he grow and prosper. I have asked some of the Great White Chiefs where they get their authority to say to the Indian that he shall stay in one place, while he sees white men going where they please. They cannot tell me.

I only ask of the Government to be treated as all other men are treated. If I cannot go to my own home, let me have a home in a country where my people will not die so fast. I would like to go to Bitter Root Valley. There my people would be happy; where they are now they are dying. Three have died since I left my camp to come to Washington.

When I think of our condition, my heart is heavy. I see men of my own race treated as outlaws and driven from country to country, or shot down like animals.

I know that my race must change. We cannot hold our own with the white men as we are. We only ask an even chance to live as other men live. We ask to be recognized as men. We ask that the same law shall work alike on all men. If an Indian breaks the law, punish him by the law. If a white man breaks the law, punish him also.

Let me be a free man, free to travel, free to stop, free to work, free to trade when I choose, free to choose my own teachers, free to follow the religion of my fathers, free to talk, think and act for myself —and I will obey every law or submit to the penalty.

Whenever the white man treats the Indian as they treat each other then we shall have no more wars. We shall be all alike—brothers of one father and mother, with one sky above us and one country around us and one government for all. Then the Great Spirit Chief who rules above will smile upon this land and send rain to wash out the bloody spots made by brothers' hands upon the face of the earth. For this time the Indian race is waiting and praying. I hope no more groans of wounded men and women will ever go to the ear of the Great Spirit Chief above, and that all people may be one people.

The Negro cannot remain half slave and half free

Twenty-one years after Congress had emancipated the slaves in the District of Columbia, Frederick Douglass marked the anniversary with a speech to the Congregational Church in Washington. No American was better qualified to estimate how the Negro stood in April of 1883. Since his escape to freedom in 1838, Frederick Douglass had swiftly risen to become the foremost abolitionist and political spokesman of his people. Almost fifty years of unrelenting struggle in the cause of freedom had won him great prestige at home and abroad. In his speeches and writings the former slave was brilliant and fearless, always saying what he thought the world should hear. In the Civil War he had seen freedom won for the Negro people, and, shortly after, laws established to guarantee their liberty. But by 1876 the Hayes-Tilden Compromise had ended Reconstruction. Soon, too, the courts had made a dead letter of the Fourteenth and Fifteenth Amendments. Not content with uttering thanksgiving for emancipation on this anniversary, Douglass went on to probe the heart of relations between Negro and white in this country.

THE SKY of the American Negro is dark, but not rayless; it is stormy, but not cheerless . . . As the war for the Union recedes into the misty shadows of the past, and the Negro is no longer needed to assault forts and stop rebel bullets, he is in some sense, of less importance. Peace with the old master class has been war to the Negro. As the one has risen, the other has fallen. The reaction has been sudden, marked, and violent. It has swept the Negro from all the legislative halls of the Southern States, and from those of the Congress of the United States. It has, in many cases, driven him from the ballot box and the jury box. The situation has much in it for serious thought, but nothing to cause despair . . .

Time and events which have done so much for us in the past, will, I trust, not do less for us in the future. The moral government of the universe is on our side, and cooperates, with all honest efforts, to lift up the down-trodden and oppressed in all lands, whether the oppressed be white or black . . .

It is his sad lot to live in a land where all presumptions are arrayed against him, unless we except the presumption of inferiority and worthlessness. If his course is downward, he meets very little resistance, but if upward, his way is disputed at every turn of the road. If he comes in rags and in wretchedness, he answers the public demand for a Negro, and provokes no anger, though he may provoke derision, but if he presumes to be a gentleman and a scholar, he is then entirely out of his place. He excites resentment and calls forth stern and bitter opposition. If he offers himself to a builder as a mechanic, to a client as a lawyer, to a patient as a physician, to a university as a professor, or to a department as a clerk, no matter what may be his ability or his attainments, there is a presumption based upon his color or his previous condition, of incompetency, and if he succeeds at all, he has to do so against this most discouraging presumption.

It is a real calamity, in this country, for any man, guilty or not guilty, to be accused of crime, but it is

Frederick Douglass, a slave on Maryland's Eastern Shore, taught himself to read and write secretly, and at twenty-one fled to freedom. He became a speaker for the abolitionists, often attacked by mobs. Interested in freedom for all, he was the only male speaker at the first woman's rights convention at Seneca Falls. He edited several influential newspapers, lectured widely, raised Negro regiments in the Civil War, campaigned successfully for Negro suffrage and civil rights. Grant made him secretary of the Santo Domingo mission in 1871 and Hayes appointed him U.S. Marshal of the District of Columbia. He died at seventy-eight, in 1895.

an incomparably greater calamity for any colored man to be so accused. Justice is often painted with bandaged eyes. She is described in forensic eloquence, as utterly blind to wealth or poverty, high or low, white or black, but a mask of iron, however thick, could never blind American justice, when a black man happens to be on trial. Here, even more than elsewhere, he will find all presumptions of law and evidence against him. It is not so much the business of his enemies to prove him guilty, as it is the business of himself to prove his innocence. The reasonable doubt which is usually interposed to save the life and liberty of a white man charged with crime, seldom has any force or effect when a colored man is accused of crime . . .

A still greater misfortune to the Negro is that the press, that engine of omnipotent power, usually tries him in advance of the courts, and when once his case is decided in the newspapers, it is easy for the jury to bring in its verdict of "guilty as indicted."

In many parts of our common country, the action of courts and juries is entirely too slow for the impetuosity of the people's justice. When the black man is accused, the mob takes the law into its own hands, and whips, shoots, stabs, hangs or burns the accused, simply upon the allegation or suspicion of crime . . .

Another feature of the situation is, that this mob violence is seldom rebuked by the press and the pulpit, in its immediate neighborhood. Because the public opinion which sustains and makes possible such outrages, intimidates both press and pulpit.

Besides, nobody expects that those who participate in such mob violence will ever be held answerable to the law, and punished. Of course, judges are not always unjust, nor juries always partial in cases of this class, but I affirm that I have here given you no picture of the fancy, and I have alleged no point incapable of proof, and drawn no line darker or denser than the terrible reality. The situation, my colored fellow citizens, is discouraging, but with all its hardships and horrors, I am neither desperate nor despairing as to the future.

One ground of hope is found in the fact referred to in the beginning and that is, the discussion concerning the Negro still goes on.

The country in which we live is happily governed by ideas as well as by laws, and no black man need despair while there is an audible and earnest assertion of justice and right on his behalf. He may be riddled with bullets, or roasted over a slow fire by the mob, but his cause cannot be shot or burned or otherwise destroyed. Like the impalpable ghost of the murdered Hamlet, it is immortal. All talk of its being a dead issue is a mistake. It may for a time be buried, but it is not dead. Tariffs, free trade, civil service, and river and harbor bills, may for a time cover it, but it will rise again, and again, and again, with increased life and vigor. Every year adds to the black man's numbers. Every year adds to his wealth and to his intelligence. These will speak for him.

There is a power in numbers, wealth and intelligence, which can never be despised nor defied. All efforts thus far to diminish the Negro's importance as a man and as a member of the American body politic, have failed . . .

Without putting my head to the ground, I can even now hear the anxious inquiry as to when this discussion of the Negro will cease. When will he cease to be a bone of contention between the two great parties? Speaking for myself I can honestly say I wish it to cease. I long to see the Negro utterly out of the whirlpool of angry political debate. No one will rejoice more heartily than I shall when this consummation is reached. I want the whole American people to unite with the sentiment of their greatest captain, U. S. Grant, and say with him on this subject, "Let us have peace." I need it; you need it; the Negro needs it; and every lover of his country should endeavor to withdraw the Negro from this angry gulf. But it is idle, utterly idle to dream of peace anywhere in this world, while any part of the human family are the victims of marked injustice and oppression.

In America, no less than elsewhere, purity must go before tranquillity. Nations, no more than individuals, can reverse this fundamental and eternal order of human relations. There is no modern Joshua who can command this resplendent orb of popular discussion to stand still. As in the past, so in the future, it will go on. It may be arrested and imprisoned for a while, but no power can permanently restrain it.

If you wish to suppress it, I counsel you, my fellow citizens, to remove its cause. The voice of popular complaint, whether it is heard in this country or in other countries, does not and can not rest upon dreams, visions, or illusions of any kind. There must be solid ground for it.

The demand for Negro rights would have ceased long since but for the existence of a sufficient and substantial cause for its continuance . . .

What Abraham Lincoln said in respect of the United States is as true of the colored people as of the relations of those States. They can not remain half slave and half free. You must give them all or take from them all. Until this half-and-half condition is ended, there will be just ground of complaint. You will have an aggrieved class, and this discussion will go on. Until the public schools shall cease to be caste schools in every part of our country, this discussion will go on. Until the colored man's pathway to the American ballot box, North and South, shall

Blanche K. Bruce was one of the two Negro Senators—both from Mississippi—elected during the Reconstruction period. After serving as tax collector in Natchez, sheriff and superintendent of schools, he was elected to the U.S. Senate. Bruce, a Virginia slave who had escaped to the North and been educated at Oberlin College, was thirty-three when he began his 1875–1881 term. The other Negro Senator, Hiram R. Revels, was elected to fill out the uncompleted term of Jefferson Davis, and served one year.

John R. Lynch represented Mississippi in Congress in 1873–77 and 1882–83. In 1872, he was Speaker of the House in his state legislature.

J. J. Wright was elected to South Carolina's Senate and was also an associate justice of the State Supreme Court.

A Union captain in the Second Louisiana Volunteers, P. B. S. Pinchback became acting governor of Louisiana in 1873. Later, he was elected to the U. S. Senate, but was never seated.

John M. Langston was in the diplomatic service from 1877 to 1885. He served as Congressman from Virginia in 1890–1891.

be as smooth and as safe as the same is for the white citizen, this discussion will go on. Until the colored man's right to practice at the bar of our courts, and sit upon juries, shall be the universal law and practice of the land, this discussion will go on. Until the courts of the country shall grant the colored man a fair trial and a just verdict, this discussion will go on. Until color shall cease to be a bar to equal participation in the offices and honors of the country, this discussion will go on. Until the trades-unions and the workshops of the country shall cease to proscribe the colored man and prevent his children from learning useful trades, this discussion will go on. Until the American people shall make character, and not color, the criterion of respectability, this discussion will go on. Until men like Bishops Payne and Campbell shall cease to be driven from respectable railroad cars at the South, this discussion will go on. In a word, until truth and humanity shall cease to be living ideas, and mankind shall sink back into moral darkness, and the world shall put evil for good, bitter for sweet, and darkness for light, this discussion will go on. Until all humane ideas and civilization shall be banished from the world, this discussion will go on . . .

What is to be the future of the colored people of this country? Some change in their condition seems to be looked for by thoughtful men everywhere; but what that change will be, no one yet has been able with certainty to predict . . .

In every great movement men are prepared by preceding events for those which are to come. We neither know the evil nor the good which may be in store for us. Twenty-five years ago the system of slavery seemed impregnable. Cotton was king, and the civilized world acknowledged his sway. Twenty-five years ago no man could have foreseen that in less than ten years from that time no master would wield a lash and no slave would clank a chain in the United States.

Who at that time dreamed that Negroes would ever be seen as we have seen them to-day marching through the streets of this superb city, the Capital of this great Nation, with eagles on their buttons, muskets on their shoulders and swords by their sides, timing their high footsteps to the Star Spangled Banner and the Red, White and Blue? Who at that time dreamed that colored men would ever sit in the House of Representatives and in the Senate of the United States?

With a knowledge of the events of the last score of years, with a knowledge of the sudden and startling changes which have already come to pass, I am not prepared to say what the future will be . . .

There is but one destiny, it seems to me, left for

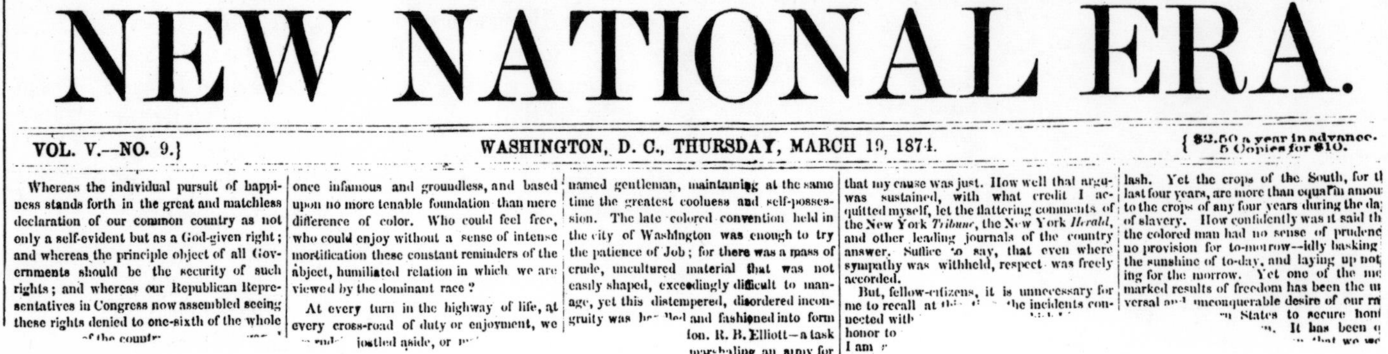

NEW NATIONAL ERA.

VOL. V.—NO. 9.} WASHINGTON, D. C., THURSDAY, MARCH 19, 1874. {$2.50 a year in advance. 5 Copies for $10.

Whereas the individual pursuit of happiness stands forth in the great and matchless declaration of our common country as not only a self-evident but as a God-given right; and whereas the principle object of all Governments should be the security of such rights; and whereas our Republican Representatives in Congress now assembled seeing these rights denied to one-sixth of the whole

once infamous and groundless, and based upon no more tenable foundation than mere difference of color. Who could feel free, who could enjoy without a sense of intense mortification these constant reminders of the abject, humiliated relation in which we are viewed by the dominant race?

At every turn in the highway of life, at every cross-road of duty or enjoyment, we jostled aside, or

named gentleman, maintaining at the same time the greatest coolness and self-possession. The late colored convention held in the city of Washington was enough to try the patience of Job; for there was a mass of crude, uncultured material that was not easily shaped, exceedingly difficult to manage, yet this distempered, disordered incongruity was and fashioned into form

Hon. R. B. Elliott—a task marshaling an army for

that my cause was just. How well that argument was sustained, with what credit I acquitted myself, let the flattering comments of the New York *Tribune*, the New York *Herald*, and other leading journals of the country answer. Suffice to say, that even where sympathy was withheld, respect was freely accorded.

But, fellow-citizens, it is unnecessary for me to recall at the incidents connected with

honor to

I am

lash. Yet the crops of the South, for the last four years, are more than equal in amount to the crops of any four years during the days of slavery. How confidently was it said that the colored man had no sense of prudence no provision for to-morrow—idly basking in the sunshine of to-day, and laying up nothing for the morrow. Yet one of the most marked results of freedom has been the universal and unconquerable desire of our race

States to secure homes

It has been

Buying the *New National Era* in 1870, Douglass became its editor and set forth a platform of "Free men, free soil, free speech, a free press, everywhere in the land. The ballot for all, education for all, fair wages for all."

us, and that is to make ourselves and be made by others a part of the American people in every sense of the word. Assimilation and not isolation is our true policy and our natural destiny. Unification for us is life: separation is death. We cannot afford to set up for ourselves a separate political party, or adopt for ourselves a political creed apart from the rest of our fellow citizens. Our own interests will be subserved by a generous care for the interests of the Nation at large. All the political, social and literary forces around us tend to unification.

I am the more inclined to accept this solution because I have seen the steps already taken in that direction. The American people have their prejudices, but they have other qualities as well. They easily adapt themselves to inevitable conditions, and all their tendency is to progress, enlightenment and to the universal.

I lift my lamp beside the golden door

Born in New York City in 1849, and educated privately, Emma Lazarus saw her first book of poems published at eighteen. She was befriended by Emerson and dedicated her next volume to him. Early in the eighteen-eighties she translated Heine's poems and ballads. When anti-Semitic persecution became widespread in Russia she organized relief for the Jews and helped fugitives from the Czar's ghettos to establish homes in America. In 1883, to assist a national campaign for funds to construct the pedestal for the Statue of Liberty, she wrote her famed sonnet, "The New Colossus." It is inscribed on a bronze tablet in the pedestal.

Emma Lazarus

In 1877, on Washington's Birthday, the colossal arm of the Statue of Liberty (right) was raised on Madison Square in New York to help spur the campaign for funds to complete the pedestal, for which America had taken the responsibility. Later, the head and shoulders of Miss Liberty (left) were exhibited in the same park. The idea of presenting the monument to the United States as a symbol of the friendship between France and America was born in 1865. The young Alsatian sculptor, Frederic Auguste Bartholdi, began the gigantic statue in 1875 and completed it ten years later, on funds contributed entirely by the French people.

You are invited to be present on the occasion of the inauguration by the President of the United States, of the Statue of Liberty Enlightening the World, on Bedloe's Island, New York Harbor, on Thursday, October 28th 1886.

On behalf of The American Committee

William M. Evarts, Chairman.
Richard Butler, Secretary.
Henry F. Spaulding, Treasurer.
Joseph W. Drexel, Parke Godwin
James W. Pinchot, V. Mumford Moore,
Frederic A. Potts.

John M. Schofield,
Major General U.S. Army
Commanding
Division of the Atlantic.

The invitation to attend the dedication of the Statue of Liberty Enlightening the World, on October 28, 1886. In the torch 300 feet aloft, Bartholdi pulled the rope that removed the French tricolor from Liberty's face, and President Grover Cleveland accepted the statue on behalf of the nation. The torch was lighted that night.

NOT like the brazen giant of Greek fame,
With conquering limbs astride from land to land;
Here at our sea-washed, sunset gates shall stand
A mighty woman with a torch, whose flame
Is the imprisoned lightning, and her name
Mother of Exiles. From her beacon hand
Glows world-wide welcome; her mild eyes command
The air-bridged harbor that twin cities frame.

"Keep, ancient lands, your storied pomp!" cries she
With silent lips, "Give me your tired, your poor,
Your huddled masses yearning to breathe free,
The wretched refuse of your teeming shore.
Send these, the homeless, tempest-tost to me,
I lift my lamp beside the golden door!"

The grievous wrongs of a suffering people

The ominously long depression, the bloody Homestead and Pullman strikes, the bread lines, unemployed marches and farm uprisings of the nineties were profoundly disturbing to the country. Was America any different from the Europe of constant wars and revolutions? many asked. In the Carnegie steel strike of 1892, the 300 Pinkerton detectives hired by the company were fired upon by strikers at Homestead (above) and 7 were killed. Two years later the great Pullman strike occurred and Federal troops were sent in by President Cleveland (below) over Illinois Governor Altgeld's protest. Both strikes were smashed.

As business and labor organized, in the generation that came after the Civil War, the farmer slowly followed their example. The railroads, the mortgage companies, the trusts and the middlemen—added to the natural calamities of drought, insect pest and plant disease—made the farmer's lot worse and worse. It was an irony hard to bear that farmers able to feed a continent and more had nothing to show for their labor.

Out of the depression of the late eighties and early nineties came new farm organizations in the South and West. Learning from the labor unions, the distressed farmers banded together in Farmers' Alliances. Their first ventures were into cooperative buying and selling, coupled with social and educational programs. But as the crisis stretched on, many farmers felt political action was needed to eliminate the unfair practices of the business interests who dominated the scene. The Southern branch of the Alliance tried at first to take over the Democratic Party, and the Western branch the Republican. Third-party advocates won out, however, and at Omaha in July, 1892, a People's or Populist Party was formally launched. Its platform denounced the old parties and called for many reforms in land, transportation, finance, and other policies. Although damned as revolutionary, most of the planks were soon to be taken over by the major parties and made into law.

Ignatius Donnelly of Minnesota, who drafted the Preamble to the Populist Party platform of 1892. His novel, *Caesar's Column,* was widely read in the nineties.

Platform of the Populist Party

(July 4, 1892)

THE CONDITIONS which surround us best justify our co-operation. We meet in the midst of a nation brought to the verge of moral, political, and material ruin. Corruption dominates the ballot box, the Legislatures, the Congress, and touches even the ermine of the Bench. The people are demoralized; most of the States have been compelled to isolate the voters at the polling places to prevent universal intimidation and bribery. The newspapers are largely subsidized or muzzled, public opinion silenced, business prostrated, homes covered with mortgages, labor impoverished, and the land concentrating in the hands of capitalists. The urban workmen are denied the right to organize for self-protection; imported pauperized labor beats down their wages, a hireling standing army, unrecognized by our laws, is established to shoot them down, and they are rapidly degenerating into European conditions. The fruits of the toil of millions are boldly stolen to build up colossal fortunes for a few, unprecedented in the history of mankind, and the possessors of these in turn despise the Republic and endanger liberty. From the same prolific womb of governmental injustice we breed the two great classes—tramps and millionaires. . . .

We have witnessed for more than a quarter of a century the struggles of the two great political parties for power and plunder, while grievous wrongs have been inflicted upon the suffering people. We charge that the controlling influences dominating both these parties have permitted the existing dreadful conditions to develop without serious effort to prevent or restrain them. Neither do they now promise us any substantial reform. . . . They propose to drown the outcries of a plundered people with the uproar of a sham battle over the tariff . . .

Our country finds itself confronted by conditions for which there is no precedent in the history of the world; our annual agricultural productions amount to billions of dollars in value, which must, within a few weeks or months, be exchanged for billions of dollars' worth of commodities consumed in their production; the existing currency supply is wholly inadequate to make this exchange; the results are falling prices, the formation of combines and rings, the impoverishment of the producing class. We pledge ourselves that if given power we will labor to correct these evils by wise and reasonable legislation, in accordance with the terms of our platform. . . .

First. . . . the union of the labor forces of the United States this day consummated shall be permanent and perpetual; . . .

General James B. Weaver, Populist candidate for the presidency in 1892. He got over a million votes, or 8.5 per cent of the ballots cast, chiefly from a few plains and mountain states, plus 6 Southern states. Although Cleveland won the presidency, the Populists elected governors in Colorado, Kansas, North Dakota, and Wyoming, sent 2 Senators and 11 Congressmen to Washington, and sat 354 representatives in 19 state legislatures.

William Jennings Bryan, the Democrat-Populist candidate who made a spectacular race for the presidency in 1896. A two-term Congressman from Nebraska, and then editor of the Omaha *World-Herald,* he won the nomination at the age of thirty-six by his famous "cross of gold" speech. As a champion of reform he led the Democratic Party from 1896 to 1912.

In the winter of 1893-1894 suffering from the depression became so widespread that bands of jobless men formed into "armies" that followed any leader who promised them relief. One of these was Jacob M. Coxey, an Ohio businessman and reformer who advocated a public works relief program of local improvements to be financed by Federal non-interest-bearing bonds. Coxey is shown (at right) leading an army of unemployed to Washington to demand Congressional aid. When some of the leaders of Coxey's Army were arrested on the Capitol grounds the men dispersed.

Second. Wealth belongs to him who creates it, and every dollar taken from industry without an equivalent is robbery. . . .

Third. We believe that the time has come when the railroad corporations will either own the people or the people must own the railroads; . . .

FINANCE: We demand a national currency, safe, sound, and flexible issued by the General Government only, a full legal tender for all debts public and private, and that without the use of banking corporations; a just, equitable, and efficient means of distribution direct to the people, at a tax not to exceed 2 per cent, per annum, to be provided as set forth in the sub-treasury plan of the Farmers' Alliance, or a better system; also by payments in discharge of its obligations for public improvements.

A. We demand free and unlimited coinage of silver and gold at the present legal ratio of 16 to 1.

B. We demand that the amount of circulating medium be speedily increased to not less than $50 per capita.

C. We demand a graduated income tax.

D. We believe that the money of the country should be kept as much as possible in the hands of the people, and hence we demand that all State and national revenues shall be limited to the necessary expenses of the government, economically and honestly administered.

E. We demand that postal savings banks be established by the government . . .

TRANSPORTATION: Transportation being a means of exchange and a public necessity, the government should own and operate the railroads in the interest of the people.

The telegraph and telephone, like the post office system, being a necessity for the transmission of news, should be owned and operated by the government in the interest of the people.

LAND: The land, including all the natural sources of wealth, is the heritage of the people, and should not be monopolized for speculative purposes, and alien ownership of land should be prohibited. . . .

Supplementary Resolutions

. . . Whereas, Other questions have been presented for our consideration, we hereby submit the following, not as a part of the platform of the People's Party but as resolutions expressive of the sentiment of this Convention.

1. *Resolved,* That we demand a free ballot and a fair count in all elections, . . . through the adoption by the States of the unperverted Australian or secret ballot system.

2. *Resolved,* That the revenue derived from a graduated income tax should be applied to the reduction of the burden of taxation now levied upon the domestic industries of this country.

3. *Resolved,* That we pledge our support to fair and liberal pensions to ex-Union soldiers and sailors.

4. *Resolved,* That we condemn the fallacy of protecting American labor under the present system, which opens our ports to the pauper and criminal classes of the world, . . . and demand the further restriction of undesirable emigration.

5. *Resolved,* That we cordially sympathize with the efforts of organized workingmen to shorten the hours of labor, and demand a rigid enforcement of the existing eight-hour law on Government work, . . .

6. *Resolved,* That we regard the maintenance of a large standing army of mercenaries, known as the Pinkerton system, as a menace to our liberties, and we demand its abolition; . . .

7. *Resolved,* That we commend to the favorable consideration of the people and the reform press the legislative system known as the initiative and referendum.

8. *Resolved,* That we favor a constitutional provision limiting the office of President and Vice-President to one term, and providing for the election of Senators of the United States by a direct vote of the people.

9. *Resolved,* That we oppose any subsidy or national aid to any private corporation for any purpose.

10. *Resolved,* That this convention sympathizes with the Knights of Labor and their righteous contest with the tyrannical combine of clothing manufacturers of Rochester, and declare it to be a duty of all who hate tyranny and oppression to refuse to purchase the goods made by the said manufacturers, or to patronize any merchants who sell such goods.

The 1896 Populist convention met in St. Louis. This unfriendly newspaper cartoon, titled "A Pitiful Spectacle," shows Free Silver Democracy appealing to the Populists for support. The Populists endorsed Bryan's candidacy on the Democratic ticket but ran their own man, Tom Watson of Georgia, for Vice President. The Republican choice, William McKinley, won with 7 million votes, defeating Bryan by half a million.

A pencil sketch of Charles Eliot Norton, made in 1902. Norton traveled widely in Europe and Asia, was a friend of Longfellow, Lowell, Carlyle, and Ruskin, and was elected first president of the Archaeological Institute of America. His speech on "True Patriotism" came in the midst of the "splendid little war," which began on May 1, 1898, and was over in ten weeks. Despite many threats of violence, Norton stood by his principles.

1898 Charles Eliot Norton: True Patriotism

The rights of individual judgement and expression

A coat of tar and feathers was a strange costume to suggest for the aristocratic and venerable Charles Eliot Norton. But popular passion over the Spanish-American War rose so high that his clear, firm voice of opposition to "this wretched, needless and iniquitous war" brought him private abuse and public denunciation. A translator of Dante, Norton held the chair of professor of the history of art at Harvard for over twenty years. His concern with teaching, art, and literature did not cut him off from the life around him. He worked for abolition of slavery, for labor and Negro education, civil service reform, and against imperialism. The mood of jingoism and expansion which seized the nation as the great depression of the nineties wore away was openly opposed by Norton, and when it culminated in the war with Spain, he did not hesitate to defend "the rights of independent individual judgement and expression" in a famous speech—"True Patriotism"—he made on June 7, 1898, to a Cambridge church group.

THERE are moments in every man's life, in the life of every nation, when, under the excitement of passion, the simple truths which in common times are the foundation upon which the right order and conduct of life depend are apt to be forgotten and disregarded. I shall venture to-night to recall to you some of these commonplace truths, which in these days of war need more than ever to be kept in mind.

There never was a land that better deserved the love of her people than America, for there never was a mother-country kinder to her children. She has given to them all that she could give. Her boundless resources have lain open to them, to use at their will. And the consequence has been that never in the history of man has there been so splendid a spectacle of widely diffused and steadily increasing material welfare as America has displayed during the last hundred years. Millions upon millions of men have lived here with more comfort, with less fear, than any such numbers elsewhere in any age have lived. Countless multitudes, whose forefathers from the beginning of human life on earth have spent weary lives in unrewarded toil, in anxiety, in helplessness, in ignorance, have risen here, in the course of even a single generation, to the full and secure enjoyment of the fruits of their labor, to confident hope, to intelligent possession of their own faculties. Is not the land to be dearly loved in which this has been possible, in which this has been achieved?

But there is a deeper source of love of country than the material advantages and benefits it may afford. It is in the character of its people, in their moral life, in the type of civilization which they exhibit. The elements of human nature are indeed so fixed that favorable or unfavorable circumstances have little effect upon its essential constitution, but prosperity or the reverse brings different traits into prominence. The conditions which have prevailed in America have, if broadly considered, tended steadily and strongly to certain good results in the national character; not, indeed, to unmixed good, but to a preponderance of good. The institutions established for self-government have been founded with intent to secure justice and independence for all. The social relations among the whole body of the people are humane and simple. The general spirit of the people is liberal, is kindly, is considerate. The ideas for the realization of which in private and public conduct there is more or less steady and consistent effort are as high and as worthy as any which men have pursued. Every genuine American holds to the ideal of justice for all men, of independence, including free speech and free action within the limits of law, of obedience to law, of universal education, of material well-being for all the well-behaving and industrious, or peace and good-will among men. These, however far short the nation may fall in expressing them in its actual life, are, no one will deny it, the ideals of our American democracy. And it is because America represents these ideals that the deepest love for his country glows in the heart of the American, and inspires him with that patriotism which counts no cost, which esteems no sacrifice too great to maintain and to increase the influence of these principles which embody themselves in the fair shape of his native land, and have their expressive symbol in her flag. The spirit of his patriotism is not an intermittent impulse; it is an abiding principle; it is the strongest motive of his life; it is his religion.

And because it is so, and just in proportion to his love of the ideals for which his country stands, is his hatred of whatever is opposed to them in private conduct or public policy. Against injustice, against dishonesty, against lawlessness, against whatever may make for war instead of peace, the good citizen is always in arms.

No thoughtful American can have watched the course of affairs among us during the last thirty years without grave anxiety from the apparent decline in power to control the direction of public and private conduct, of the principles upon regard for which the permanent and progressive welfare of America depends; and especially the course of events during the last few months and the actual condition of the country to-day, should bring home to every man the question whether or not the nation is true to one of the chief of the ideals to which it has professed allegiance. A generation has grown up that has known nothing of war. The blessings of peace have been poured out upon us. We have congratulated ourselves that we were free from the misery and the burdens that war and standing armies have brought upon the nations of the Old World. "Their fires"—I cite a fine phrase of Sir Philip Sidney in a letter to Queen Elizabeth—"Their fires have given us light to see our own quietness." And now of a sudden, without cool deliberation, without prudent preparation, the nation is hurried into war, and America, she who more than any other land was pledged to peace and good-will on earth, unsheathes her sword, compels a weak and unwilling nation to a fight, rejecting without due considera-

Punch's caricaturist suspected the United States's intentions in the war with Spain. In this 1898 cartoon entitled "The Prize Brand," Cousin Jonathan is saying, "These look very nice! I wonder if they'll be the better for *keeping*?"

In the fighting in the Philippines during the Spanish-American War, American troops were accused by many outstanding citizens of following the same "inhuman methods" that Spain had practiced when she too had attempted to suppress the independence movement. This drawing from life made early in 1899 shows the 20th Kansas Volunteers, under Colonel Frederick Funston, marching through villages they had devastated.

tion her earnest and repeated offers to meet every legitimate demand of the United States. It is a bitter disappointment to the lover of his country; it is a turning-back from the path of civilization to that of barbarism.

"There never was a good war," said Franklin. There have indeed been many wars in which a good man must take part, and take part with grave gladness to defend the cause of justice, to die for it if need be, a willing sacrifice, thankful to give life for what is dearer than life, and happy that even by death in war he is serving the cause of peace. But if a war be undertaken for the most righteous end, before the resources of peace have been tried and proved vain to secure it, that war has no defence; it is a national crime. And however right, however unavoidable a war may be, and those of us who are old enough to remember the war for the Union know that war may be right and unavoidable, yet, I repeat the words of Franklin, "There never was a good

war." It is evil in itself, it is evil in its never-ending train of consequences. No man has known the nature of war better than General Sherman, and in his immortal phrase he has condensed its description—"War is hell." "From the earliest dawnings of policy to this day," said Edmund Burke, more than a hundred years ago, "the invention of men has been sharpening and improving the mystery of murder, from the first rude essays of clubs and stones to the present perfection of gunnery, cannoneering, bombarding, mining, and all these species of artificial, learned and refined cruelty in which we are now so expert, and which make a principal part of what politicians have taught us to believe is our principal glory." And it is now, at the end of this century, the century in which beyond any other in history knowledge has increased and the arts of peace have advanced, that America has been brought by politicians and writers for the press, faithless to her noble ideals, against the will of every right-minded citizen, to resort to these cruel arts, these arts of violence, these arts which rouse the passions of the beast in man, before the resources of peace have been fairly tested and proved insufficient to secure the professed ends, which, however humane and desirable, afford no sufficient justification for resorting to the dread arbitrament of arms.

There are, indeed, many among us who find justification of the present war in the plea that its motive is to give independence to the people of Cuba, long burdened by the oppressive and corrupt rule of Spain, and especially to relieve the suffering of multitudes deprived of their homes and of means of subsistence by the cruel policy of the general who exercised for a time a practical dictatorship over the island. The plea so far as it is genuine deserves the respect due to every humane sentiment. But independence secured for Cuba by forcible overthrow of the Spanish rule means either practical anarchy or the substitution of the authority of the United States for that of Spain. Either alternative might well give us pause. And as for the relief of suffering, surely it is a strange procedure to begin by inflicting worse suffering still. It is fighting the devil with his own arms. That the end justifies the means is a dangerous doctrine, and no wise man will advise doing evil for the sake of an uncertain good. But the plea that the better government of Cuba and the relief of the reconcentrados could only be secured by war is the plea either of ignorance or of hypocrisy.

But the war is declared; and on all hands we hear the cry that he is no patriot who fails to shout for it, and to urge the youth of the country to enlist, and to rejoice that they are called to the service of their native land. The sober counsels that were appropriate before the war was entered upon must give way to blind enthusiasm, and the voice of condemnation must be silenced by the thunders of the guns and the hurrahs of the crowd. Stop! A declaration of war does not change the moral law. "The ten commandments will not budge" at a joint resolve of Congress. Was James Russell Lowell aught but a good patriot when during the Mexican war he sent the stinging shafts of his matchless satire at the heart of the monstrous iniquity, or when, years afterward, he declared, that he thought at the time and that he still thought the Mexican war was a national crime? Did John Bright ever render greater service to his country than when, during the Crimean war, he denounced the Administration which had plunged England into it, and employed his magnificent power of earnest and incisive speech in the endeavor to repress the evil spirit which it evoked in the heart of the nation? No! the voice of protest, of warning, of appeal is never more needed than when the clamor of fife and drum, echoed by the press and too often by the pulpit, is bidding all men fall in and keep step and obey in silence the tyrannous word of command. Then, more than ever, it is the duty of the good citizen not to be silent, and spite of obloquy, misrepresentation and abuse, to insist on being heard, and with sober counsel to maintain the everlasting validity of the principles of the moral law.

So confused are men by false teaching in regard to national honor and the duty of the citizen that it is easy to fall into the error of holding a declaration of war, however brought about, as a sacred decision of the national will, and to fancy that a call to arms from the Administration has the force of a call from the lips of the country, of the America to whom all her sons are ready to pay the full measure of devotion. This is indeed a natural and for many a youth not a discreditable error. But if the nominal, though authorized, representatives of the country have brought us into a war that might and should have been avoided, and which consequently is an un-

When 32-year-old William Randolph Hearst bought the New York *Journal* in 1895 it had a circulation of 30,000. His sensational campaign to line up public opinion for intervention in the conflict between Cuban rebels and their Spanish rulers shoved circulation up to 400,000 daily by 1897. When the war came, lurid coverage boomed readership to over a million. One example of Hearst's tactics was this sketch by Frederic Remington, based not on fact but on Hearst's fancy.

A DEFENCE OF GENERAL FUNSTON.

BY MARK TWAIN.

I.

February 22. To-day is the great Birth-Day; and it was observed so widely in the earth that differences in longitudinal time made curious work with some of the cabled testimonies of respect paid to the sublime name which the date calls up in our minds; for, although they were all being offered at about the same hour, several of them were yesterday to us and several were to-morrow.

There was a reference in the papers to General Funston.

Neither Washington nor Funston was made in a day. It took a long time to accumulate the materials. In each case, the basis or moral skeleton of the man was inborn disposition—a thing which is as permanent as rock, and never undergoes any actual and genuine change between cradle and grave. In each case, the moral flesh-bulk (that is to say, *character*) was built and shaped around the skeleton by training, association and circumstances. Given a crooked-disposition skeleton, no power nor influence in the earth can mould a permanently shapely form around it. Training, association and circumstances

"I am an anti-imperialist. I am opposed to having the eagle put its talons on any other land," Mark Twain said in 1900. Many other writers felt the same way: William Dean Howells, Henry and William James, William Vaughn Moody, Carl Schurz, Hamlin Garland, Thomas Wentworth Higginson, Ambrose Bierce, Finley Peter Dunne, Edgar Lee Masters, Edwin Arlington Robinson. Like Twain they vigorously opposed militarism and interference in the affairs of other nations. Twain's "Defense of General Funston" was a savage condemnation of America's behavior in the Philippines. Many of these writers were denounced as "traitors" for exercising their freedom of speech and conscience.

righteous war, then, so long as the safety of the State is not at risk, the duty of the good citizen is plain. He is to help to provide the Administration responsible for the conduct of the war with every means that may serve to bring it to the speediest end. He is to do this alike that the immediate evils of the war may be as brief and as few as possible, and also that its miserable train of after evils may be diminished and the vicious passions excited by it be the sooner allayed. Men, money, must be abundantly supplied. But must he himself enlist or quicken the ardent youth to enter service in such a cause? The need is not yet. The country is in no peril. There is always in a vast population like ours an immense, a sufficient supply of material of a fighting order, often of a heroic courage, ready and eager for the excitement of battle, filled with the old notion that patriotism is best expressed in readiness to fight for our country, be she right or wrong. Better the paying of bounties to such men to fill the ranks than that they should be filled by those whose higher duty is to fit themselves for the service of their country in the patriotic labors of peace. We mourn the deaths of our noble youth fallen in the cause of their country when she stands for the right; but we may mourn with a deeper sadness for those who have fallen in a cause which their generous hearts mistook for one worthy of the last sacrifice.

My friends, America has been compelled against the will of all her wisest and best to enter into a path of darkness and peril. Against their will she has been forced to turn back from the way of civilization to the way of barbarism, to renounce for the time her own ideals. With grief, with anxiety must the lover of his country regard the present aspect and the future prospect of the nation's life. With serious purpose, with utter self-devotion he should prepare himself for the untried and difficult service to which it is plain he is to be called in the quick-coming years.

Two months ago America stood at the parting of the ways. Her first step is irretrievable. It depends on the virtue, on the enlightened patriotism of her children whether her future steps shall be upward to the light or downward to the darkness.

"Nil desperandum de republica."

Theodore Roosevelt, Harvard graduate, historian, and at 42 the 26th President of the U.S. Promoted to the Vice-Presidency by political bosses who thought they were penning a maverick in a safe corral, he reached the chief office on McKinley's death and was elected in his own right in 1904. Despite a Congress unsympathetic to his liberal ideas, he was able to maneuver the passage of the Pure Food and Drug Act, and laws designed to conserve the nation's depleted natural resources, and to regulate the railroads.

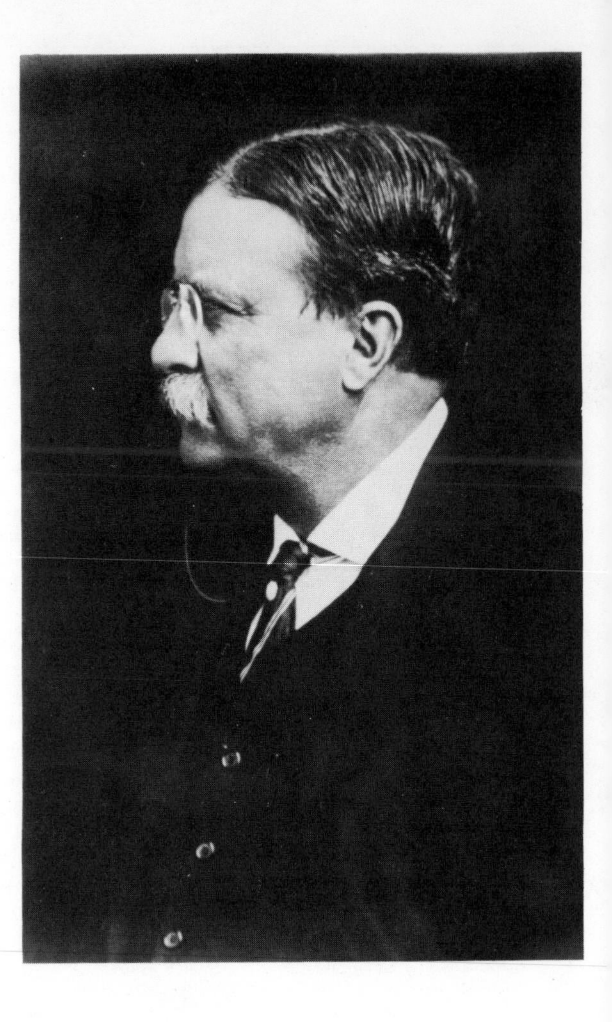

1901 Theodore Roosevelt: First Annual Message

Trusts must be regulated for the public welfare

A trust agreement signed in 1879 made Standard Oil the controller of 95 per cent of America's refined oil. Rapidly sugar, salt, whiskey, lead, beef, and a host of other commodity interests followed Standard Oil's successful pattern, using several organizational and legal devices to concentrate their economic power.

The trusts, an investigating committee said in 1888, have "spread like a disease through the commercial system of this country." Under public pressure, the states soon made attempts to restrain the monopolies in national necessities. But government action on this limited scale proved difficult. Finally, in 1890, Congress adopted the Sherman Antitrust Act, branding as illegal trusts or conspiracies in restraint of trade or commerce, among the states or with foreign nations.

The Supreme Court's interpretation severely curbed the law's effectiveness. From 1890 until Theodore Roosevelt took presidential office, the act was not vigorously enforced. To many Americans, by the turn of the century the private power of the corporations loomed vaster than the public power of government. Already the trusts and banking houses were buying up political support wherever they needed it. American democracy would fail, Theodore Roosevelt felt, unless the power of the state were kept above big business, subordinating its special interests to the public welfare.

In his first annual message to Congress, on December 3, 1901, the dynamic young President spoke out against the predatory misuse of monopoly power. His successful antitrust action against the Northern Securities railway merger earned him his "trustbuster" title but only a few of the twenty-five indictments subsequently pressed by his Department of Justice were won. It was an inevitable record of failure. Modern organization of business could not be turned back to the conditions of earlier generations. But what Theodore Roosevelt helped establish was that the affairs of big business were the concern of all the people, and violations of the public interest should be exposed and punished.

How one cartoonist analyzed the workings of the trusts.

THE TREMENDOUS and highly complex industrial development which went on with ever accelerated rapidity during the latter half of the nineteenth century brings us face to face at the beginning of the twentieth, with very serious social problems. The old laws, and the old customs which had almost the binding force of law, were once quite sufficient to regulate the accumulation and distribution of wealth. Since the industrial changes which have so enormously increased the productive power of mankind, they are no longer sufficient.

The growth of cities has gone on beyond comparison faster than the growth of the country, and the upbuilding of the great industrial centers has meant a startling increase, not merely in the aggregate of wealth, but in the number of very large individual, and especially of very large corporate, fortunes. The creation of these great corporate fortunes has not been due to the tariff nor to any other governmental action, but to natural causes in the business world, operating in other countries as they operate in our own.

The process has aroused much antagonism, a great part of which is wholly without warrant. It is not true that as the rich have grown richer the poor have grown poorer. On the contrary, never before has the average man, the wage-worker, the farmer, the small trader, been so well off as in this country and at the present time. There have been abuses connected with the accumulation of wealth; yet it remains true that a fortune accumulated in legitimate business can be accumulated by the person specially benefited only on condition of conferring immense incidental benefits upon others. Successful enterprise, of the type which benefits all mankind, can only exist if the conditions are such as to offer great prizes as the rewards of success.

The captains of industry who have driven the railway systems across this continent, who have built up our commerce, who have developed our manufactures, have on the whole done great good to our people. Without them the material development of which we are so justly proud could never have taken place. Moreover, we should recognize the immense importance in this material development of leaving as unhampered as is compatible with the public good the strong and forceful men upon whom the success of business operations inevitably rests. The slightest study of business conditions will satisfy anyone capable of forming a judgment that the personal equation is the most important factor in a business operation; that the business ability of the man at the head of any business concern, big or little, is usually the factor which fixes the gulf between striking success and hopeless failure.

An additional reason for caution in dealing with corporations is to be found in the international commercial conditions of today. The same business conditions which have produced the great aggregations of corporate and individual wealth have made them

Theodore Roosevelt's failure to make much headway against the monopolies was satirized in this 1903 cartoon, captioned "Bronco busting in the west—'Amuses us and don't hurt the hoss.' "

very potent factors in international commercial competition. Business concerns which have the largest means at their disposal and are managed by the ablest men are naturally those which take the lead in the strife for commercial supremacy among the nations of the world. America has only just begun to assume that commanding position in the international business world which we believe will more and more be hers. It is of the utmost importance that this position be not jeopardized, especially at a time when the overflowing abundance of our own natural resources and the skill, business energy, and mechanical aptitude of our people make foreign markets essential. Under such conditions it would be most unwise to cramp or to fetter the youthful strength of our Nation.

Moreover, it cannot too often be pointed out that to strike with ignorant violence at the interests of one set of men almost inevitably endangers the interests of all. The fundamental rule in our national life—the rule which underlies all others—is that, on the whole, and in the long run, we shall go up or down together. There are exceptions; and in times of prosperity some will prosper far more, and in times of adversity, some will suffer far more, than others; but speaking generally, a period of good times means that all share more or less in them, and in a period of hard times all feel the stress to a greater or less degree. It surely ought not to be necessary to enter into any proof of this statement; the memory of the lean years which began in 1893 is still vivid, and we can contrast them with the conditions in this very year which is now closing. Disaster to great business enterprises can never have its effects limited to the men at the top. It spreads throughout, and while it is bad for everybody, it is worst for those farthest down. The capitalist may be shorn of his luxuries; but the wage-worker may be deprived of even bare necessities.

The mechanism of modern business is so delicate that extreme care must be taken not to interfere with it in a spirit of rashness or ignorance. Many of those who have made it their vocation to denounce the great industrial combinations which are popularly, although with technical inaccuracy, known as "trusts," appeal especially to hatred and fear. These are precisely the two emotions, particularly when combined with ignorance, which unfit men for the exercise of cool and steady judgment. In facing new industrial conditions, the whole history of the world shows that legislation will generally be both unwise and ineffective unless undertaken after calm inquiry and with sober self-restraint. Much of the legislation directed at the trusts would have been exceedingly mischievous had it not also been entirely ineffective. In accordance with a well-known sociological law, the ignorant or reckless agitator has been the really effective friend of the evils which he has been nominally opposing. In dealing with business interests, for the Government to undertake by crude and ill-considered legislation to do what may turn out to be bad, would be to incur the risk of such far-reaching national disaster that it would be preferable to undertake nothing at all. The men who demand the impossible or the undesirable serve as the allies of the forces with which they are nominally at war, for they hamper those who would endeavor to find out in rational fashion what the wrongs really are and to what extent and in what manner it is practicable to apply remedies.

All this is true; and yet it is also true that there are real and grave evils, one of the chief being over-capitalization because of its many baleful consequences; and a resolute and practical effort must be made to correct these evils.

There is a widespread conviction in the minds of the American people that the great corporations known as trusts are in certain of their features and tendencies hurtful to the general welfare. This springs from no spirit of envy or uncharitableness, nor lack of pride in the great industrial achievements that have placed this country at the head of the nations struggling for commercial supremacy. It does not rest upon a lack of intelligent appreciation of the necessity of meeting changing and changed conditions of trade with new methods, nor upon ignorance of the fact that combination of capital in the effort to accomplish great things is necessary when the world's progress demands that great things be done. It is based upon sincere conviction that combination and concentration should be, not prohibited, but supervised and within reasonable limits controlled; and in my judgment this conviction is right.

It is no limitation upon property rights or freedom of contract to require that when men receive from Government the privilege of doing business under corporate form, which frees them from individual responsibility, and enables them to call into their enterprises the capital of the public, they shall do so upon absolutely truthful representations as to the value of the property in which the capital is to be invested. Corporations engaged in interstate commerce should be regulated if they are found to exercise a license working to the public injury. It should be as much the aim of those who seek for social betterment to rid the business world of crimes of cunning as to rid the entire body politic of crimes of violence. Great corporations exist only because they are created and safeguarded by our institutions; and

"The Bosses of the Senate," an 1889 cartoon by Joseph Keppler in *Puck*. As wealthy men moved directly into the seats of power the Senate became known as the millionaires' club. "Shall the will of the monopolies take the place of the Government of the people?" was the warning of former President Rutherford B. Hayes, who watched the Senate dispense lavish favors to the great trusts.

it is therefore our right and our duty to see that they work in harmony with these institutions.

The first essential in determining how to deal with the great industrial combinations is knowledge of the facts—publicity. In the interest of the public, the Government should have the right to inspect and examine the workings of the great corporations engaged in interstate business. Publicity is the only sure remedy which we can now invoke. What further remedies are needed in the way of governmental regulation, or taxation, can only be determined after publicity has been obtained, by process of law, and in the course of administration. The first requisite is knowledge, full and complete—knowledge which may be made public to the world.

Artificial bodies, such as corporations and joint stock or other associations, depending upon any statutory law for their existence or privileges, should be subject to proper governmental supervision, and full and accurate information as to their operations should be made public regularly at reasonable intervals.

The large corporations, commonly called trusts, though organized in one State, always do business in many States, often doing very little business in the State where they are incorporated. There is utter lack of uniformity in the State laws about them; and as no State has any exclusive interest in or power over their acts, it has in practice proved impossible to get adequate regulation through State action. Therefore, in the interest of the whole people, the Nation should, without interfering with the power of the States in the matter itself, also assume power of supervision and regulation over all corporations doing an interstate business. This is especially true where the corporation derives a portion of its wealth from the existence of some monopolistic element or tendency in its business. There would

New York American

PART II. MAIN SHEET

ROOSEVELT SCOLDS CRITICS OF GRAFT IN HIS "MUCK-RAKE" SPEECH.

Expresses the Fear That Too Much Light on Corruption Impairs the Public Eyesight.

URGES NEW KIND OF TAXATION ON ALL IMMENSE FORTUNES.

Suggests a Progressive Levy So No One Can Inherit More Than a Certain Amount.

HISTORIC GAVEL IS USED

George Washington Employed It for the Capitol Corner-stone 113 Years Ago.

THE MUCK RAKE AND SOME OF THE MUCK.

ROOSEVELT'S ADVERTISED SPEECH FULL OF PLATITUDES

Julian Hawthorne Says It Is a Thing of Copybook Maxims Fit for Children.

The press headlines Theodore Roosevelt's attack of April 14, 1906, upon the "muckrakers," the reporter-reformers whose exposes of greed and corruption in business and politics aroused public opinion. Irritated by the crusaders' tactics, TR denounced them as "muckrakers," a label they were proud to wear. National magazines boomed their circulation by featuring the sensational disclosures. Stars of the muckraking era (1904–10) included such writers as Ida Tarbell, Lincoln Steffens, Upton Sinclair, David Graham Phillips, and Ray Stannard Baker.

Ida Tarbell in 1904, the year her *History of the Standard Oil Company,* exposing the methods by which the Rockefeller empire had been built, was published.

Lincoln Steffens, whose *Shame of the Cities* indicted not only the corrupt politicians, but those who corrupted them.

The Jungle, written by Upton Sinclair, was a passionate condemnation of labor conditions in the meat-packing industry. This is Art Young's drawing of the crusading novelist.

McClure's built vast circulation in publishing the muckrakers' unappetizing truths about the social evils of the first decade of 20th century America. The ties between corrupt politics and the economic jungle were the center of their attack.

be no hardship in such supervision; banks are subject to it, and in their case it is now accepted as a simple matter of course. Indeed, it is probable that supervision of corporations by the National Government need not go so far as is now the case with the supervision exercised over them by so conservative a State as Massachusetts, in order to produce excellent results.

When the Constitution was adopted, at the end of the eighteenth century, no human wisdom could foretell the sweeping changes, alike in industrial and political conditions, which were to take place by the beginning of the twentieth century. At that time it was accepted as a matter of course that the several States were the proper authorities to regulate, so far as was then necessary, the comparatively insignificant and strictly localized corporate bodies of the day. The conditions are now wholly different and wholly different action is called for. I believe that a law can be framed which will enable the National Government to exercise control along the lines above indicated; profiting by the experience gained through the passage and administration of the Interstate-Commerce Act. If, however, the judgment of the Congress is that it lacks the constitutional power to pass such an act, then a constitutional amendment should be submitted to confer the power.

There should be created a Cabinet officer, to be known as Secretary of Commerce and Industries, as provided in the bill introduced at the last session of the Congress. It should be his province to deal with commerce in its broadest sense; including among many other things whatever concerns labor and all matters affecting the great business corporations and our merchant marine.

The course proposed is one phase of what should be a comprehensive and far-reaching scheme of constructive statesmanship for the purpose of broadening our markets, securing our business interests on a safe basis, and making firm our new position in the international industrial world; while scrupulously safeguarding the rights of wage-worker and capitalist, of investor and private citizen, so as to secure equity as between man and man in this Republic. . . .

Government at the service of humanity

When Woodrow Wilson was pushed out of Princeton's presidential chair the trustees did not expect the momentum would land their victim in the White House. Wilson was the son of a Virginia minister; he had earned degrees at Princeton and Johns Hopkins. Twenty years of teaching and writing had established his high reputation as an authority in government and won him the presidency of Princeton. To the great displeasure of the trustees and alumni, however, he pressed relentlessly for democratizing reforms. Forced to resign in 1910, he was conveniently available to the Democratic bosses of New Jersey as a "safe" candidate for governor. In two years in office the scholar proved he could put the bosses down and put reform up. A leader, he had told his classes, could be as big a man as he chose; his capacity was his limit. Using press and public opinion masterfully, he put through the legislature of a state known as the "home of the trusts" a spectacular series of reform measures that made him a national figure.

In a four-cornered contest for President in 1912, Wilson defeated Roosevelt, Taft, and Debs. His "New Freedom" campaign speeches were an eloquent expression of progressive political thought, whose ideas differed not markedly from those of Roosevelt and Bryan. Riding the crest of the insurgent wave, Wilson made his inaugural address a statement of dedication to the needs not of a party, but of humanity. From promise to performance he moved with dazzling speed. In three years every proposal outlined in the inaugural had been made into law. The Underwood Tariff, the Federal Reserve Act, the Clayton Antitrust Act, and the Federal Trade Commission Act were milestones in an era of reform that World War I was soon to end.

My Fellow Citizens:

THERE HAS BEEN a change of government. It began two years ago, when the House of Representatives became Democratic by a decisive majority. It has now been completed. The Senate about to assemble will also be Democratic. The offices of President and Vice-President have been put into the hands of Democrats. What does the change mean? That is the question that is uppermost in our minds to-day. That is the question I am going to try to answer, in order, if I may, to interpret the occasion.

It means much more than the mere success of a party. The success of a party means little except when the Nation is using that party for a large and definite purpose. No one can mistake the purpose for which the Nation now seeks to use the Democratic Party. It seeks to use it to interpret a change in its own plans and point of view. Some old things with which we had grown familiar, and which had begun to creep into the very habit of our thought and of our lives, have altered their aspect as we have latterly looked critically upon them with fresh awakened eyes; have dropped their disguises and shown themselves alien and sinister. Some new things, as we look frankly upon them, willing to comprehend their real character, have come to assume the aspect of things long believed in and familiar, stuff of our own convictions. We have been refreshed by a new insight into our own life.

We see that in many things that life is very great.

"All the News That's Fit to Print."

The New York Times.

THE WEATHER.

Probably snow this morning, fair colder by afternoon; fair, warmer Thursday; wind variable.
For full weather report see Page 23.

VOL. LXII...NO. 20,129. NEW YORK, WEDNESDAY, MARCH 5, 1913.—TWENTY-EIGHT PAGES. ONE CENT In Greater New York, Jersey City and Newark. | Elsewhere, TWO CENTS

DUAL SUBWAY NOW ADOPTED

Chairman McCall Accepts Willcox Draft—Objections Only from ...nd Cram.

THE COLONEL, TOO, ON PAGE 1

Third-Term Futurist Consults Third-Dimension Oracles on Inaugural Day.

Just at noon yesterday, when President Taft, retiring, was turning over the reins of the National Government to the incoming President, Mr. Wilson, in Washington, Col. Roosevelt took the time to view the collection of paintings of the Futurists at the Sixty-ninth Regiment Armory, Lexington Avenue and Twenty-fifth Street. It will be remembered that up ... Roosevelt had

Inauguration Pictures.

Two pages of photographs of yesterday's scenes in Washington will be found on Pages 6 and 7 of this issue of The Times.

Special Half-Tone Section

A special half-tone section, on fine paper, devoted entirely to pictures of Mr. Wilson's inauguratio...

WILSON SWORN IN AS PRESIDENT; PLEDGES HIMSELF TO JUSTICE; BIGGEST INAUGURAL THRONG

Sun Burstin...

It is incomparably great in its material aspects, in its body of wealth, in the diversity and sweep of its energy, in the industries which have been conceived and built up by the genius of individual men and the limitless enterprise of groups of men. It is great, also, very great, in its moral force. Nowhere else in the world have noble men and women exhibited in more striking forms the beauty and the energy of sympathy and helpfulness and counsel in their efforts to rectify wrong, alleviate suffering, and set the weak in the way of strength and hope. We have built up, moreover, a great system of government, which has stood through a long age as in many respects a model for those who seek to set liberty upon foundations that will endure against fortuitous change, against storm and accident. Our life contains every great thing, and contains it in rich abundance.

But the evil has come with the good, and much fine gold has been corroded. With riches has come inexcusable waste. We have squandered a great part of what we might have used, and have not stopped to conserve the exceeding bounty of nature, without which our genius for enterprise would have been worthless and impotent, scorning to be careful, shamefully prodigal as well as admirably efficient. We have been proud of our industrial achievements, but we have not hitherto stopped thoughtfully enough to count the human cost, the cost of lives snuffed out, of energies overtaxed and broken, the fearful physical and spiritual cost to the men and women and children upon whom the dead weight and burden of it all has fallen pitilessly the years through. The groans and agony of it all had not yet reached our ears, the solemn, moving undertone of our life, coming up out of the mines and factories and out of every home where the struggle had its intimate and familiar seat. With the great Government went many deep secret things which we too long delayed to look into and scrutinize with candid, fearless eyes. The great Government we loved has too often been made use of for private and selfish purposes, and those who used it had forgotten the people.

At last a vision has been vouchsafed us of our life as a whole. We see the bad with the good, the debased and decadent with the sound and vital. With this vision we approach new affairs. Our duty is to cleanse, to reconsider, to restore, to correct the evil without impairing the good, to purify and humanize every process of our common life without weakening or sentimentalizing it. There has been something crude and heartless and unfeeling in our haste to succeed and be great. Our thought has been "Let every man look out for himself, let every generation look out for itself," while we reared giant machinery which made it impossible that any but those who stood at the levers of control should have a chance to look out for themselves. We had not forgotten our morals. We remembered well enough that we had set up a policy which was meant to serve the humblest as well as the most powerful, with an eye single to the standards of justice and fair play, and remembered it with pride. But we were very heedless and in a hurry to be great.

We have come now to the sober second thought. The scales of heedlessness have fallen from our eyes. We have made up our minds to square every process of our national life again with the standards we so proudly set up at the beginning and have always carried at our hearts. Our work is a work of restoration.

We have itemized with some degree of particularity the things that ought to be altered, and here are some of the chief items: A tariff which cuts us off from our proper part in the commerce of the world, violates the just principles of taxation, and makes the Government a facile instrument in the hands of private interests; a banking and currency system based upon the necessity of the Government to sell its bonds 50 years ago and perfectly adapted to concentrating cash and restricting credits; an industrial

Woodrow Wilson in his first campaign for the Presidency. "This country from one end to the other believes that something is wrong," he told his audiences. "Society is looking itself over, in our day, from top to bottom; is making fresh and critical analysis of its very elements; is questioning its oldest practices as freely as its newest, scrutinizing every arrangement and motive of its life; and it stands ready to attempt nothing less than a radical reconstruction . . . in its economic and political practice."

system which, take it on all sides, financial as well as administrative, holds capital in leading strings, restricts the liberties and limits the opportunities of labor, and exploits without renewing or conserving the natural resources of the country; a body of agricultural activities never yet given the efficiency of great business undertakings or served as it should be through the instrumentality of science taken directly to the farm, or afforded the facilities of credit best suited to its practical needs; water-courses undeveloped, waste places unreclaimed, forests untended, fast disappearing without plan or prospect of renewal, unregarded waste heaps at every mine. We have studied as perhaps no other nation has the most effective means of production, but we have not studied cost or economy as we should either as organizers of industry, as statesmen, or as individuals.

Nor have we studied and perfected the means by which government may be put at the service of humanity, in safeguarding the health of the Nation, the health of its men and its women and its children, as well as their rights in the struggle for existence. This is no sentimental duty. The firm basis of government is justice, not pity. These are matters of justice. There can be no equality or opportunity, the first essential of justice in the body politic, if men and women and children be not shielded in their lives, their very vitality, from the consequences of great industrial and social processes which they can not alter, control, or singly cope with. Society must see to it that it does not itself crush or weaken or damage its own constituent parts. The first duty of law is to keep sound the society it serves. Sanitary laws, pure-food laws, and laws determining conditions of labor which individuals are powerless to determine for themselves are intimate parts of the very business of justice and legal efficiency.

These are some of the things we ought to do, and not leave the others undone, the old-fashioned, never-to-be-neglected, fundamental safeguarding of property and of individual right. This is the high enterprise of the new day: To lift everything that concerns our life as a Nation to the light that shines from the hearthfire of every man's conscience and vision of the right. It is inconceivable that we should do this as partisans; it is inconceivable we should do in it ignorance of the facts as they are or in blind haste. We shall restore, not destroy. We shall deal with our economic system as it is and as it may be modified, not as it might be if we had a clean sheet of paper to write upon; and step by step we shall make it what it should be, in the spirit of those who question their own wisdom and seek counsel and knowledge, not shallow self-satisfaction or the excitement of excursions whither they can not tell. Justice, and only justice, shall always be our motto.

And yet it will be no cool process of mere science. The Nation has been deeply stirred, stirred by a solemn passion, stirred by the knowledge of wrong, of ideals lost, of government too often debauched and made an instrument of evil. The feelings with which we face this new age of right and opportunity sweep across our heartstrings like some air out of God's own presence, where justice and mercy are reconciled and the judge and the brother are one. We know our task to be no mere task of politics but a task which shall search us through and through, whether we be able to understand our time and the need of our people, whether we be indeed their spokesmen and interpreters, whether we have the pure heart to comprehend and the rectified will to choose our high course of action.

This is not a day of triumph; it is a day of dedication. Here muster, not the forces of party, but the forces of humanity. Men's hearts wait upon us; men's lives hang in the balance; men's hopes call upon us to say what we will do. Who shall live up to the great trust? Who dares fail to try? I summon all honest men, all patriotic, all forward-looking men, to my side. God helping me, I will not fail them, if they will but counsel and sustain me!

President Wilson leading the draft parade in Washington on September 4, 1917, five months after the U.S. declaration of war on Germany. In October the first American troops moved up to the front in France. From a first inaugural address that had never mentioned anything but domestic problems, Wilson had moved to an exclusive concern with foreign affairs.

Fourteen points for peace

Hardly eighteen months after Wilson took office the German armies began marching over Europe. The President asked America to be "impartial in thought as well as in action," but he could not keep the country isolated. A popular sympathy for the Allies, heavy war trade and vast profits, and finally the torpedoing of the Lusitania by a German submarine accelerated the drift towards American participation.

In 1916, running on the "He kept us out of war" slogan, Wilson squeaked through over Hughes by a bare electoral majority. Convinced that the war in Europe was senseless and futile, he hoped to bring about its end by a compromise peace. After the election he urged both sides to make a "peace without victory," but neither side would give up hope of forcing its demands upon the other.

When Germany turned to unrestricted submarine warfare against all ships including the neutrals, the United States entered the war against her. America's aim, Wilson said, was to vindicate "the principles of peace and justice in the life of the world as against selfish and autocratic power." To make the world safe for democracy, he continued, the United States would seek no indemnity and no material compensation.

In a speech to Congress on January 8, 1918, Wilson outlined his peace terms in brief paragraphs that became known as the "Fourteen Points." They were the President's concept of a just and lasting peace.

"All the News That's Fit to Print."

The New [...]

VOL. LXVII...NO. 21,900. NEW YORK, WEDNESDAY, J[...]

PRESIDENT SPECIFIES TERMS A[...]
ASKS JUSTICE FOR ALSAC[...]
TELLS GERMANY SHE MAY[...]

TROTZKY DISTRUSTS ALLIES

Thinks They Want Him to Give In to Berlin and Make Peace.

THUS HELPING THEIR ENDS

Germans Starve by Hundreds; Vorwaerts Sees Catastrophe

Special Cable to THE NEW YORK TIMES.

AMSTERDAM, Jan. 8. (Dispatch to The London Daily Express.)—"What was uncertain last year has now become a bitter reality. It can no longer be denied that people are starving by the hundreds in Germany."

This statement was made today by a Dutchman who has just [...]

LONDON SEES NO PEACE

Fierce Fighting Ahead Despite the Lloyd George Statement.

NECESSITY PROMPTED IT

Text

WASHINGT[...]

Gentlemen of the Congress

Once more, as repeated[...] men of the Central Empir[...] desire to discuss the objec[...] possible basis of a general[...] been in progress at Brest-[...]slan repre[...]

Before a special session of Congress on April 2, 1917, Wilson read his message calling the German submarine policy "warfare against mankind." He asked Congress for a declaration of war, and on the 6th of April he signed the Joint Resolution which had passed the Senate, 82–6, and the House, 373–50.

S. J. Res. 1. (PUBLIC RESOLUTION NO. 1 65th CONGRESS.)

RECEIVED APR 6 1917

Sixty-fifth Congress of the United States of America;

At the First Session,

Begun and held at the City of Washington on Monday, the second day of April, one thousand nine hundred and seventeen.

JOINT RESOLUTION

Declaring that a state of war exists between the Imperial German Government and the Government and the people of the United States and making provision to prosecute the same.

Whereas the Imperial German Government has committed repeated acts of war against the Government and the people of the United States of America: Therefore be it

Resolved by the Senate and House of Representatives of the United States of America in Congress assembled, That the state of war between the United States and the Imperial German Government which has thus been thrust upon the United States is hereby formally declared; and that the President be, and he is hereby, authorized and directed to employ the entire naval and military forces of the United States and the resources of the Government to carry on war against the Imperial German Government; and to bring the conflict to a successful termination all of the resources of the country are hereby pledged by the Congress of the United States.

Champ Clark,

Speaker of the House of Representatives.

Thos. R. Marshall

Vice President of the United States and President of the Senate.

Approved 6 April, 1917

Woodrow Wilson

Spread swiftly abroad, they would, he hoped, cripple the German will to fight and insipre the peoples behind the warring governments with the ideal of a peace without vengeance, annexations, or reparations. In the Fourteen Points speech is Wilson's dream of a weaponless world, a world of equal and friendly nations. It was a dream that the Treaty of Versailles almost wrecked. All it left of Wilson's hopes was the proposal for a League of Nations. In November, 1919, the United States Senate rejected the Treaty and with it American participation in the instrument Wilson had hoped would introduce justice into international relations.

ork Times.

THE WEATHER
Fair today; Thursday snow; diminishing northwest to north winds.
For full weather report see Page 23.

9, 1918.—TWENTY-FOUR PAGES.

ONE CENT In Greater New York. | TWO CENTS Within Commuting Distance. | THREE CENTS Elsewhere.

ASIS FOR WORLD PEACE;)RRAINE, APPLAUDS RUSSIA, AN EQUAL BUT NOT A MASTER

President Wilson's Speech

The President in his address to Congress today spoke as follows:

okes- their d the have Rus- of the

There is, moreover, a voice calling for these definitions of principle and of purpose which is, it seems to me, more thrilling and more compelling than any of the many moving voices with which the troubled air of the world is filled. It is the voice of the Russian people. They are prostrate and all but helpless, it would seem, be- the grim pow

attempt to limit the sovereignty which she enjoys in common with all other free nations. No other single act will serve as this will serve to restore confidence among the nations in the laws which they have themselves set and determined for the government of their relations with one another. Without this healing act the whole structure and validity of international law

APPEALS TO GERMAN PEOPLE

Wilson Declares We Must Know for Whom Their Rulers Speak.

READY TO FIGHT TO END

The Fourteen Points

(January 8, 1918)

Gentlemen of the Congress,

. . . IT WILL BE our wish and purpose that the processes of peace, when they are begun, shall be absolutely open and that they shall involve and permit henceforth no secret understandings of any kind. The day of conquest and aggrandizement is gone by; so is also the day of secret covenants entered into in the interest of particular governments and likely at some unlooked-for moment to upset the peace of the world. . . .

We entered this war because violations of right had occurred which touched us to the quick and made the life of our own people impossible unless they were corrected and the world secured once for all against their recurrence. What we demand in this war, therefore, is nothing peculiar to ourselves. It is that the world be made fit and safe to live in; and particularly that it be made safe for every peace-loving nation which, like our own, wishes to live its own life, determine its own institutions, be assured of justice and fair dealing by the other peoples of the world as against force and selfish aggression. All the peoples of the world are in effect partners in this interest, and for our own part we see very clearly that unless justice be done to others it will not be done to us. The program of the world's peace, therefore, is our program; and that program, the only possible program, as we see it, is this:

I. Open covenants of peace, openly arrived at, after which there shall be no private international understandings of any kind but diplomacy shall proceed always frankly and in the public view.

II. Absolute freedom of navigation upon the seas, outside territorial waters, alike in peace and in war, except as the seas may be closed in whole or in part by international action for the enforcement of international covenants.

III. The removal, so far as possible, of all eco-

President Wilson and Ray Stannard Baker in Paris during the peace negotiations that followed the Armistice of November 11, 1918.

The major decisions at the peace conference were made by the "Big Four" (above): Vittorio Orlando of Italy, Lloyd George of Great Britain, Georges Clemenceau of France, and Woodrow Wilson. Negotiations began in Paris in January, 1919, and Wilson, hoping to win his goal of a League of Nations, made several concessions on his other points. The Treaty of Versailles was signed by the Germans on July 10. Bitter division occurred in the U.S. Senate over the League of Nations issue and Wilson took his case to the country that September, making thirty-seven speeches in twenty-nine cities. Late in the month he broke down, suffering a paralytic stroke from which he never recovered. Unwilling to compromise with his opponents, Wilson met defeat in his attempt to establish his own blueprint for the machinery of international cooperation. His failure meant that for many years the United States was to live by the policy of isolationism.

nomic barriers and the establishment of an equality of trade conditions among all the nations consenting to the peace and associating themselves for its maintenance.

IV. Adequate guarantees given and taken that national armaments will be reduced to the lowest point consistent with domestic safety.

V. A free, open-minded, and absolutely impartial adjustment of all colonial claims, based upon a strict observance of the principle that in determining all such questions of sovereignty the interests of the populations concerned must have equal weight with the equitable claims of the government whose title is to be determined.

VI. The evacuation of all Russian territory and such a settlement of all questions affecting Russia as will secure the best and freest co-operation of the other nations of the world in obtaining for her an unhampered and unembarrassed opportunity for the independent determination of her own political development and national policy and assure her of a sincere welcome into the society of free nations under institutions of her own choosing; and, more than a welcome, assistance also of every kind that she may need and may herself desire. The treatment accorded Russia by her sister nations in the months to come will be the acid test of their good will, of their comprehension of her needs as distinguished from their own interests, and of their intelligent and unselfish sympathy.

VII. Belgium, the whole world will agree, must be evacuated and restored, without any attempt to limit the sovereignty which she enjoys in common with all other free nations. No other single act will serve as this will serve to restore confidence among the nations in the laws which they have themselves set and determined for the government of their relations with one another. Without this healing act the whole structure and validity of international law is forever impaired.

VIII. All French territory should be freed and the invaded portions restored, and the wrong done to France by Prussia in 1871 in the matter of Alsace-Lorraine, which has unsettled the peace of the world for nearly fifty years, should be righted, in order that peace may once more be made secure in the interest of all.

IX. A readjustment of the frontiers of Italy should be effected along clearly recognizable lines of nationality.

X. The peoples of Austria-Hungary, whose place among the nations we wish to see safeguarded and assured, should be accorded the freest opportunity of autonomous development.

XI. Rumania, Serbia, and Montenegro should be evacuated; occupied territories restored; Serbia accorded free and secure access to the sea; and the relations of the several Balkan states to one another determined by friendly counsel along historically established lines of allegiance and nationality; and international guarantees of the political and economic independence and territorial integrity of the several Balkan states should be entered into.

XII. The Turkish portions of the present Ottoman Empire should be assured a secure sovereignty, but the other nationalities which are now under Turkish rule should be assured an undoubted security of life and an absolutely unmolested opportunity of autonomous development, and the Dardanelles should be permanently opened as a free passage to the ships and commerce of all nations under international guarantees.

XIII. An independent Polish state should be erected which should include the territories inhabited by indisputably Polish populations, which should be assured a free and secure access to the sea, and whose political and economic independence and territorial integrity should be guaranteed by international covenant.

XIV. A general association of nations must be formed under specific covenants for the purpose of affording mutual guarantees of political independence and territorial integrity to great and small states alike. . . .

For such arrangements and covenants we are willing to fight and to continue to fight until they are achieved; but only because we wish the right to prevail and desire a just and stable peace such as can be secured only by removing the chief provocations to war, which this program does not remove. We have no jealousy of German greatness, and there is nothing in this program that impairs it. We grudge her no achievement or distinction of learning or of pacific enterprise such as have made her record very bright and very enviable. We do not wish to injure her or to block in any way her legitimate influence or power. We do not wish to fight her either with arms or with hostile arrangements of trade if she is willing to associate herself with us and the other peace-loving nations of the world in covenants of justice and law and fair dealing. We wish her only to accept a place of equality among the peoples of the world,—the new world in which we now live,—instead of a place of mastery. . . .

We have spoken now, surely, in terms too concrete to admit of any further doubt or question. An evident principle runs through the whole program I have outlined. It is the principle of justice to all peoples and nationalities, and their right to live on equal terms of liberty and safety with one another, whether they be strong or weak. Unless this principle be made its foundation no part of the structure of international justice can stand. The people of the United States could act upon no other principle; and to the vindication of this principle they are ready to devote their lives, their honor, and everything that they possess. The moral climax of this the culminating and final war for human liberty has come, and they are ready to put their own strength, their own highest purpose, their own integrity and devotion to the test.

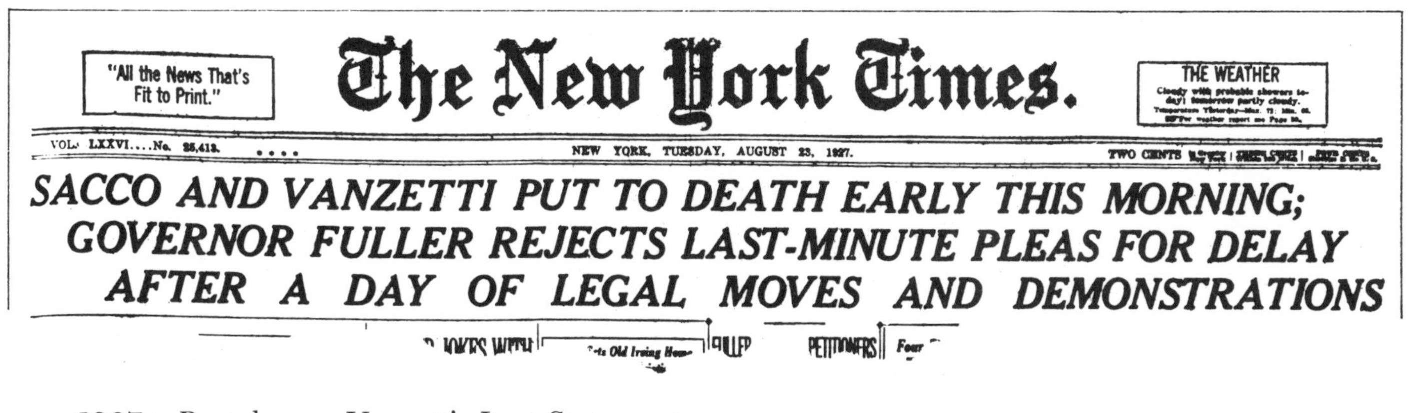

"All the News That's Fit to Print."

The New York Times.

THE WEATHER

VOL. LXXVI....No. 25,413. NEW YORK, TUESDAY, AUGUST 23, 1927. TWO CENTS

SACCO AND VANZETTI PUT TO DEATH EARLY THIS MORNING; GOVERNOR FULLER REJECTS LAST-MINUTE PLEAS FOR DELAY AFTER A DAY OF LEGAL MOVES AND DEMONSTRATIONS

1927 Bartolomeo Vanzetti: Last Statement

I would live again to do what I have done already

From the shabby ending of the crusade for world democracy America turned to a mood of "normalcy." The Harding and Coolidge administrations looked back to McKinley's day; the Roosevelt and Wilson programs of progressivism gave way to conservatism in domestic politics and isolationism in foreign affairs. It was a time of big money and high living, with most of the country preferring to ignore the pockets of unemployment and the distress of the farmers.

The repressive measures adopted during the war to secure military ends continued into the twenties. Radicals, pacifists, and aliens of suspicious leanings were hounded, jailed, deported. Free criticism of political and economic institutions was penalized as disloyalty to the "American" way of life. Nevertheless, through the babble of conformity and intolerance voices of dissent continued to be heard.

Early in the postwar decade the paymaster of a Massachusetts shoe factory was robbed and shot by two men who fled in a car. Nicola Sacco and Bartolomeo Vanzetti, a shoe-worker and a fish-peddler, were charged with the crime. The two Italian immigrants, who were pacifists and philosophical anarchists, were convicted in 1921 on evidence which many distinguished lawyers, conservative as well as liberal, regarded as insubstantial. Liberals and radicals at home and abroad charged that the two men were being tried for their radical views rather than for any crime. The tragic miscarriage of justice became a cause célèbre, *stirring deep emotion and arousing mass protest around the world. The issue dragged on for seven fatal years, until Sacco and Vanzetti were executed on August 23, 1927.*

Knowing almost no English when imprisoned, the two friends studied in jail. Their letters from prison were eloquent with courage. Vanzetti's last statement before sentence of death was pronounced (quoted here) speaks the mind and spirit of men whose passion for justice is never silenced.

Bartolomeo Vanzetti (middle) and Nicola Sacco (right) in the fourth year of their imprisonment.

Edna St. Vincent Millay, one of the principal poets of the post World War I period, joined scores of other artists and writers who picketed in protest against the execution of the two anarchists.

YES. What I say is that I am innocent, not only of the Braintree crime, but also of the Bridgewater crime. That I am not only innocent of these two crimes, but in all my life I have never stolen and I have never killed and I have never spilled blood. That is what I want to say. And it is not all. Not only am I innocent of these two crimes, not only in all my life I have never stole, never killed, never spilled blood, but I have struggled all my life, since I began to reason, to eliminate crime from the earth.

Everybody that knows these two arms knows very well that I did not need to go in between the street and kill a man to take money. I can live with my two arms and live well. But besides that, I can live even without work with my arm for other people. . . .

Well, I want to reach a little point farther, and it is this, that not only have I not been trying to steal in Bridgewater, not only have I not been in Braintree to steal and kill and have never steal or kill or spilt blood in all my life, not only have I struggled hard against crimes, but I have refused myself the commodity or glory of life, the pride of life of a good position because in my consideration it is not right to exploit man. . . .

Now, I should say that I am not only innocent of all these things, not only have I never committed a real crime in my life—though some sins, but not crimes—not only have I struggled all my life to eliminate crimes that the official law and the official moral condemns, but also the crime that the official moral and the official law sanctions and sanctifies,—the exploitation and the oppression of the man by the man, and if there is a reason why I am here as a guilty man, if there is a reason why you in a few minutes can doom me, it is this reason and none else.

There is the best man I ever cast my eyes upon since I lived, a man that will last and will grow always more near and more dear to the people, as far as into the heart of the people, so long as admiration for goodness and for sacrifice will last. I mean Eugene Debs. . . . He know, and not only he but every man of understanding in the world, not only in this country but also in the other countries, men that we have provided a certain amount of a record of the times, they all stick with us, the flower of mankind of Europe, the better writers, the greatest thinkers, of Europe, have pleaded in our favor. The scientists, the greatest scientists, the greatest states-

Eight years of trials, petitions, and hearings, in what became the *cause célèbre* of the nineteen-twenties failed to change the order for the execution, and vast throngs of men and women in cities around the world met in the summer of 1927 to demonstrate against the death of Sacco and Vanzetti. This photo shows part of the crowd in New York's Union Square on August 9.

men of Europe, have pleaded in our favor. The people of foreign nations have pleaded in our favor.

Is it possible that only a few on the jury, a handful of men of the jury, who would condemn their mother for worldly honor and for earthly fortune; is it possible that they are right against what the world, the whole world has say it is wrong and that I know that it is wrong? If there is one that I should know it, if it is right or if it is wrong, it is I and this man. You see it is seven years that we are in jail. What we have suffered during those years no human tongue can say, and yet you see me before you, not trembling, you see me looking you in your eyes straight, not blushing, not changing color, not ashamed or in fear. . . .

We have proven that there could not have been another Judge on the face of the earth more prejudiced and more cruel than you have been against us. We have proven that. Still they refuse the new trial. We know, and you know in your heart, that you have been against us from the very beginning, before you see us. Before you see us you already know that we were radicals, that we were underdogs, that we were the enemy of the institution that you can believe in good faith in their goodness—I don't want to condemn that—and that it was easy on the time of the first trial to get a verdict of guiltiness.

We know that you have spoken yourself and have spoke your hostility against us, and your despisement against us with friends of yours on the train, at the University Club, of Boston, on the Golf Club of Worcester. I am sure that if the people who know all what you say against us would have the civil courage to take the stand, maybe your Honor—I am sorry to say this because you are an old man, and

Shortly after midnight of August 22, 1927, the two men went to their death in Charlestown State Prison. Later, a silent cortege escorted the bodies to the crematory through eight miles of Boston's streets as thousands looked on.

I have an old father—but maybe you would be beside us in good justice at this time. . . .

This is what I say: I would not wish to a dog or to a snake, to the most low and misfortunate creature on the earth—I would not wish to any of them what I have had to suffer for things that I am not guilty of. I am suffering because I am a radical and indeed I am a radical; I have suffered because I was an Italian, and indeed I am an Italian; I have suffered more for my fmily and for my beloved than for myself; but I am so convinced to be right that if you could execute me two times, and if I could be reborn two other times, I would live again to do what I have done already. I have finished. Thank you.

Judge Webster B. Thayer, the trial judge in the Sacco-Vanzetti case, to whom Vanzetti made his famous last address before the sentence of death was pronounced.

Vanzetti and Sacco near the end of their fight for justice.

"IF it had not been for these thing, I might have live out my life talking at street corners to scorning men. I might have die, unmarked, unknown, a failure. Now we are not a failure. This is our career and our triumph. Never in our full life could we hope to do such work for tolerance, for justice, for man's understanding of man as now we do by accident. Our words—our lives—our pains—nothing! The taking of our lives—lives of a good shoemaker and a poor fish-peddler—all! That last moment belongs to us—that agony is our triumph."

—Vanzetti's reported statement after receiving sentence, April 9, 1927.

1933 Franklin D. Roosevelt: First Inaugural Address

The only thing we have to fear is fear itself

"We in America," Herbert Hoover proclaimed, "are nearer to the final triumph over poverty than ever before in the history of our land." Hardly six months after he had entered the White House the prophet of permanent prosperity was abruptly confronted with the worst crisis the country had known since the Civil War. On October 29, 1929, came the great stock market crash and the onset of a depression that spiralled downward to incredible disaster.

As Secretary of Commerce under both Harding and Coolidge, Hoover had been the chief architect of a program of "rugged individualism" that had given generous government aid to business but turned its back upon hard pressed farmers and workers. Faced with the collapse of the economy and mass poverty and distress, the Administration's approach to government's responsibility remained the same. Little more than the slogan, "Prosperity is just around the corner," was thrown up against the tidal wave of panic and depression.

By 1932 over twelve million unemployed were in the streets, and five thousand banks had shut their doors. Farm prices had hit bottom, business failures were wholesale, production had dropped 60 per cent in three years. Nominated once again by the Republican chiefs, Hoover ran against the liberal Governor of New York, Franklin Delano Roosevelt. Promising a "new deal," Roosevelt swept into office with a majority of seven million votes.

Basing himself upon the first Roosevelt's Square Deal and Wilson's New Freedom, the new president extended their liberal reforms into a continuous program of governmental responsibility for the social and economic well-being of the people. In his First Inaugural Address of March 4, 1933, he bolstered public confidence in the nation's ability to endure and to prosper, and dedicated himself to a bold series of measures to meet the crisis.

"All the News That's Fit to Print."

The New York Times.

Copyright, 1929, by The New York Times Company.

THE WEATHER
Cloudy, probably rain today and to-morrow; warmer tomorrow.

VOL. LXXIX....No. 26,212. NEW YORK, WEDNESDAY, OCTOBER 30, 1929. TWO CENTS

STOCKS COLLAPSE IN 16,410,030-SHARE DAY, BUT RALLY AT CLOSE CHEERS BROKERS; BANKERS OPTIMISTIC, TO CONTINUE AID

GRUNDY FOR CURBING 'BACKWARD STATES' ON THE TARIFF BILL

Veteran Republican Lobbyist Tells Senate Inquiry the West Needs "Silencing."

PENNSYLVANIA KNOWS BEST

Von Opel, Rocket Flier, Weds Woman Pilot Who Advised Him

Wireless to THE NEW YORK TIMES.

BERLIN, Oct. 29.—Fritz von Opel, the first to fly a rocket plane, and who intends to sail for New York the beginning of November to study and work at General Motors plants, was married on Saturday to Frau Sellnik, née Loewenstein, the former wife of a Wiesbaden actor. For many months she has been von Opel's professional adviser on aviation and she herself is one of Germany's six woman pilots, flying her Handley Page plane with the greatest skill.

Frau von Opel, who is also a daring automobilist, is handsome, slender and blonde. When the airman landed safely from his rocket flig...

KAHN REFUSES POST IN SENATE CAMPAIGN; CALLS CHOICE UNWISE

He Writes to Moses to Withhold His Name for Treasurer Due to 'Divided Reception.'

WAS RELUCTANT, HE SAYS

Newark Man, 4 Feet 10, Says He Was Smallest in A. E. F.

WASHINGTON, Oct. 29 (AP).—Nicholas Casale of Newark, N. J., wants to be known as the smallest man who went to France with the American Expeditionary Forces.

He has appealed to Representative Hartley of Kearny to establish that fact. Casale recently secured an affidavit from the Veterans' Bureau certifying that he was 4 feet 10 inches tall and weighed 106 pounds when he enlisted. The bureau has refused to declare him the "smallest man," saying it would require months for clerks to scan the record of every man who served with the...

LEADERS SEE FEAR WANING

Point to 'Lifting Spells'

240 Issues Lose $15,894,818,894 in Month; Slump in Full Exchange List Vastly Larger

The drastic effects of Wall Street's October bear market is shown by valuation tables prepared last night by THE NEW YORK TIMES, which place the decline...

CLOSING RALLY VIGOROUS

Leading Issues Regain

October 29, 1929: "From every point of view, in the extent of losses sustained, in total turnover, in the number of speculators wiped out, the day was the most disastrous in Wall Street's history," said *The New York Times* in reporting the stock market's collapse. Hysteria swept the country. Millions of investors lost their life savings, businesses shut down, factories locked their gates, hundreds of thousands were evicted from their homes, millions of jobless hunted desperately for work. Apple-selling on street corners became the symbol of the times.

I AM CERTAIN that my fellow Americans expect that on my induction into the Presidency I will address them with a candor and a decision which the present situation of our nation impels. This is pre-eminently the time to speak the truth, the whole truth, frankly and boldly. Nor need we shrink from honestly facing conditions in our country to-day. This great Nation will endure as it has endured, will revive and will prosper. So, first of all, let me assert my firm belief that the only thing we have to fear is fear itself—nameless, unreasoning, unjustified terror which paralyzes needed efforts to convert retreat into advance. In every dark hour of our national life a leadership of frankness and vigor has met with that understanding and support of the people themselves which is essential to victory. I am convinced that you will again give that support to leadership in these critical days.

In such a spirit on my part and on yours we face our common difficulties. They concern, thank God, only material things. Values have shrunken to fantastic levels; taxes have risen; our ability to pay has fallen; government of all kinds is faced by serious curtailment of income; the means of exchange are

Section 1

"All the News That's Fit to Print."

The New York Times.

LATE CITY EDITION

Section 1

Copyright, 1933, by The New York Times Company.

VOL. LXXXII....No. 27,434. NEW YORK, SUNDAY, MARCH 5, 1933. TEN CENTS

ROOSEVELT INAUGURATED, ACTS TO END THE NATIONAL BANKING CRISIS QUICKLY; WILL ASK WAR-TIME POWERS IF NEEDED

PLAN TO USE SCRIP HERE

Bankers Ready to Issue Clearing House Paper at End of Holiday.

WILL MEET WOODIN TODAY

Checks Still Accepted Here For Federal Income Taxes

Collectors of Internal Revenue in New York City were still accepting checks yesterday in payment of Federal income taxes, and it was said that checks would continue to be accepted during the bank holiday.

No consideration was yet being given to possible postponement of payments, due on March 15. This could only be granted by the Secretary of the Treasury or Commissioner of Internal Rev- ... Washington, althou- ... individual

READY TO CALL CONGRESS

President Probably Will Summon Extra Session for Wednesday.

WORKS ON LEGISLATION

... Meet With

THE NEW PRESIDENT TAKING THE OATH OF OFFICE.

100,000 AT INAUGURATION

President, Grim, Terse, Pledges 'Adequate but Sound Currency.'

SCORES 'MONEY-CHANGERS'

"ROOSEVELT ACTS" was the key phrase in the headlines describing the new President's inaugural address. Taking office at the bottom of the depression, FDR pushed through a mass of legislation to provide immediate relief for the homeless, the starving, the needy, pillars for a collapsing economic system, and reforms for government administration.

frozen in the currents of trade; the withered leaves of industrial enterprise lie on every side; farmers find no markets for their produce; the savings of many years in thousands of families are gone.

More important, a host of unemployed citizens face the grim problem of existence, and an equally great number toil with little return. Only a foolish optimist can deny the dark realities of the moment.

Yet our distress comes from no failure of substance. We are stricken by no plague of locusts. Compared with the perils which our forefathers conquered because they believed and were not afraid, we have still much to be thankful for. Nature still offers her bounty and human efforts have multiplied it. Plenty is at our doorstep, but a generous use of it languishes in the very sight of the supply. Primarily this is because the rulers of the exchange of mankind's goods have failed through their own stubbornness and their own incompetence, have admitted their failure and abdicated. Practices of the unscrupulous money changers stand indicted in the court of public opinion, rejected by the hearts and minds of men.

True they have tried, but their efforts have been cast in the pattern of an outworn tradition. Faced by failure of credit, they have proposed only the lending of more money.

Stripped of the lure of profit by which to induce our people to follow their false leadership, they have resorted to exhortations, pleading tearfully for restored confidence. They know only the rules of a generation of self-seekers. They have no vision, and when there is no vision the people perish.

The money changers have fled from their high seats in the temple of our civilization. We may now restore that temple to the ancient truths. The measure of the restoration lies in the extent to which we apply social values more noble than mere monetary profit.

Happiness lies not in the mere possession of money; it lies in the joy of achievement, in the thrill of creative effort. The joy and moral stimulation of work no longer must be forgotten in the mad chase of evanescent profits. These dark days will be worth all they cost us if they teach us that our true destiny is not to be ministered unto but to minister to ourselves and to our fellow men.

Recognition of the falsity of material wealth as the standard of success goes hand in hand with the abandonment of the false belief that public office and high political position are to be valued only by the standards of pride of place and personal profit; and there must be an end to a conduct in banking and in business which too often has given to a sacred trust the likeness of callous and selfish wrongdoing. . . .

Restoration calls, however, not for changes in ethics alone. This Nation asks for action, and action now.

Our greatest primary task is to put people to work. This is no unsolvable problem if we face it wisely and courageously.

President Roosevelt during one of his frequent "fireside chats." He used the radio networks to reach people everywhere with messages that explained his plans and fired enthusiasm for getting them through Congress.

It can be accomplished in part by direct recruiting by the Government itself, treating the task as we would treat the emergency of a war, but at the same time, through this employment, accomplishing greatly needed projects to stimulate and reorganize the use of our natural resources. . . .

The task can be helped by definite efforts to raise the values of agricultural products and with this the power to purchase the output of our cities. It can be helped by preventing realistically the tragedy of the growing loss, through foreclosure, of our small homes and our farms. It can be helped by insistence that the Federal, State and local governments act forthwith on the demand that their cost be drastically reduced. It can be helped by the unifying of relief activities which to-day are often scattered, uneconomical, and unequal. It can be helped by national planning for and supervision of all forms of transportation and of communications

With millions unemployed in the great depression, long lines of hungry people formed across the country to get food handouts. Typical were these destitute people (in top photo) gathering potatoes from a federal relief agency in Cleveland. To provide jobs quickly, Roosevelt launched several work programs. Among the first, set up in 1933 by the famous "100 days" Congress, was the Civilian Conservation Corps. Single, unemployed youths seventeen to twenty-three (bottom picture) were given uniforms and put to work at reforestation and road-building on public lands.

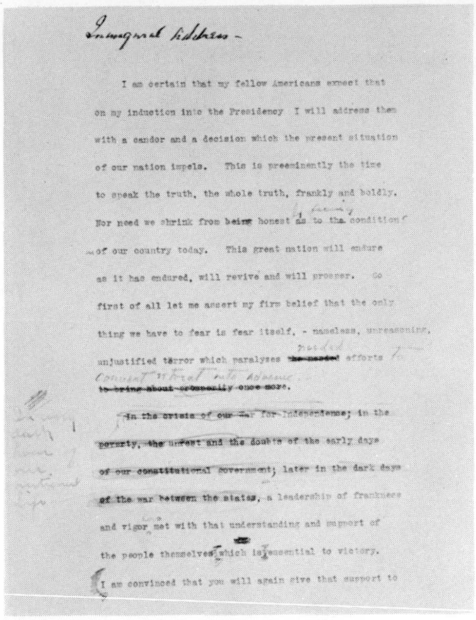

and other utilities which have a definitely public character. There are many ways in which it can be helped, but it can never be helped merely by talking about it. We must act, and act quickly.

Finally, in our progress toward a resumption of work we require two safeguards against a return of the evils of the old order; there must be a strict supervision of all banking and credits and investments; there must be an end to speculation with other people's money, and there must be provision for an adequate but sound currency.

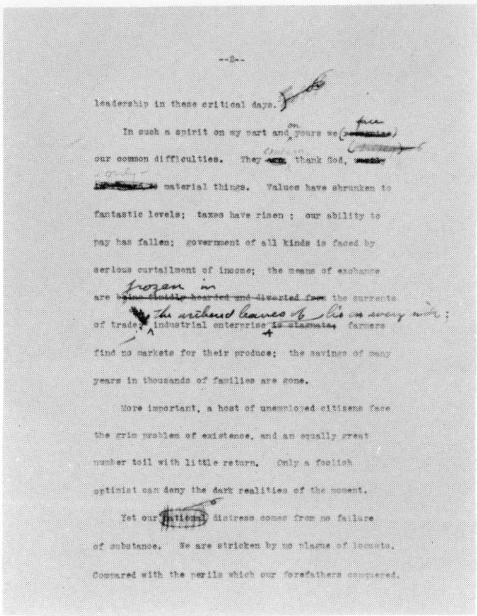

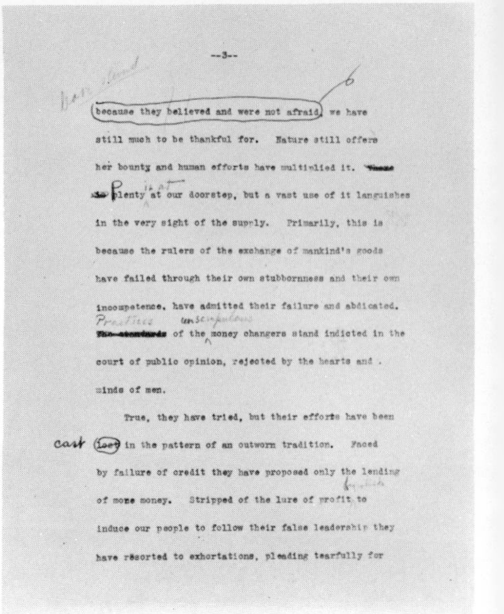

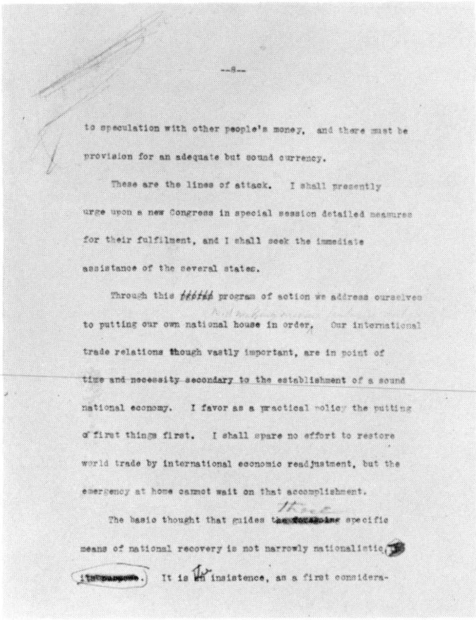

These are the lines of attack. I shall presently urge upon a new Congress in special session detailed measures for their fulfillment, and I shall seek the immediate assistance of the several States.

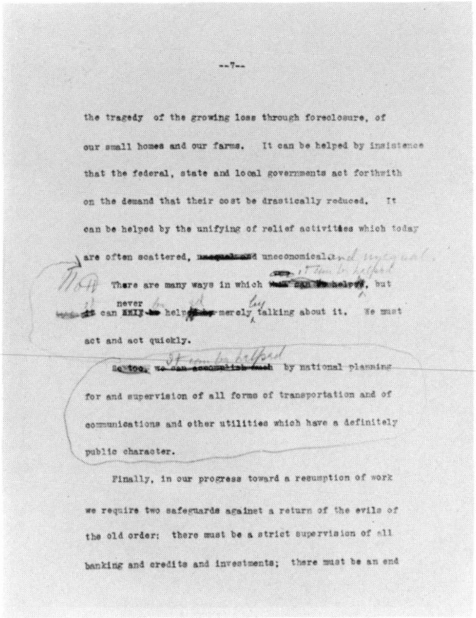

Through this program of action we address ourselves to putting our own national house in order and making income balance outgo. . . .

I favor as a practical policy the putting of first things first. I shall spare no effort to restore world trade by international economic readjustment, but the emergency at home cannot wait on that accomplishment.

The basic thought that guides these specific means of national recovery is not narrowly nationalistic. It is the insistence, as a first consideration, upon the interdependence of the various elements in and parts of, the United States—a recognition of the old and permanently important manifestation of the American spirit of the pioneer. It is the way to recovery. It is the immediate way. It is the strongest assurance that the recovery will endure.

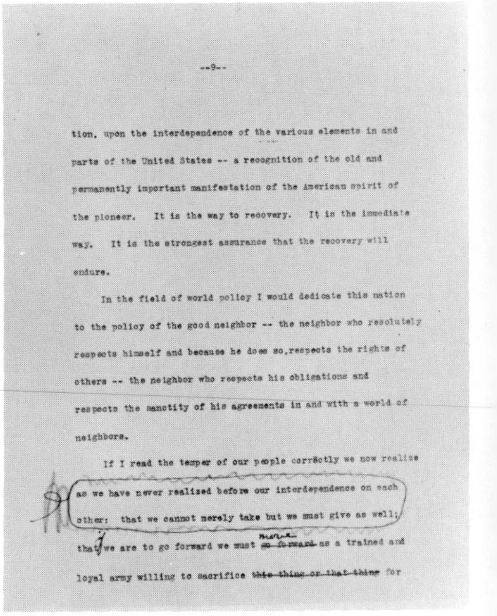

--4--

restored confidence. They know only the rules of a generation of self-seekers. They have no vision, and when there is no vision the people perish. The money changers have fled from their high seats in the temple of our civilization.

We may now restore that temple to the ancient truths. The measure of the restoration lies in the extent to which we apply social values more noble than mere monetary profit.

Happiness lies not in the mere possession of money; it lies in the joy of achievement, in the thrill of creative effort. The moral stimulation of work must no longer be forgotten in the mad chase of evanescent profits. These dark days will be worth all they cost us if they teach us that our true destiny is not to be ministered unto but to

--5--

minister to ourselves and to our fellowmen.

Recognition of the falsity of material wealth as the standard of success goes hand in hand with the abandonment of the false belief that public office and high political position are to be valued only by the standards of pride of place and personal profit; and there must be an end to a conduct in banking and in business which too often has given to a sacred trust the likeness of callous and selfish wrongdoing. Small wonder that confidence languishes, for it thrives only on honesty, on honor, on the sacredness of obligations, on faithful protection, on unselfish performance; without them it cannot live.

Restoration calls, however, not for changes in ethics alone. This nation asks for action, and action now.

--6--

Our greatest primary task is to put people to work. This is no unsolvable problem if we face it wisely and courageously. It can be accomplished in part by direct recruiting by the government itself, treating the task as we would treat the emergency of a war, but at the same time through this employment accomplishing greatly needed projects to stimulate and reorganize the use of our natural resources.

Hand in hand with this we must frankly recognize the overbalance of population in our industrial centers and by engaging on a national scale in a redistribution, endeavor to provide a better use of the land for those best fitted for the land. The task can be helped by definite efforts to raise the values of agricultural products and with this the power to purchase the output of our cities. It can be helped by preventing realistically

--10--

the good of a common discipline, because without such discipline no progress is made, no leadership becomes effective. We are, I know, ready and willing to submit our lives and property to such discipline because it makes possible a leadership which aims at a larger good. This I propose to offer, pledging that the larger purposes will bind upon us all as a sacred obligation with a unity of duty hitherto evoked only in time of armed strife.

With this pledge taken, I assume unhesitatingly the leadership of this great army of our people dedicated to a disciplined attack upon our common problems.

Action in this image and to this end is feasible under the form of government which we have inherited from our ancestors. Our constitution is so simple and practical that it is possible always to meet extraordinary needs by changes in emphasis and arrangement without loss of essential form. That is why our constitutional system

--11--

has proved itself the most superbly enduring political mechanism the modern world has produced. It has met every stress of vast expansion of territory, of foreign wars, of bitter internal strife, of world relations.

It is to be hoped that the normal balance of executive and legislative authority may be wholly adequate to meet the unprecedented task before us. But it may be that an unprecedented demand and need for undelayed action may call for temporary departure from that normal balance of public procedure.

I am prepared under my constitutional duty to recommend the measures that a stricken nation in the midst of a stricken world may require. These measures, or such other measures as the Congress may build out of their experience and wisdom, I shall seek, within my constitutional authority, to bring to speedy adoption.

--12--

But in the event that the Congress shall fail to take one of these two courses, and in the event that the national emergency is still critical, I shall not evade the clear course of duty that will then confront me. I shall ask the Congress for the one remaining instrument to meet the crisis -- broad executive power to wage a war against the emergency, as great as the power that would be given to me if we were in fact invaded by a foreign foe.

For the trust reposed in me I will return the courage and the devotion that befit the time. I can do no less.

We face the arduous days that lie before us in the warm courage of national unity; with the clear consciousness of seeking old and precious moral values; with the clean satisfaction that comes from the stern performance of duty by old and young alike. We aim at the assurance of a rounded and permanent national life.

We do not distrust the future of essential democracy. The people of the United States have not failed. In their

--13--

need they have registered a mandate that they want direct vigorous action. They have asked for discipline and direction under leadership. They have made me the present instrument of their wishes. In the spirit of the gift I take it.

In this dedication of a nation we humbly ask the blessing of God. May he protect each and every one of us. May he guide me in the days to come.

This was the final draft of the Inaugural at Hyde Park – Wed. March 1st 1933

Franklin D. Roosevelt

The last draft of FDR's first inaugural address, with corrections in the President's hand.

In the field of world policy I would dedicate this Nation to the policy of the good neighbor—the neighbor who resolutely respects himself and, because he does so, respects the rights of others—the neighbor who respects his obligations and respects the sanctity of his agreements in and with a world of neighbors.

If I read the temper of our people correctly, we now realize as we have never before our interdependence on each other; that we cannot merely take but we must give as well; that if we are to go forward we must move as a trained and loyal army willing to sacrifice for the good of a common discipline, because without such discipline no progress is made, no leadership becomes effective. We are, I know, ready and willing to submit our lives and property to such discipline, because it makes possible a leadership which aims at a larger good. This I propose to offer, pledging that the larger purposes will bind upon us all as a sacred obligation with a unity of duty hitherto evoked only in time of armed strife.

With this pledge taken, I assume unhesitatingly the leadership of this great army of our people, dedicated to a disciplined attack upon our common problems.

Action in this image and to this end is feasible under the form of government which we have inherited from our ancestors. Our Constitution is so simple and practical that it is possible always to meet extraordinary needs by changes in emphasis and arrangement without loss of essential form. That is why our constitutional system has proved itself the most superbly enduring political mechanism the modern world has produced. It has met every stress of vast expansion of territory, of foreign wars, of bitter internal strife, of world relations.

It is to be hoped that the normal balance of executive and legislative authority may be wholly adequate to meet the unprecedented task before us.

But it may be that an unprecedented demand and need for undelayed action may call for temporary departure from that normal balance of public procedure.

I am prepared under my constitutional duty to recommend the measures that a stricken nation in the midst of a stricken world may require. These measures, or such other measures as the Congress may build out of its experience and wisdom, I shall seek, within my constitutional authority, to bring to speedy adoption.

But in the event that the Congress shall fail to take one of these two courses, and in the event that the national emergency is still critical, I shall not evade the clear course of duty that will then confront me. I shall ask the Congress for the one remaining instrument to meet the crisis—broad executive power to wage a war against the emergency, as great as the power that would be given me if we were in fact invaded by a foreign foe.

For the trust reposed in me I will return the courage and the devotion that befit the time. I can do no less.

We face the arduous days that lie before us in the warm courage of national unity; with the clear consciousness of seeking old and precious moral values; with the clean satisfaction that comes from the stern performance of duty by old and young alike. We aim at the assurance of a rounded and permanent national life.

We do not distrust the future of essential democracy. The people of the United States have not failed. In their need they have registered a mandate that they want direct, vigorous action. They have asked for discipline and direction under leadership. They have made me the present instrument of their wishes. In the spirit of the gift I take it. In this dedication of a Nation we humbly ask the blessing of God. May He protect each and every one of us. May He guide me in the days to come.

1939 Walter Lippmann: The Indispensable Opposition

The liberties of other men are our own vital necessity

In 1939, the Atlantic Monthly *carried an article by Walter Lippmann on the nature of political freedom. A New Yorker, Lippmann was a graduate of Harvard, where he had been strongly influenced by the pragmatist philosophy of William James From campus politics he moved swiftly into the sphere of world politics. He served a while as an assistant to Lincoln Steffens, was an associate editor of the* New Republic, *and when America was drawn into the First World War, became Woodrow Wilson's Assistant Secretary of War. In the twenties he was an editor of the liberal* New York World. *Since 1931 he has been a syndicated columnist for the New York* Herald Tribune.

Lippmann's commentary has shown a brilliant skill in dissecting complex national and international problems, penetrating through layers of prejudice and propaganda until the essential issue is revealed. In this essay he demonstrates that the civil liberties we proclaim are not to be dismantled at the first sign of disorder. Freedom of speech and press, the right to criticize, are rooted in the practical necessity of finding the truth—without which we cannot flourish, nor even survive.

WERE THEY PRESSED hard enough, most men would probably confess that political freedom—that is to say the right to speak freely and to act in opposition—is a noble ideal rather than a practical necessity. As the case for freedom is generally put today, the argument lends itself to this feeling. It is made to appear that, whereas each man claims his freedom as a matter of right, the freedom he accords to other men is a matter of toleration. Thus, the defense of freedom of opinion tends to rest not on its substantial, beneficial, and indispensable consequences, but on a somewhat eccentric, a rather vaguely benevolent, attachment to an abstraction.

It is all very well to say with Voltaire, "I wholly disapprove of what you say, but will defend to the death your right to say it," but as a matter of fact most men will not defend to the death the rights of other men: if they disapprove sufficiently what other men say, they will somehow suppress those men if they can.

So, if this is the best that can be said for liberty of opinion, that a man must tolerate his opponents because every one has a "right" to say what he pleases, then we shall find that liberty of opinion is a luxury, safe only in pleasant times when men can be tolerant because they are not deeply and vitally concerned.

Yet actually, as a matter of historic fact, there is a much stronger foundation for the great constitutional right of freedom of speech, and as a matter of practical human experience there is a much more compelling reason for cultivating the habits of free men. We take, it seems to me, a naively self-righteous view when we argue as if the right of our opponents to speak were something that we protect because we are magnanimous, noble, and unselfish. The compelling reason why, if liberty of opinion did not exist, we should have to invent it, why it will eventually have to be restored in all civilized countries where it is now suppressed, is that we must protect the right of our opponents to speak because we must hear what they have to say.

We miss the whole point when we imagine that we tolerate the freedom of our political opponents as we tolerate a howling baby next door, as we put up with the blasts from our neighbor's radio because we are too peaceable to heave a brick through the window. If this were all there is to freedom of opinion, that we are too good-natured or too timid to do anything about our opponents and our critics except to let them talk, it would be difficult to say whether we are tolerant because we are magnanimous or because we are lazy, because we have strong principles or because we lack serious convictions, whether we have the hospitality of an inquiring mind or the indifference of an empty mind. And so, if we truly wish to understand why freedom is necessary in a civilized society, we must begin by realizing that, because freedom of discussion improves our own opinions, the liberties of other men are our own vital necessity.

We are much closer to the essence of the matter, not when we quote Voltaire, but when we go to the doctor and pay him to ask us the most embarrassing questions and to prescribe the most disagreeable diet. When we pay the doctor to exercise complete freedom of speech about the cause and cure of our stomach-ache, we do not look upon ourselves as tolerant and magnanimous, and worthy to be admired by ourselves. We have enough common sense to know that if we threaten to put the doctor in jail because we do not like the diagnosis and the prescription it will be unpleasant for the doctor, to be sure, but equally unpleasant for our own stomach-ache. That is why even the most ferocious dictator would rather be treated by a doctor who was free to think and speak the truth than by his own Minister of Propaganda. For there is a point, the point at which things really matter, where the freedom of others is no longer a question of their right but of our own need.

The point at which we recognize this need is much higher in some men than in others. The totalitarian rulers think they do not need the freedom of an opposition: they exile, imprison, or shoot their opponents. We have concluded on the basis of practical experience, which goes back to Magna Carta and beyond, that we need the opposition. We pay the opposition salaries out of the public treasury.

In so far as the usual apology for freedom of speech ignores this experience, it becomes abstract and eccentric rather than concrete and human. The emphasis is generally put on the right to speak, as if all that mattered were that the doctor should be free to go out into the park and explain to the vacant air why I have a stomach-ache. Surely that is a miserable caricature of the great civic right which men have bled and died for. What really matters is that the doctor should tell me what ails me, that I should listen to him; that if I do not like what he says I should be free to call in another doctor; and that then the first doctor should have to listen to the second doctor; and that out of all the speaking and listening, the give-and-take of opinions, the truth should be arrived at.

This is the creative principle of freedom of speech, not that it is a system for the tolerating of error, but that it is a system for finding the truth. It may not produce the truth, or the whole truth all the time, or often, or in some cases ever. But if the truth can be found, there is no other system which will normally and habitually find so much truth. Until we have thoroughly understood this principle, we shall not know why we must value our liberty, or how we can protect and develop it . . .

The only reason for dwelling on all this is that if we are to preserve democracy we must understand its principles. And the principle which distinguishes it from all other forms of government is that in a democracy the opposition not only is tolerated as constitutional but must be maintained because it is in fact indispensable.

The democratic system cannot be operated without effective opposition. For, in making the great experiment of governing people by consent rather than by coercion, it is not sufficient that the party in power should have a majority. It is just as necessary that the party in power should never outrage the minority. That means that it must listen to the minority and be moved by the criticisms of the minority. That means that its measures must take account of the minority's objections, and that in administering measures it must remember that the minority may become the majority.

The opposition is indispensable. A good statesman, like any other sensible human being, always learns more from his opponents than from his fervent supporters. For his supporters will push him to disaster unless his opponents show him where the dangers are. So if he is wise he will often pray to be delivered from his friends, because they will ruin him. But, though it hurts, he ought also to pray never to be left without opponents; for they keep him on the path of reason and good sense.

The national unity of a free people depends upon a sufficiently even balance of political power to make it impracticable for the administration to be arbitrary and for the opposition to be revolutionary and irreconcilable. Where that balance no longer exists, democracy perishes. For unless all the citizens of a state are forced by circumstances to compromise, unless they feel that they can affect policy but that no one can wholly dominate it, unless by habit and necessity they have to give and take, freedom cannot be maintained.

"All the News That's Fit to Print."

The New York Times.

LATE CITY EDITION

VOL. XC..No. 30,299. NEW YORK, TUESDAY, JANUARY 7, 1941. THREE CENTS

ROOSEVELT ASKS ALL-OUT AID TO DEMOCRACIES; TO SEND THEM SHIPS, PLANES, TANKS AND GUNS; BRITISH MOVING ON TOBRUK; NAZIS STIR BALKANS

The International Situation

SOFIA HOLDS STAGE CAPITAL EXPECTANT

Defying the dictators and denouncing the appeasers, Roosevelt called for material aid to the democracies resisting Hitler's aggression and then outlined his four-point program for a peace to be built upon "essential human freedoms." This "moral order" for peace, the President said, was directly opposed to the "new order of tyranny."

1941 Franklin D. Roosevelt: "Four Freedoms" speech

A world founded upon four freedoms

Franklin D. Roosevelt's annual message to Congress on January 6, 1941, came sixteen months after the outbreak of World War II and almost a year before the Japanese attack upon Pearl Harbor. The United States was not neutral, he said in this speech: "The future and the safety of our country and of our democracy are overwhelmingly involved." After outlining the progress of the war that was being waged on four continents, he expressed his convictions on the nature and the meaning of the democracy whose life was threatened by fascism's advancing armies. This excerpt from what came to be known as the "Four Freedoms" speech voiced America's goal for the postwar world.

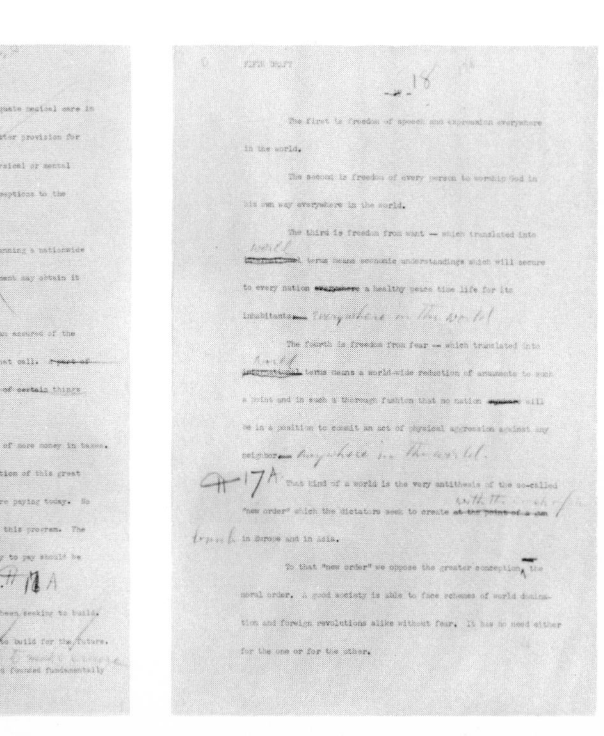

FIFTH DRAFT 17

We should widen the opportunities for adequate medical care in many parts of the country. With it we must make better provision for the care of those who are handicapped in life by physical or mental causes or by personal conditions which make them exceptions to the normal.

We must go further than ever before in planning a nationwide system by which all persons desiring gainful employment may obtain it in private or in government work.

I have called for personal sacrifice. I am assured of the willingness of almost all Americans to respond to that call. ~~A part of the response involves harder work and the giving up of certain things in life which are not essentials.~~

A part of the sacrifice means the payment of more money in taxes. In my budget message I recommend that a greater portion of this great defense program be paid for from taxation than we are paying today. No person should try, or be allowed, to get rich out of this program. The principle of tax payments in accordance with ability to pay should be constantly before our eyes to guide our legislation. 17A

That is the kind of system which we have been seeking to build. That is the kind of system which we shall continue to build for the future.

In the future, we look forward to a world founded fundamentally upon four essential human freedoms.

FIFTH DRAFT 18

The first is freedom of speech and expression everywhere in the world.

The second is freedom of every person to worship God in his own way everywhere in the world.

The third is freedom from want — which translated into world ~~international~~ terms means economic understandings which will secure to every nation ~~everywhere~~ a healthy peace time life for its inhabitants — everywhere in the world

The fourth is freedom from fear — which translated into world ~~international~~ terms means a world-wide reduction of armaments to such a point and in such a thorough fashion that no nation ~~anywhere~~ will be in a position to commit an act of physical aggression against any neighbor — anywhere in the world.

17A That kind of a world is the very antithesis of the so-called "new order" which the dictators seek to create ~~at the point of a gun~~ in Europe and in Asia.

To that "new order" we oppose the greater conception, the moral order. A good society is able to face schemes of world domination and foreign revolutions alike without fear. It has no need either for the one or for the other.

Pages 17 and 18 of President Roosevelt's reading copy of his annual message to Congress. Although labeled the "fifth draft," it was the sixth. The section on the Four Freedoms begins at the bottom of page 17.

Ten months after the Four Freedoms speech, Japan attacked Pearl Harbor and the next day, December 8, 1941, President Roosevelt addressed a joint session of Congress, asking the legislators to declare that a state of war existed between the United States and the Japanese empire. Seated at right is the President's son James, then a Captain in the Marine Corps. Above at left is Vice President Henry A. Wallace, presiding over the Senate, and at right, Speaker of the House Sam Rayburn of Texas.

As MEN do not live by bread alone, they do not fight by armaments alone. Those who man our defenses, and those behind them who build our defenses, must have the stamina and courage which come from an unshakable belief in the manner of life which they are defending. The mighty action which we are calling for cannot be based on a disregard of all things worth fighting for.

There is nothing mysterious about the foundations of a healthy and strong democracy. The basic things expected by our people of their political and economic systems are simple.

They are:

Equality of opportunity for youth and for others.

Jobs for those who can work.

Security for those who need it.

The ending of special privilege for the few.

The preservation of civil liberties for all.

The enjoyment of the fruits of scientific progress in a wider and constantly rising standard of living.

These are the simple and basic things that must never be lost sight of in the turmoil and unbelievable complexity of our modern world. The inner and abiding strength of our economic and political systems is dependent upon the degree to which they fulfill these expectations. . . .

I have called for personal sacrifice. I am assured of the willingness of almost all Americans to respond to that call.

In the future days, which we seek to make secure, we look forward to a world founded upon four essential human freedoms.

The first is freedom of speech and expression, everywhere in the world.

The second is freedom of every person to worship God in his own way, everywhere in the world.

The third is freedom from want, which, translated into world terms, means economic understandings which will secure to every nation a healthy peace time life for its inhabitants, everywhere in the world.

The fourth is freedom from fear—which, translated into world terms, means a world-wide reduction of armaments to such a point and in such a thorough fashion that no nation will be in a position to commit an act of physical aggression against any neighbor—anywhere in the world.

That is no vision of a distant millennium. It is a definite basis for a kind of world attainable in our own time and generation. That kind of world is the very antithesis of the so-called new order of tyranny which the dictators seek to create with the crash of a bomb.

To that new order we oppose the greater conception—the moral order. A good society is able to face schemes of world domination and foreign revolutions alike without fear.

Since the beginning of our American history we have been engaged in change—in a perpetual peaceful revolution—a revolution which goes on steadily, quietly adjusting itself to changing conditions—without the concentration camp or the quick lime in the ditch. The world order which we seek is the cooperation of free countries, working together in a friendly, civilized society.

This Nation has placed its destiny in the hands and heads and hearts of its millions of free men and women; and its faith in freedom under the guidance of God. Freedom means the supremacy of human rights everywhere. Our support goes to those who struggle to gain those rights or keep them. Our strength is in our unity of purpose.

To that high concept there can be no end save victory.

So that all men in all lands may live out their lives in freedom from fear and want

On August 14, 1941 President Roosevelt and British Prime Minister Winston Churchill met secretly aboard ship off Newfoundland and drafted an "Atlantic Charter." The document was a brief and simple declaration of the broad postwar goals of the United States and Great Britain. Within a month, fifteen nations (including the Soviet Union) had endorsed the Atlantic Charter. In this statement of principles Roosevelt and Churchill gave encouragement to the idea of a new international organization to ensure a peaceful and stable world.

In secret meetings aboard the U.S. cruiser *Augusta* and the British battleship *Prince of Wales,* Roosevelt and Churchill worked out the draft of the Atlantic Charter. Support for isolationism had faded rapidly with the coming of the war in Europe, and the new document signed at sea was a reflection of America's change of mind and heart.

"All the News That's Fit to Print."

The New York Times.

LATE CITY EDITION
Cloudy and somewhat warmer today with occasional showers. Tomorrow showers, moderately warm.
Temperatures Yesterday—Max., 76; Min., 56

VOL. XC....No. 30,519. Entered as Second-Class Matter, Postoffice, New York, N. Y. NEW YORK, FRIDAY, AUGUST 15, 1941. THREE CENTS NEW YORK CITY and Vicinity

ROOSEVELT, CHURCHILL DRAFT 8 PEACE AIMS, PLEDGING DESTRUCTION OF NAZI TYRANNY; JOINT STEPS BELIEVED CHARTED AT PARLEY

. . . FIRST, THEIR COUNTRIES seek no aggrandizement, territorial or other;

Second, they desire to see no territorial changes that do not accord with the freely expressed wishes of the peoples concerned;

Third, they respect the right of all peoples to choose the form of government under which they will live; and they wish to see sovereign rights and self-government restored to those who have been forcibly deprived of them;

Fourth, they will endeavor, with due respect for their existing obligations, to further the enjoyment by all States, great or small, victor or vanquished, of access, on equal terms, to the trade and to the raw materials of the world which are needed for their economic prosperity;

Fifth, they desire to bring about the fullest collaboration between all nations in the economic field with the object of securing, for all, improved labor standards, economic advancement and social security;

Sixth, after the final destruction of the Nazi tyranny, they hope to see established a peace which will afford to all nations the means of dwelling in safety within their own boundaries, and which will afford assurance that all the men in all the lands may live out their lives in freedom from fear and want;

Seventh, such a peace should enable all men to traverse the high seas and oceans without hindrance;

Eighth, they believe that all of the nations of the world, for realistic as well as spiritual reasons, must come to the abandonment of the use of force. Since no future peace can be maintained if land, sea or air armaments continue to be employed by nations which threaten, or may threaten, aggression outside of their frontiers, they believe, pending the establishment of a wider and permanent system of general security, that the disarmament of such nations is essential. They will likewise aid and encourage all other practicable measures which will lighten for peace-loving peoples the crushing burden of armaments.

Separate educational facilities are inherently unequal

Speaking for a unanimous Supreme Court, the Chief Justice of the United States declared on May 17, 1954, that segregation of Negro and white children in the public schools is unconstitutional. The Court thereby reversed its "separate but equal" doctrine of 1896 which took the position that segregation is permissible when equal facilities are provided for Negro and white. In that 1896 case of Plessy v. Ferguson, *Justic John Marshall Harlan, in a strong dissent from the majority decision, had argued that "our Constitution is color-blind, and neither knows nor tolerates classes among citizens."*

Now, fifty-eight years later, the Court had come unanimously to agreement with that position, expressing it in Chief Justice Earl Warren's words: "Separate educational facilities are inherently unequal."

The ruling was followed with another on May 31, 1955, directing that educational desegregation be achieved "with all deliberate speed," based on equitable principles and a "practical flexibility." Again, on March 5, 1956, the Court said that tax-supported colleges and universities came within its ban on segregation.

The concept of equality, at the very heart of the Declaration of Independence, serving as a guide for the public conscience, was bringing America, however slowly and painfully, nearer to that ideal state of democracy in which all men would be free, equal, and independent.

The Supreme Court's members who voted unanimously in 1954 that America's public schools must admit all without regard to color. Seated front, from left, are Justices Felix Frankfurter, Hugo L. Black, Chief Justice Earl Warren, Stanley F. Reed, and William O. Douglas. Standing are Justices Tom C. Clark, Robert H. Jackson, Harold H. Burton, and Sherman Minton.

"All the News That's Fit to Print"

The New York Times.

LATE CITY EDITION

Temperatures Yesterday—Max., 69; Min., 61

VOL. CIII...No. 35,178.

Copyright, 1954, by The New York Times Company.

NEW YORK, TUESDAY, MAY 18, 1954.

FIVE CENTS

HIGH COURT BANS SCHOOL SEGREGATION; 9-TO-0 DECISION GRANTS TIME TO COMPLY

McCarthy Hearing Off a Week as Eisenhower Bars Report

1896 RULING UPSET

'Separate but Equal' Doctrine Held Out of

At the time of the Supreme Court's 1954 decision, seventeen states and the District of Columbia required racial separation in the public schools. In the two years that followed, the Upper South undertook fairly speedy and voluntary desegregation. At Fort Myer, Virginia (above), the school doors were promptly opened to Negro children as the fall term of 1954 began. In 1956, suits initiated by Negro parents in communities within the Old Confederacy brought Federal court orders to compel desegregation, as in New Orleans and Little Rock (below), on which international attention was focused.

Lunch counter sitdown strikes by Negro students in the South who sought equal access to these public accommodations began early in 1960. At first some managers closed their counters, as above, but in many places restaurants, swimming pools, parks, golf courses, theatres, bus terminals, and other facilities were soon desegregated.

Brown v. Board of Education of Topeka

(May 17, 1954)

. . . THESE CASES come to us from the States of Kansas, South Carolina, Virginia, and Delaware. They are premised on different facts and different local conditions, but a common legal question justifies their consideration together in this consolidated opinion.

In each of the cases, minors of the Negro race, through their legal representatives, seek the aid of the courts in obtaining admission to the public schools of their community on a nonsegregated basis. In each instance, they have been denied admission to schools attended by white children under laws requiring or permitting segregation according to race. This segregation was alleged to deprive the plaintiffs of the equal protection of the laws under the Fourteenth Amendment. . . .

The plaintiffs contend that segregated public schools are not "equal" and cannot be made "equal," and that hence they are deprived of the equal protection of the laws. Because of the obvious importance of the question presented, the Court took jurisdiction. Argument was heard in the 1952 Term, and reargument was heard this Term on certain questions propounded by the Court.

Reargument was largely devoted to the circumstances surrounding the adoption of the Fourteenth Amendment in 1868. It covered exhaustively consideration of the Amendment in Congress, ratification by the states, then existing practices in racial segregation, and the views of proponents and opponents of the Amendment. This discussion and our own investigation convince us that, although these sources cast some light, it is not enough to resolve the problem with which we are faced. At best, they are inconclusive. The most avid proponents of the post-War Amendments undoubtedly intended them to remove all legal distinctions among "all persons born or naturalized in the United States." Their opponents, just as certainly, were antagonistic to both the letter and the spirit of the Amendments and wished them to have the most limited effect. What others in Congress and the state legislatures had in mind cannot be determined with any degree of certainty.

An additional reason for the inconclusive nature of the Amendment's history, with respect to segregated schools, is the status of public education at that time. In the South, the movement toward free common schools, supported by general taxation, had not yet taken hold. Education of white children was largely in the hands of private groups. Education of Negroes was almost nonexistent, and practically all of the race were illiterate. . . . In fact, any education of Negroes was forbidden by law in some states. Today, in contrast, many Negroes have achieved outstanding success in the arts and sciences as well as in the business and professional world. It is true that public education had already advanced further in the North, but the effect of the Amendment on Northern States was generally ignored in the congressional debates. Even in the North, the conditions of public education did not approximate those existing today. The curriculum was usually rudimentary; ungraded schools were common in rural areas; the school term was but three months a year in many states; and compulsory school attendance was virtually unknown. As a consequence, it is not surprising that there should be so little in the history of the Fourteenth Amendment relating to its intended effect on public education.

In the first cases in this Court construing the Fourteenth Amendment, decided shortly after its adoption, the Court interpreted it as proscribing all state-imposed discriminations against the Negro race. The doctrine of "separate but equal" did not make its appearance in this Court until 1896 in the case of Plessy v. Ferguson, supra, involving not education but transportation. American courts have since labored with the doctrine for over half a century. . . .

In appoaching this problem, we cannot turn the clock back to 1868 when the Amendment was adopted, or even to 1896 when Plessy v. Ferguson was written. We must consider public education in the light of its full development and its present place in American life throughout the Nation. Only in this way can it be determined if segregation in public schools deprives these plaintiffs of the equal protection of the laws.

Today, education is perhaps the most important function of state and local governments. Compulsory school attendance laws and the great expenditures for education both demonstrate the recognition of the importance of education to our democratic society. It is required in the performance of our most basic public responsibilities, even service in the armed forces. It is the very foundation of good citizenship. Today it is a principal instrument in awakening the child to cultural values, in preparing him for later professional training, and in helping him to adjust normally to his environment. In these days, it is doubtful that any child may reasonably be expected to succeed in life if he is denied the opportunity of an education. Such an opportunity, where the state has undertaken to provide it, is a right which must be made available to all on equal terms.

We come then to the question presented: Does segregation of children in public schools solely on the basis of race, even though the physical facilities and other "tangible" factors may be equal, deprive the children of the minority group of equal educational opportunities? We believe that it does.

In Sweatt v. Painter supra, in finding that a segregated law school for Negroes could not provide them equal educational opportunities, this Court relied in large part on "those qualities which are incapable of objective measurement but which make for greatness in a law school." In McLaurin v. Oklahoma State Regents supra, the Court, in requiring that a Negro admitted to a white graduate school be treated like all other students, again resorted to intangible considerations: ". . . his ability to study, to engage in discussions and exchange views with other students, and, in general, to learn his profession." Such considerations apply with added force to children in grade and high schools. To separate them from others of similar age and qualifications solely because of their race generates a feeling of inferiority as to their status in the community that may affect their hearts and minds in a way unlikely ever to be undone. . . .

We conclude that in the field of public education the doctrine of "separate but equal" has no place. Separate educational facilities are inherently unequal. Therefore, we hold that the plaintiffs and others similarly situated for whom the actions have been brought are, by reason of the segregation complained of, deprived of the equal protection of the laws guaranteed by the Fourteenth Amendment. . . .

Our Disarmament Doctrine —

"Mankind must put an end to war - or war will put an end to mankind."

Partial text of President Kennedy's address to the United Nations General Assembly Sept. 26, 1961.

WE MEET in an hour of grief and challenge. Dag Hammarskjold is dead. But the United Nations lives on. His tragedy is deep in our hearts, but the task for which he died is at the top of our agenda.

A noble servant of peace is gone. But the quest for peace lies before us.

The problem is not death of one man—the problem is the life of this organization. It will either grow to meet the challenge of our age—or it will be gone with the wind, without influence, without force, without respect.

Were we to let it die—to enfeeble its vigor—to cripple its powers—we would condemn the future.

For in the development of this organization rests the only true alternative to war—and war appeals no longer as a rational alternative.

Unconditional war can no longer lead to unconditional victory. It can no longer serve to settle disputes. It can no longer be of concern to great powers alone.

For a nuclear disaster, spread by winds and waters and fear, would well engulf the great and small, the rich and the poor, the committed and the uncommitted alike. *Mankind must put an end to war—or war will put an end to mankind.*

So let us here resolve that Dag Hammarskjold did not live—or die—in vain. Let us call a truce to terror. Let us invoke the blessings of peace.

And, as we build an international capacity to keep peace, let us join in dismantling the national capacity to wage war.

This will require new strength and new roles for a new United Nations. For disarmament without checks is but a shadow—and a community without law is but a shell.

Already the United Nations has become both the measure and the vehicle of man's most generous impulses. Already it has provided—in the Middle East, in Africa, in Asia—a means of holding violence within bounds.

But the great question which confronted this body in 1945 is still before us—whether man's cherished hopes for progress and freedom are to be destroyed by tactics of terror and disruption—whether the "foul winds of war" can be tamed in time to free the cooling winds of reason—and whether the pledges of our charter are to be fulfilled or defied: pledges to secure peace, progress, human rights and respect for world law.

In this hall there are not three forces, but only two. One is composed of those who are trying to build the kind of world described in Articles I and II of the charter. The other, seeking a different world, would undermine this organization in the process.

Today of all days our dedication to that charter must be strengthened.

It must be strengthened first of all, by the selection of an outstanding civil servant to carry forward the responsibilities of the secretary general—a man endowed with both the wisdom and the power to make meaningful the moral force of the world community.

The late secretary general nutured and sharpened the United Nations' obligations to act. But he did not invent it. It was there in the charter. It is still here in the charter.

• • • • •

The secretary general, in a very real sense, is the servant of this Assembly. Diminish his authority and you diminish the authority of the only body where all nations, regardless of power, are equal and sovereign.

The United Nations protects the weak

Until all the powerful are just, the weak will be secure only in the strength of this Assembly.

Effective and independent executive action is not the same question as balanced representation.

In view of the enormous change in the membership of this body since its founding, the American delegation will join in any effort for the prompt review and revision of the composition of United Nations bodies.

But to give this organization three drivers—to permit each great power in effect to decide its own case—would entrench the Cold War in the headquarters of peace.

Whatever advantages such a plan holds out to my country, as one of the great powers, we reject it. For we far prefer world law, in the age of self-determination, to world war, in the age of mass extermination.

Today, every inhabitant of this planet must contemplate the day when it may no longer be habitable.

Every man, woman and child lives under a nuclear sword of Damocles, hanging by the slenderest of threads, capable of being cut at any moment by accident, miscalculation or madness. *The weapons of war must be abolished before they abolish us.*

Men no longer debate whether armaments are a symptom or cause of tension.

The mere existence of modern weapons—10,000,000 times more destructive than anything the world has ever known, and only minutes away from any target on earth—is a source of horror, of discord and distrust.

Men no longer maintain that disarmament must await the settlement of all disputes—for disarmament must be a part of any permanent settlement.

And men no longer pretend that the quest for disarmament is a sign of weakness—for in a spiraling arms race, a nation's security may well be shrinking even as its arms increase.

A matter of life – or death

For 15 years this organization has sought the reduction and destruction of arms. Now that goal is no longer a dream—it is a practical matter of life or death. The risks inherent in disarmament pale in comparison to the risks inherent in an unlimited arms race.

It is in this spirit that the recent Belgrade confer-

President Kennedy turns to leave rostrum after addressing the United Nations General Assembly.

ence—recognizing that this is no longer a Soviet problem or an American problem, but a human problem—endorsed a program of "general, complete and strictly and internationally controlled disarmament."

It is in this same spirit that we in the United States have labored this year, with a new urgency, and with a new, now-statutory agency fully endorsed by the Congress, to find an approach to disarmament which would be so far-reaching yet realistic, so mutually balanced and beneficial, that it could be accepted by every nation.

And it is in this spirit that we have presented to the Soviet Union—under the label both nations now accept of "general and complete disarmament"—a statement of newly agreed principles for negotiation.

But we are well aware that all issues of principle are not settled—and that principles alone are not enough.

Our intention is complete disarmament

It is therefore our intention to challenge the Soviet Union, not to an arms race, but to a peace race—to advance with us step by step, stage by stage, until general and complete disarmament has actually been achieved.

We invite them now to go beyond agreement in principle to reach agreement on actual plans.

The program to be presented to this Assembly—for general and complete disarmament under effective international control—moves to bridge the gap between those who insist on a gradual approach and those who talk only of the final and total achievement.

It would create machinery to keep the peace as it destroys the machines of war. It would proceed through balanced and safeguarded stages designed to give no state a military advantage over another.

It would place the final responsibility for verification and control where it belongs—not with the big powers alone, not with one's adversary or one's self—but in an international organization within the framework of the United Nations itself.

It would assure that indispensable condition of disarmament—true inspection— in stages proportionate to the stage of disarmament. It would cover delivery systems as well as weapons. It would ultimately halt their production as well as their testing, their transfer as well as their possession.

It would achieve, under the eye of an international disarmament organization, a steady reduction in forces, both nuclear and conventional, until it has abolished all armies and all weapons except those needed for internal order and a new United Nations peace force.

And it starts that process now, today, even as the talks begins.

Our disarmament proposals

But to halt the spread of these terrible weapons, to halt the contamination of the air, to halt the spiraling nuclear arms race, we remain ready to seek new avenues of agreement. Our new disarmament program thus includes the following proposals:

—First, signing the test-ban treaty, by all nations. This can be done now. Test ban negotiations need not and should not await general disarmament talks.

—Second, stopping the production of fissionable materials for use in weapons and preventing their transfer to any nation now lacking nuclear weapons.

—Third, prohibiting the transfer of control over nuclear weapons to states that do not now own them.

—Fourth, keeping nuclear weapons from seeding new battlegrounds in outer space.

—Fifth, gradually destroying existing nuclear weapons and converting their materials to peaceful uses; and . . .

—Finally, halting the unlimited testing and production of strategic nuclear delivery vehicles, and gradually destroying them as well.

To destroy arms, however, is not enough, we must create even as we destroy—creating worldwide law and law enforcement as we outlaw worldwide war and weapons.

In the world we seek, United Nations emergency forces which have been hastily assembled, uncertainly supplied and inadequately financed will never be enough.

Therefore, the United States recommends that all member nations earmark special peace-keeping units in their armed forces—to be on call to the United Nations—to be specially trained and quickly available—and with advance provision for financial and logistic support.

In addition, the American delegation will suggest a series of steps to improve the United Nations' machinery for the peaceful settlement of disputes—for on-the-spot fact-finding, mediation and adjudication —for extending the rule of international law.

For peace is not solely a military or technical problem—it is primarily a problem of politics and people.

And unless man can match his strides in weaponry and technology with equal strides in social and political development, our great strength, like that of the dinosaur, will become incapable of proper control—and man, like the dinosaur, will decline and disappear.

Man's new domain: outer space

As we extend the rule of law on earth, so must we also extend it to man's new domain: outer space.

All of us salute the brave cosmonauts of the Soviet Union. The new horizons of outer space must not be riven by the old bitter concepts of imperialism and sovereign claims. The cold reaches of the universe must not become the new arena of an even colder war.

To this end, we shall urge proposals extending the United Nations charter to the limits of man's exploration in the universe, reserving outer space for peaceful use, prohibiting weapons of mass destruction in space or on celestial bodies and opening the mysteries and benefits of space to every nation.

We shall further propose cooperative efforts in weather prediction and eventually weather control.

We shall propose, finally, a global system of communications satellites linking the whole world in telegraph, telephone, radio and television.

The day need not be far away when such a system will televise the proceedings of this body to every corner of the world.

But the mysteries of outer space must not divert our eyes or our energies from the harsh realities that face our own fellow men.

Political sovereignty is but a mockery without the means to meet poverty, illiteracy and disease. Self-determination is but a slogan if the future holds no hope.

That is why my nation—which has freely shared its capital and its technology to help others help themselves—now proposes officially designating this decade of the 1960s as the UN Decade of Development.

'. . . Shall Now Also Be Equal . . .'

On July 2, 1964, the most sweeping civil rights bill in 100 years was signed into law by President Lyndon B. Johnson. "The purpose of this law is simple," the President said. "It does not restrict the freedom of any American so long as he respects the rights of others. It does not give special treatment to any citizen. It does say the only limit to a man's hope for happiness and for the future of his children shall be his own ability.

"It does say that those who are equal before God shall now be equal in the polling booths, in the classrooms, in the factories, and in hotels and restaurants and movie theatres, and other places that provide service to the public."

The long and difficult passage of the bill marked the arrival of the Negro as a major force in American political life. At the same time, it was a demonstration of the power of national conscience awakened after a long, long sleep by the Negro freedom movement which engulfed a thousand towns and cities.

It was on the hundredth anniversary of Lincoln's Emancipation Proclamation that the Negro revolution began. Emancipation—a proclamation, but not a fact—was followed by the 13th Amendment to the Constitution abolishing slavery but giving the Negro little more than his physical freedom. The 14th Amendment promised equality to the Negro by giving Federal protection to his rights as a citizen. The 15th extended that protection to his franchise. Congress crowned these measures by the Civil Rights Act of 1875, banning discrimination in all public accommodations.

But very shortly after America declared its intention to guarantee Negro equality, the obligation was shrugged off and all but forgotten for almost a century. Supreme Court decisions said the new statutes and amendments did not mean what they seemed to mean, nor what the legislators thought they meant. In the words of Mr. Justice John M. Harlan's famous dissenting opinion of 1883, the constitutional commitments made after the Civil War had been turned into "splendid baubles, thrown out to delude those who deserved fair and generous treatment at the hands of the nation."

It was his dissent that the Civil Rights Act of 1964 now made into law.

Lyndon B. Johnson signs the Civil Rights Bill as Senators Everett Dirkson and Hubert Humphrey, Representative Charles Halleck, and others look on.

HR 7152—AN ACT

To enforce the constitutional right to vote, to confer jurisdiction upon the district courts of the United States to provide injunctive relief against discrimination in public accommodations, to authorize the Attorney General to institute suits to protect constitutional rights in public facilities and public education, to extend the Commission on Civil Rights, to prevent discrimination in federally assisted programs, to establish a Commission on Equal Employment Opportunity, and for other purposes.

Be it enacted by the Senate and House of Representatives of the United States of America in Congress assembled, That this Act may be cited as **"The Civil Rights Act of 1964."**

TITLE I—VOTING RIGHTS

SEC. 101. Section 2004 of the Revised Statutes (42 U.S.C. 1971), as amended by section 131 of the Civil Rights Act of 1957 (71 Stat. 637), and as further amended by section 601 of the Civil Rights Act of 1960 (74 Stat. 90), is further amended as follows:

(a) Insert "1" after "(a)" in subsection (a) and add at the end of subsection (a) the following new paragraphs:

"(2) No person acting under color of law shall

"(A) in determining whether any individual is qualified under State law or laws to vote in any Federal election, apply any standard, practice, or procedure different from the standards, practices, or procedures applied under such law or laws to other individuals within the same county, parish, or similar political subdivision who have been found by State officials to be qualified to vote;

"(B) deny the right of any individual to vote in any Federal election because of an error or omission of such individual on any record or paper relating to any application, registration, payment of poll tax, or other act requisite to voting, if such error or omission is not material in determining whether such individual is qualified under State law to vote in such election; or

"(C) employ any literacy test as a qualification for voting in any Federal election unless (i) such test is administered to each individual wholly in writing except where an individual requests and State law authorizes a test other than in writing, and (ii) a certified copy of the test whether written or oral and of the answers given by the individual is furnished to him within twenty-five days of the submission of his request made within the period of time during which records and papers are required to be retained and preserved pursuant to title III of the Civil Rights Act of 1960 (42 U.S.C. 1974 74c; 74 Stat. 88).

"(3) For purposes of this subsection

"(A) the term 'vote' shall have the same meaning as in subsection (e) of this section;

"(B) the phrase 'literacy test' includes any test of the ability to read, write, understand, or interpret any matter."

(b) Insert immediately following the period at the end of the first sentence of subsection (c) the following new sentence: "If in any such proceeding literacy is a relevant fact there shall be a rebuttable presumption that any person who has not been adjudged an incompetent and who has completed the sixth grade in a public school in, or a private school accredited by, any State or territory, the District of Columbia or the Commonwealth of Puerto Rico where instruction is carried on predominantly in the English language, possesses sufficient literacy, comprehension, and intelligence to vote in any Federal election."

(c) Add the following subsection "(f)" and designate the present subsection "(f)" as subsection "(g)":

"(f) When used in subsections (a) or (c) of this section, the words 'Federal election' shall mean any general, special, or primary election held solely or in part for the purpose of electing or selecting any candidate for the office of President, Vice President, presidential elector, Member of the Senate, or Member of the House of Representatives."

(d) Add the following subsection "(h)":

"(h) In any proceeding instituted in any district court of the United States under this section the Attorney General or any defendant in the proceeding may file with the clerk of such court a request that a court of three judges be convened to hear and determine the case. A copy of the request shall be immediately furnished by such clerk to the chief judge of the circuit (or in his absence, the presiding circuit judge) of the circuit in which the case is pending. Upon receipt of the copy of such request it shall be the duty of the chief judge of the circuit or the presiding circuit judge, as the case may be, to designate immediately three judges in such circuit, of whom at least one shall be a circuit judge and another of whom shall be a district judge of the court in which the proceeding was instituted, to hear and determine such case, and it shall be the duty of the judges so designated to assign the case for hearing at the earliest practicable date, to participate in the hearing and determination thereof, and to cause the case to be in every way expedited. An appeal from the final judgment of such court will lie to the Supreme Court.

"In the event the Attorney General fails to file such a request in any such proceeding, it shall be the duty of the chief judge of the district (or in his absence, the acting chief judge) in which the case is pending immediately to designate a judge in such district to hear and determine the case. In the event that no judge in the district is available to hear and determine the case, the chief judge of the district, or the acting chief judge, as the case may be, shall certify this fact to the chief judge of the circuit (or in his absence, the acting chief judge) who shall then designate a district or circuit judge of the circuit to hear and determine the case.

"It shall be the duty of the judge designated pursuant to this section to assign the case for hearing at the earliest practicable date and to cause the case to be in every way expedited."

TITLE II INJUNCTIVE RELIEF AGAINST DISCRIMINATION IN PLACES OF PUBLIC ACCOMMODATION

SEC. 201. (a) All persons shall be entitled to the full and equal enjoyment of the goods, services, facilities, privileges, advantages, and accommodations of any place of public accommodation, as defined in this section, without discrimination or segregation on the ground of race, color, religion, or national origin.

Each of the following establishments which serves the public is a place of public accommodation within the meaning of this title if its operations affect commerce, or if discrimination or segregation by it is supported by State action:

(1) any inn, hotel, motel, or other establishment which provides lodging to transient guests, other than an establishment located within a building which contains more than five rooms for rent or hire and which is actually occupied by the proprietor of such establishment as his residence;

(2) any restaurant, cafeteria, lunch room, lunch counter, soda fountain, or other facility principally engaged in selling food for consumption on the premises, including, but not limited to, any such facility located on the premises of any retail establishment; or any gasoline station;

(3) any motion picture house, theater, concert hall, sports arena, stadium or other place of exhibition or entertainment; and

(4) any establishment (A) which is physically located within the premises of any establishment otherwise covered by this subsection, or within the premises of which is physically located any such covered establishment, and (B) which holds itself out as serving patrons of such covered establishment.

(c) The operations of an establishment affect commerce within the meaning of this title if (1) it is one of the establishments described in paragraph (1) of subsection (b); (2) in the case of an establishment described in paragraph (2) of subsection (b), it serves or offers to serve interstate travelers or a substantial portion of the food which it serves, or gasoline or other products which it sells, has moved in commerce; (3) in the case of an establishment described in paragraph (3) of subsection (b), it customarily presents films, performances, athletic teams, exhibitions, or other sources of entertainment which move in commerce; and (4) in the case of an establishment described in paragraph (4) of subsection (b), it is physically located within the premises of, or there is physically located within its premises, an establishment the operations of which affect commerce within the meaning of this subsection. For purposes of this section, "commerce" means travel, trade, traffic, commerce, transportation or communication among the several States, or between the District of Columbia and any State, or between any foreign country or any territory or possession and any State or the District of Columbia, or between points in the same State but through any other State or the

District of Columbia or a foreign country.

(d) Discrimination or segregation by an establishment is supported by State action within the meaning of this title if such discrimination or segregation (1) is carried on under color of any law, statute, ordinance or regulation; or (2) is carried on under color of any custom or usage required or enforced by officials of the State or political subdivision thereof; or (3) is required by action of a State or political subdivision thereof.

(c) The provisions of this title shall not apply to a bona fide private club or other establishment not open to the public, except to the extent that the facilities of such establishment are made available to the customers or patrons of an establishment within the scope of subsection (b).

SEC. 202. All persons shall be entitled to be free, at any establishment or place, from discrimination or segregation of any kind on the ground of race, color, religion, or national origin, if such discrimination or segregation is or purports to be required by any law, statute, ordinance, regulation, rule or order, of a State or any agency or political subdivision thereof.

SEC. 203. No person shall (a) withhold, deny, or attempt to withhold or deny, or deprive or attempt to deprive, any person of any right or privilege secured by section 201 or 202, or (b) intimidate, threaten, or coerce, or attempt to intimidate, threaten, or coerce any person with the purpose of interfering with any right or privilege secured by section 201 or 202, or (c) punish or attempt to punish any person for exercising or attempting to exercise any right or privilege secured by section 201 or 202.

SEC. 204 (a) Whenever any person has engaged or there are reasonable grounds to believe that any person is about to engage in any act or practice prohibited by section 203, a civil action for preventive relief, including an application for a permanent or temporary injunction, restraining order, or other order, may be instituted (1) by the person aggrieved, or (2) by the Attorney General for or in the name of the United States if he satisfies himself that the purposes of this title will be materially furthered by the filing of an action.

(b) In any action commenced pursuant to this title, the court, in its discretion, may allow the prevailing party, other than the United States, a reasonable attorney's fees as part of the costs, and the United States shall be liable for costs the same as a private person.

(c) In case of any complaint received by the Attorney General alleging a violation or threatened violation of section 203 in a place where State or local laws or regulations forbid the act or practice involved, the Attorney General shall notify the appropriate State or local officials and, upon request, afford them a reasonable time to act under such State or local laws or regulations before he institutes an action.

(d) In the case of any complaint received by the Attorney General alleging a violation or threatened violation of section 203, the Attorney General, before instituting an action, may utilize the services of any Federal, State, or local agency or instrumentality which may be available to attempt to secure compliance with the provisions of this title by voluntary procedures.

(e) Compliance with the foregoing provisions of subsection (c) shall not be required if the Attorney General shall file with the court a certificate that the delay consequent upon compliance with such provisions in the particular case would adversely affect the interests of the United States, or that in the particular case compliance with such provisions would prove ineffective.

SEC. 205. (a) The district courts of the United States shall have jurisdiction of proceedings instituted pursuant to this title and shall exercise the same without regard to whether the aggrieved party shall have exhausted any administrative or other remedies that may be provided by law.

(b) The remedies provided in this title shall be the exclusive means of enforcing the rights hereby created, but nothing in this title shall preclude any individual or any State or local agency from asserting any right created by any other Federal or State law not inconsistent with this title, including any statute or ordinance requiring nondiscrimination in public establishments or accommodations, or from pursuing any remedy, civil or criminal, which may be available for the vindication or enforcement of such right.

(c) Proceedings for contempt arising under the provisions of this title shall be subject to the provisions of section 151 of the Civil Rights Act of 1957 (71 Stat. 638).

TITLE III DESEGREGATION OF PUBLIC FACILITIES

SEC. 301. (a) Whenever the Attorney General receives a complaint signed by an individual to the effect that he is being deprived of or threatened with the loss of his right to the equal protection of the laws, on account of his race, color, religion, or national origin, by being denied access to or full and complete utilization of any public facility which is owned, operated, or managed by or on behalf of any State or subdivision thereof, other than a public school or public college as defined in section 401 of title IV hereof, and the Attorney General certifies that the signer or signers of such complaint are unable, in his judgment, to initiate and maintain appropriate legal proceedings for relief and that the institution of an action will materially further the public policy of the United States favoring the orderly progress of desegregation in public facilities, the Attorney General is authorized to institute for or in the name of the United States a civil action in any appropriate district court of the United States against such parties and for such relief as may be appropriate, and such court shall have and shall exercise jurisdiction of proceedings instituted pursuant to this section. The Attorney General may implead as defendants such additional parties as are or become necessary to the grant of effective relief hereunder.

(b) The Attorney General may deem a person or persons unable to initiate and maintain appropriate legal proceedings within the meaning of subsection (a) of this section when such person or persons are unable, either directly or through other interested persons or organizations, to bear the expense of the litigation or to obtain effective legal representation; or whenever he is satisfied that the institution of such litigation would jeopardize the employment or economic standing of, or might result in injury or economic damage to, such person or persons, their families, or their property.

SEC. 302. Whenever an action has been commenced in any court of the United States seeking relief from the denial of equal protection of the laws on account of race, color, religion, or national origin, the Attorney General for or in the name of the United States may intervene in such action. In such an action the United States shall be entitled to the same relief as if it had instituted the action.

SEC. 303. In any action or proceeding under this title the United States shall be liable for costs, including a reasonable attorney's fee, the same as a private person.

SEC. 304. Nothing in this title shall affect adversely the right of any person to sue for or obtain relief in any court against discrimination in any facility covered by this title.

TITLE IV DESEGREGATION OF PUBLIC EDUCATION

Definitions

SEC. 401. As used in this title

(a) "Commissioner" means the Commissioner of Education.

(b) "Desegregation" means the assignment of students to public schools and within such schools without regard to their race, color, religion, or national origin, but "desegregation" shall not mean the assignment of students to public schools in order to overcome racial imbalance.

(c) "Public school" means any elementary or secondary educational institution, and "public college" means any institution of higher education or any technical or vocational school above the secondary school level, operated by a State, subdivision of a State, or governmental agency within a State, or operated wholly or predominantly from or through the use of governmental funds or property, or funds or property derived from a governmental source.

(d) "School board" means any agency or agencies which administer a system of one or more public schools and any other agency which is responsible for the assignment of students to or within such system.

Survey and Report of Educational Opportunities

SEC. 402. The Commissioner shall conduct a survey and make a report to the President and the Congress, within two years of the enactment of this title, concerning the lack of availability of equal educational opportunities for individuals by reason of race, color, religion, or national origin in public educational institutions at all levels in the United States, its territories and possessions, and the District of Columbia.

Technical Assistance

SEC. 403. The Commissioner is authorized, upon the application of any school board, State, municipality, school district, or other governmental unit legally responsible for operating a public school or schools, to render technical assistance to such applicant in the preparation, adoption, and implementation of plans for the desegregation of public schools. Such technical assistance, may among other activities, include making available to such agencies information regarding effective methods of coping with special educational problems occasioned by desegregation, and making available to such agencies personnel of the Office of Education or other persons specially equipped to advise and assist them in coping with such problems.

Training Institutes

SEC. 404. The Commissioner is authorized to arrange, through grants or contracts, with institutions of higher education for the operation of short-term or regular session institutes for special training designed to improve the ability of teachers, supervisors, counselors, and other elementary or secondary school personnel to deal effectively with special educational problems occasioned by desegregation. Individuals who attend such an institute may be paid stipends for the period of their attendance at such institute in amounts specified by the Commissioner in regulations, including allowances for dependents and including allowances for travel to attend such institute.

Grants

SEC. 405 (a) The Commissioner is authorized, upon application of a school board, to make grants to such board to pay, in whole or in part, the cost of

(1) giving the teachers and other school personnel inservice training in dealing with problems incident to desegregation, and

(2) employing specialists to advise in problems incident to desegregation.

(b) In determining whether to make a grant, and in fixing the amount thereof and the terms and conditions on which it will be made, the Commissioner shall take into consideration the amount available for grants under this section and the other applications which are pending before him; the financial condition of the applicant and the other resources available to it; the nature, extent, and gravity of its problems incident to desegregation; and such other factors as he finds relevant.

With pen in hand, President Lyndon B. Johnson pauses after signing the Civil Rights Bill.

Courtesy Library of Congress

Presidential Elections

Year	*Candidates*	*Parties*	*Popular vote*	*Electoral vote*
1789	GEORGE WASHINGTON (Va.)			69
	John Adams *			34
	Others *			35
1792	GEORGE WASHINGTON (Va.)			132
	John Adams *			77
	George Clinton *			50
	Others *			5
1796	JOHN ADAMS (Mass.)	Federalist		71†
	Thomas Jefferson	Democratic-Republican		68
	Thomas Pinckney	Fed.		59
	Aaron Burr	Dem.-Rep.		30
	Others			48
1800	THOMAS JEFFERSON (Va.)	Dem.-Rep.		73†
	Aaron Burr	Dem.-Rep.		73
	John Adams	Fed.		65
	C. C. Pinckney	Fed.		64
	John Jay	Fed.		1
1804	THOMAS JEFFERSON (Va.)	Dem.-Rep.		162
	C. C. Pinckney	Fed.		14

* In 1789 and 1792 Washington ran without opposition for the Presidency. Electoral votes cast for other candidates were intended for the election of the Vice President. (See Constitution, article II, section 1, in effect until 1804.)

† Elected by House of Representatives, no candidate having had a majority in the electoral college. (See Constitution, article II, section 1, replaced by Amendment XII in 1804.)

Year	*Candidates*	*Parties*	*Popular vote*	*Electoral vote*
1808	James Madison (Va.)	Dem.-Rep.		122
	C. C. Pinckney	Fed.		47
	George Clinton	Dem.-Rep.		6
1812	James Madison (Va.)	Dem.-Rep.		128
	De Witt Clinton	Fed.		89
1816	James Monroe (Va.)	Dem.-Rep.		183
	Rufus King	Fed.		34
1820	James Monroe (Va.)	Dem.-Rep.		231
	John Quincy Adams	Dem.-Rep.		1
1824	John Q. Adams (Mass.)	Dem.-Rep.	108,740	84†
	Andrew Jackson	Dem.-Rep.	153,544	99
	William H. Crawford	Dem.-Rep.	46,618	41
	Henry Clay	Dem.-Rep.	47,136	37
1828	Andrew Jackson (Tenn.)	Democratic	647,231	178
	John Q. Adams	National Republican	509,097	83
1832	Andrew Jackson (Tenn.)	Dem.	687,502	219
	Henry Clay	Nat. Rep.	{ 530,189	49
	William Wirt	Anti-Mason		7
	John Floyd	Dem. (S.C.)	‡	11
1836	Martin Van Buren (N.Y.)	Dem.	761,549	170
	William H. Harrison	Whig	549,000	73
	Hugh L. White	Whig	146,000 { 736,656	26
	Daniel Webster	Whig	41,000	14
	W. P. Mangum	Dem. (S.C.)	‡	11
1840	William Henry Harrison (Ohio)	Whig	1,275,016	234
	Martin Van Buren	Dem.	1,129,102	60
	James G. Birney	Liberty	7,059	
1844	James K. Polk (Tenn.)	Dem.	1,337,243	170
	Henry Clay	Whig	1,299,062	105
	James G. Birney	Liberty	62,300	
1848	Zachary Taylor (La.)	Whig	1,360,099	163
	Lewis Cass	Dem.	1,220,544	127
	Martin Van Buren	Free Soil	291,263	
1852	Franklin Pierce (N.H.)	Dem.	1,601,274	254
	Winfield Scott	Whig	1,386,580	42
	John P. Hale	Free Soil	155,825	
1856	James Buchanan (Pa.)	Dem.	1,838,169	174
	John C. Frémont	Republican	1,341,264	114
	Millard Fillmore	American ("Know-Nothing")	874,534	8

‡ South Carolina electoral votes determined by state legislature.

Year	Candidates	Parties	Popular vote	Electoral vote
1860	ABRAHAM LINCOLN (Ill.)	Rep.	1,866,452	180
	Stephen A. Douglas	Dem.	1,375,157	12
	John C. Breckenridge	Dem.	847,953	72
	John Bell	Constitutional Union	590,631	39
1864	ABRAHAM LINCOLN (Ill.)	Rep.	2,213,665	212
	George B. McClellan	Dem.	1,802,237	21
1868	ULYSSES S. GRANT (Ohio)	Rep.	3,012,833	214
	Horatio Seymour	Dem.	2,703,249	80
1872	ULYSSES S. GRANT (Ohio)	Rep.	3,597,132	286
	Horace Greeley	Dem. and Liberal Republican	2,834,125	66
1876	RUTHERFORD B. HAYES (Ohio)	Rep.	4,036,298	185
	Samuel J. Tilden	Dem.	4,300,590	184
	Others	Greenback, etc.	93,898	
1880	JAMES A. GARFIELD (Ohio)	Rep.	4,454,416	214
	Winfield S. Hancock	Dem.	4,442,952	155
	James B. Weaver	Greenback	308,578	
1884	GROVER CLEVELAND (N.Y.)	Dem.	4,874,986	219
	James G. Blaine	Rep.	4,851,981	182
	Benjamin F. Butler	Greenback & Anti-Monopoly	175,370	
	John P. St. John	Prohibition	150,369	
1888	BENJAMIN HARRISON (Ind.)	Rep.	5,439,853	233
	Grover Cleveland	Dem.	5,540,309	168
	C. B. Fisk	Prohib.	249,506	
	A. J. Streeter	Union Labor	146,935	
1892	GROVER CLEVELAND (N.Y.)	Dem.	5,556,918	277
	Benjamin Harrison	Rep.	5,176,108	145
	James B. Weaver	Populist	1,041,028	22
	John Bidwell	Prohib.	264,133	
1896	WILLIAM MCKINLEY (Ohio)	Rep.	7,104,779	271
	William Jennings Bryan	Dem.-Populist	6,502,925	176
	John M. Palmer	Nat. Dem.	133,148	
	Others	Prohib., etc.	182,250	
1900	WILLIAM MCKINLEY (Ohio)	Rep.	7,207,923	292
	William Jennings Bryan	Dem.	6,358,133	155
	John C. Woolley	Prohib.	208,914	
	Others	Socialist, etc.	101,270	
1904	THEODORE ROOSEVELT (N.Y.)	Rep.	7,623,486	336
	Alton B. Parker	Dem.	5,077,911	140
	Eugene V. Debs	Soc.	402,283	
	S. C. Swallow	Prohib.	258,536	
	Others	People's, etc.	149,432	

Year	*Candidates*	*Parties*	*Popular vote*	*Electoral vote*
1908	WILLIAM HOWARD TAFT (Ohio)	Rep.	7,678,908	321
	William Jennings Bryan	Dem.	6,409,104	162
	Eugene V. Debs	Soc.	420,793	
	E. W. Chafin	Prohib.	253,840	
	Others	(Misc.)	126,493	
1912	WOODROW WILSON (N.J.)	Dem.	6,293,454	435
	Theodore Roosevelt	Progressive	4,119,538	88
	William Howard Taft	Rep.	3,484,980	8
	Eugene V. Debs	Soc.	900,672	
	E. W. Chafin	Prohib.	206,275	
1916	WOODROW WILSON (N.J.)	Dem.	9,129,606	277
	Charles Evans Hughes	Rep.	8,538,221	254
	A. L. Benson	Soc.	585,113	
	J. F. Hanly	Prohib.	220,506	
	Others	Soc-Labor, etc.	126,493	
1920	WARREN G. HARDING (Ohio)	Rep.	16,152,200	404
	James M. Cox	Dem.	9,147,353	127
	Eugene Debs	Soc.	919,799	
	P. P. Christensen	Farmer-Labor	265,411	
	Others	Prohib., etc.	274,960	
1924	CALVIN COOLIDGE (Mass.)	Rep.	15,725,016	382
	John W. Davis	Dem.	8,386,503	136
	Robert M. La Follette	Prog.	4,822,856	13
	W. Z. Foster	Workers' (Communist)	36,386	
	Others	(Misc.)	119,177	
1928	HERBERT C. HOOVER (Calif.)	Rep.	21,391,381	444
	Alfred E. Smith	Dem.	15,016,443	87
	Others	Workers', etc.	69,280	
1932	FRANKLIN D. ROOSEVELT (N.Y.)	Dem.	22,821,857	472
	Herbert Hoover	Rep.	15,761,841	59
	Norman Thomas	Soc.	881,951	
	W. Z. Foster	Communist	102,785	
	Others	Prohib., etc.	175,699	
1936	FRANKLIN D. ROOSEVELT (N.Y.)	Dem.	27,751,597	523
	Alfred M. Landon	Rep.	16,679,583	8
	William Lemke	Union	882,479	
	Norman Thomas	Soc.	187,720	
	Earl Browder	Comm.	80,159	
	Others	Prohib., etc.	50,624	
1940	FRANKLIN D. ROOSEVELT (N.Y.)	Dem.	27,244,160	449
	Wendell Willkie	Rep.	22,305,198	82
	Norman Thomas	Soc.	99,557	
	Earl Browder	Comm.	46,251	
	Roger Q. Babson	Prohib.	57,812	

Year	*Candidates*	*Parties*	*Popular vote*	*Electoral vote*
1944	FRANKLIN D. ROOSEVELT (N.Y.)	Dem.	25,602,504	432
	Thomas E. Dewey	Rep.	22,006,285	99
	Others	Soc., etc.	336,051	
1948	HARRY S. TRUMAN (Mo.)	Dem.	24,105,695	303
	Thomas E. Dewey	Rep.	21,969,170	189
	Henry A. Wallace	Progr.	1,156,103	
	J. Strom Thurmond	States' Rights	1,169,021	39
	Norman Thomas	Soc.	139,009	
	Others	Prohibition, etc.	149,391	
1952	DWIGHT D. EISENHOWER (Kans.)	Rep.	33,824,351	442
	Adlai E. Stevenson	Dem.	27,314,987	89
	Others	Progr., etc.	412,640	
1956	DWIGHT D. EISENHOWER (Pa.)	Rep.	35,581,003	457
	Adlai E. Stevenson	Dem.	25,738,765	73
	Others		707,272	1
1960	JOHN F. KENNEDY (Mass.)	Dem.	34,226,925	300
	Richard M. Nixon	Rep.	34,108,662	223
1964	LYNDON B. JOHNSON (Texas)	Dem.	43,126,218	486
	Barry M. Goldwater	Rep.	27,174,898	52

Entrance of States into Union

Constitutional Convention, Kansas Territory.

State	Entered Union	State	Entered Union
Delaware	December 7, 1787	Michigan	January 26, 1837
Pennsylvania	December 12, 1787	Florida	March 3, 1845
New Jersey	December 18, 1787	Texas	December 29, 1845
Georgia	January 2, 1788	Iowa	December 28, 1846
Connecticut	January 9, 1788	Wisconsin	May 29, 1848
Massachusetts	February 6, 1788	California	September 9, 1850
Maryland	April 2, 1788	Minnesota	May 11, 1858
South Carolina	May 23, 1788	Oregon	February 14, 1859
New Hampshire	June 21, 1788	Kansas	January 29, 1861
Virginia	June 26, 1788	West Virginia	June 19, 1863
New York	July 26, 1788	Nevada	October 31, 1864
North Carolina	November 21, 1789	Nebraska	March 1, 1867
Rhode Island	May 29, 1790	Colorado	August 1, 1876
Vermont	March 4, 1791	North Dakota	November 2, 1889
Kentucky	June 1, 1792	South Dakota	November 2, 1889
Tennessee	June 1, 1796	Montana	November 8, 1889
Ohio	March 1, 1803	Washington	November 11, 1889
Louisiana	April 30, 1812	Idaho	July 3, 1890
Indiana	December 11, 1816	Wyoming	July 10, 1890
Mississippi	December 10, 1817	Utah	January 4, 1896
Illinois	December 3, 1818	Oklahoma	November 16, 1907
Alabama	December 14, 1819	New Mexico	January 6, 1912
Maine	March 15, 1820	Arizona	February 14, 1912
Missouri	August 10, 1821	Alaska	January 3, 1959
Arkansas	June 15, 1836	Hawaii	August 21, 1959

Presidents and Cabinets

WASHINGTON AND HIS CABINET.

Dates for Cabinet members indicate year they assumed office. Where no date is indicated the tenure of the official coincides with that of the President.

George Washington		1789–1797
V.P.	John Adams	
Sec. of State	Thomas Jefferson	1789
	Edmund Randolph	1794
	Timothy Pickering	1795
Sec. of Treas.	Alexander Hamilton	1789
	O. Wolcott	1795
Sec. of War	H. Knox	1789
	Timothy Pickering	1795
	J. McHenry	1796
P.M. Gen.	Samuel Osgood	1789
	Timothy Pickering	1791
	Joseph Habersham	1795
Att. Gen.	Edmund Randolph	1789
	William Bradford	1794
	Charles Lee	1795

John Adams		1797–1801
V.P.	Thomas Jefferson	
Sec. of State	John Marshall	1800
Sec. of Treas.	Samuel Dexter	1801
Sec. of War	John Marshall	1800
	Samuel Dexter	1800
	R. Griswold	1801
Sec. of Navy (Est. 1798)	B. Stoddert	
P.M. Gen.	Joseph Habersham	
Att. Gen.	Theophilus Parsons	1801

Thomas Jefferson		1801–1809
V.P.	Aaron Burr	1801
	George Clinton	1805
Sec. of State	James Madison	
Sec. of Treas.	Albert Gallatin	
Sec. of War	H. Dearborn	
Sec. of Navy	Robert Smith	1801
	J. Crowninshield	1805
P.M. Gen.	Gideon Granger	
Att. Gen.	Levi Lincoln	1801
	Robert Smith	1805
	J. Breckenridge	1805
	C. A. Rodney	1807

James Madison		1809–1817
V.P.	George Clinton	1809
	Elbridge Gerry	1813
Sec. of State	Robert Smith	1809
	James Monroe	1811
Sec. of Treas.	G. W. Campbell	1814
	Alexander J. Dalbs	1814
	William H. Crawford	1816
Sec. of War	William Eustis	1809
	J. Armstrong	1813
	James Monroe	1814
	William H. Crawford	1815
	I. Shelby	1817
Sec. of Navy	P. Hamilton	1809
	W. Jones	1813
	B. Williams	1814
P.M. Gen.	R. J. Meigs, Jr.	1814
Att. Gen.	William Pinkney	1811
	Richard Rush	1814

James Monroe 1817–1825

V.P.	D. D. Tompkins	
Sec. of State	John Quincy Adams	
Sec. of Treas.	William H. Crawford	
Sec. of War	George Graham	1817
	John C. Calhoun	1817
Sec. of Navy	S. Thompson	1818
	S. L. Southard	1823
P.M. Gen.	John McLean	1823
Att. Gen.	William Wirt	

John Quincy Adams 1825–1829

V.P.	John C. Calhoun	
Sec. of State	Henry Clay	
Sec. of Treas.	Richard Rush	
Sec. of War	J. Barbour	1825
	P. B. Porter	1828
Sec. of Navy	S. L. Southard	
P.M. Gen.	John McLean	
Att. Gen.	William Wirt	

Andrew Jackson 1829–1837

V.P.	John C. Calhoun	1829–1833
V.P.	Martin Van Buren	1833
Sec. of State	Martin Van Buren	1829
	E. Livingston	1831
	L. McLane	1833
	J. Forsyth	1834
Sec. of Treas.	S. D. Ingham	1829
	Louis McLane	1831
	W. J. Duane	1833
	Roger B. Taney	1833
	Levi Woodbury	1834
Sec. of War	J. H. Eaton	1829
	Lewis Cass	1831
	Benjamin F. Butler	1837
Sec. of Navy	J. Branch	1829
	Levi Woodbury	1831
	M. Dickerson	1834
P.M. Gen.	William T. Barry	1829
	Amos Kendall	1835
Att. Gen.	John M. Berrien	1829
	Roger B. Taney	1831
	Benjamin F. Butler	1833

Martin Van Buren 1837–1841

V.P.	R. M. Johnson	
Sec. of State	J. Forsyth	
Sec. of Treas.	Levi Woodbury	
Sec. of War	J. R. Poinsett	
Sec. of Navy	J. K. Paulding	
P.M. Gen.	John M. Niles	1840
Att. Gen.	Felix Grundy	1838
	H. D. Gilpin	1840

William Henry Harrison 1841

V.P.	John Tyler	
Sec. of State	Daniel Webster	
Sec. of Treas.	Thomas Ewing	
Sec. of War	John Bell	
Sec. of Navy	George E. Badger	
P.M. Gen.	Francis Granger	
Att. Gen.	J. J. Crittenden	

John Tyler 1841–1845

V.P.	——	
Sec. of State	H. S. Legaré	1843
	A. P. Upshur	1843
	John C. Calhoun	1844
Sec. of Treas.	Walter Forward	1841
	John C. Spencer	1843
	George M. Bibb	1844
Sec. of War	J. McLean	1841
	John C. Spencer	1841
	J. M. Porter	1843
	William Wilkins	1844
Sec. of Navy	A. P. Upshur	1841
	D. Henshaw	1843
	T. W. Gilmer	1844
	John Y. Mason	1844
P.M. Gen.	Francis Granger	1841
	C. A. Wickliff	1841
Att. Gen.	H. S. Legaré	1841
	John Nelson	1843

James K. Polk 1845–1849

V.P.	George M. Dallas	
Sec. of State	James Buchanan	
Sec. of Treas.	Robert J. Walker	
Sec. of War	William L. Marcy	
Sec. of Navy	G. Bancroft	1845
	John Y. Mason	1846
P.M. Gen.	Cave Johnson	
Att. Gen.	John Y. Mason	1845
	Nathan Clifford	1846
	Isaac Toucey	1848

Zachary Taylor 1849–1850

V.P.	Millard Fillmore	
Sec. of State	John M. Clayton	
Sec. of Treas.	W. M. Meredith	
Sec. of War	G. W. Crawford	1849
	Edward Bates	1850
Sec. of Navy	W. B. Preston	
Sec. of Inter. *(Est. 1849)*	Thomas Ewing	
P.M. Gen.	J. Collamer	
Att. Gen.	Reverdy Johnson	

Millard Fillmore		1850–1853
V.P.	——	
Sec. of State	Daniel Webster	1850
	Edward Everett	1852
Sec. of Treas.	Thomas Corwin	
Sec. of War	Charles M. Conrad	
Sec. of Navy	William A. Graham	1850
	J. P. Kennedy	1852
Sec. of Inter.	James A. Pearce	1850
	T. M. T. McKennan	1850
	A. H. H. Stuart	1850
P.M. Gen.	Nathan K. Hall	1850
	S. D. Hubbard	1852
Att. Gen.	J. J. Crittenden	

Franklin Pierce		1853–1857
V.P.	William R. King	
Sec. of State	William L. Marcy	
Sec. of Treas.	James Guthrie	
Sec. of War	Jefferson Davis	
Sec. of Navy	J. C. Dobbin	
Sec. of Inter.	Robert McClelland	
P.M. Gen.	James Campbell	
Att. Gen.	Caleb Cushing	

James Buchanan		1857–1861
V.P.	J. C. Breckenridge	
Sec. of State	Lewis Cass	1857
	J. S. Black	1860
Sec. of Treas.	Howell Cobb	1857
	Philip F. Thomas	1860
	John A. Dix	1861
Sec. of War	John B. Floyd	1857
	Joseph Holt	1861
Sec. of Navy	Isaac Toucey	
Sec. of Inter.	Jacob Thompson	
P.M. Gen.	A. V. Brown	1857
	Joseph Holt	1859
	Horatio King	1861
Att. Gen.	J. S. Black	1857
	Edwin M. Stanton	1860

Abraham Lincoln		1861–1865
V.P.	Hannibal Hamlin	1861
	Andrew Johnson	1865
Sec. of State	William H. Seward	
Sec. of Treas.	Salmon P. Chase	1861
	W. P. Fessenden	1864
	Hugh McCulloch	1865
Sec. of War	Simon Cameron	1861
	Edwin M. Stanton	1862
Sec. of Navy	Gideon Welles	
Sec. of Inter.	Caleb B. Smith	1861
	John P. Usher	1863

Abraham Lincoln *(cont.)*		1861–1865
P.M. Gen.	Montgomery Blair	1861
	William Dennison	1864
Att. Gen.	Edward Bates	1861
	T. J. Coffey	1863
	James Speed	1864

Andrew Johnson		1865–1869
V.P.	——	
Sec. of State	William H. Seward	
Sec. of Treas.	Hugh McCulloch	
Sec. of War	Edwin M. Stanton	1865
	U. S. Grant	1867
	L. Thomas	1868
	J. M. Schofield	1868
Sec. of Navy	Gideon Welles	1865
Sec. of Inter.	John P. Usher	1865
	James Harlan	1865
	O. H. Browning	1866
P.M. Gen.	William Dennison	1865
	A. W. Randall	1866
Att. Gen.	James Speed	1865
	Henry Stanbery	1866
	William M. Evarts	1868

Ulysses S. Grant		1869–1877
V.P.	Schuyler Colfax	1869
	Henry Wilson	1873
Sec. of State	E. B. Washburne	1869
	Hamilton Fish	1869
Sec. of Treas.	George S. Boutwell	1869
	W. A. Richardson	1873
	Benjamin H. Bristow	1874
	Lot M. Morrill	1876
Sec. of War	J. A. Rawlins	1869
	W. T. Sherman	1869
	W. W. Belknap	1869
	Alphonso Taft	1876
	J. D. Cameron	1876
Sec. of Navy	Adolph E. Borie	1869
	George M. Robeson	1869
Sec. of Inter.	Jacob D. Cox	1869
	C. Delano	1870
	Zachary Chandler	1875
P.M. Gen.	J. A. J. Creswell	1869
	James W. Marshall	1874
	Marshall Jewell	1874
	James N. Tyner	1876
Att. Gen.	E. R. Hoar	1869
	A. T. Ackerman	1870
	George H. Williams	1871
	Edward Pierrepont	1875
	Alphonso Taft	1876

Rutherford B. Hayes		1877–1881
V.P.	William A. Wheeler	
Sec. of State	William M. Evarts	
Sec. of Treas.	John Sherman	
Sec. of War	G. W. McCrary	1877
	Alexander Ramsey	1879
Sec. of Navy	R. W. Thompson	1877
	Nathan Goff, Jr.	1881
Sec. of Inter.	Carl Schurz	
P.M. Gen.	David M. Key	1877
	Horace Maynard	1880
Att. Gen.	Charles Devens	

James Garfield		1881
V.P.	Chester A. Arthur	
Sec. of State	James G. Blaine	
Sec. of Treas.	William Windom	
Sec. of War	R. T. Lincoln	
Sec. of Navy	W. H. Hunt	
Sec. of Inter.	S. J. Kirkwood	
P.M. Gen.	T. L. James	
Att. Gen.	W. MacVeagh	

Chester A. Arthur		1881–1885
V.P.	——	
Sec. of State	F. T. Frelinghuysen	
Sec. of Treas.	Charles J. Folger	1881
	W. Q. Gresham	1884
	Hugh McCulloch	1884
Sec. of War	R. T. Lincoln	
Sec. of Navy	W. E. Chandler	
Sec. of Inter.	Henry M. Teller	
P.M. Gen.	T. O. Howe	1881
	W. Q. Gresham	1883
	Frank Hatton	1884
Att. Gen.	B. H. Brewster	

Grover Cleveland		1885–1889
V.P.	T. A. Hendricks	
Sec. of State	Thomas F. Bayard	
Sec. of Treas.	Daniel Manning	1885
	Charles S. Fairchild	1887
Sec. of War	W. C. Endicott	
Sec. of Navy	W. C. Whitney	
Sec. of Inter.	L. Q. C. Lamar	1885
	William F. Vilas	1888
P.M. Gen.	William F. Vilas	1885
	D. M. Dickinson	1888
Att. Gen.	A. H. Garland	
Sec. of Agric. (Est. 1889)	N. J. Colman	

Benjamin Harrison		1889–1893
V.P.	Levi P. Morton	
Sec. of State	James G. Blaine	1889
	John W. Foster	1892

Benjamin Harrison *(cont.)*		1893–1897
Sec. of Treas.	William Windom	1889
	Charles Foster	1891
Sec. of War	R. Proctor	1889
	S. B. Elkins	1891
Sec. of Navy	Benjamin F. Tracy	
Sec. of Inter.	John W. Noble	
P.M. Gen.	J. Wanamaker	1889
Att. Gen.	W. H. H. Miller	
Sec. of Agric.	J. M. Rusk	

Grover Cleveland		1893–1897
V.P.	Adlai E. Stevenson	
Sec. of State	W. Q. Gresham	1893
	Richard Olney	1895
Sec. of Treas.	John G. Carlisle	
Sec. of War	D. S. Lamont	
Sec. of Navy	Hillary A. Herbert	
Sec. of Inter.	Hoke Smith	1893
	D. R. Francis	1896
P.M. Gen.	W. S. Bissell	1893
	W. L. Wilson	1895
Att. Gen.	Richard Olney	1893
	J. Harmon	1895
Sec. of Agric.	J. S. Morton	

William McKinley		1897–1901
V.P.	Garret A. Hobart	1897
	Theodore Roosevelt	1901
Sec. of State	John Sherman	1897
	William R. Day	1897
	John Hay	1898
Sec. of Treas.	Lyman J. Gage	
Sec. of War	R. A. Alger	1897
	Elihu Root	1899
Sec. of Navy	John D. Long	
Sec. of Inter.	C. N. Bliss	1897
	E. A. Hitchcock	1899
P.M. Gen.	James A. Gary	1897
	Charles E. Smith	1898
Att. Gen.	J. McKenna	1897
	J. W. Griggs	1897
	P. C. Knox	1901
Sec. of Agric.	James Wilson	

Theodore Roosevelt		1901–1909
V.P.	C. W. Fairbanks	1905
Sec. of State	John Hay	1901
	Elihu Root	1905
	Robert Bacon	1909
Sec. of Treas.	Lyman J. Gage	1901
	Leslie M. Shaw	1902
	G. B. Cortelyou	1907

THEODORE ROOSEVELT *(cont.)*		1901–1909
Sec. of War	Elihu Root	1901
	William H. Taft	1904
	Luke E. Wright	1908
Sec. of Navy	John D. Long	1901
	William H. Moody	1902
	Paul Morton	1904
	C. J. Bonaparte	1905
	Victor H. Metcalf	1907
	T. H. Newberry	1908
Sec. of Inter.	E. A. Hitchcock	1901
	J. R. Garfield	1907
P.M. Gen.	Charles E. Smith	1901
	Henry C. Payne	1902
	Robert J. Wynne	1904
	G. B. Cortelyou	1905
	G. von L. Meyer	1907
Att. Gen.	P. C. Knox	1901
	W. H. Moody	1904
	C. J. Bonaparte	1907
Sec. of Agric.	James Wilson	
Sec. of Com.	G. B. Cortelyou	1903
and Labor	V. H. Metcalf	1904
(Est. 1903)	O. S. Strauss	1907
WILLIAM H. TAFT		1909–1913
V.P.	James S. Sherman	
Sec. of State	P. C. Knox	
Sec. of Treas.	F. MacVeagh	
Sec. of War	J. M. Dickinson	1909
	H. L. Stimson	1911
Sec. of Navy	G. von L. Meyer	
Sec. of Inter.	R. A. Ballinger	1909
	W. L. Fisher	1911
P.M. Gen.	F. H. Hitchcock	
Att. Gen.	G. W. Wickersham	
Sec. of Agric.	James Wilson	
Sec. of Com.	Charles Nagel	1909
and Labor		
(Divided 1913)		
WOODROW WILSON		1913–1921
V.P.	Thomas R. Marshall	
Sec. of State	William J. Bryan	1913
	Robert Lansing	1915
	Bainbridge Colby	1920
Sec. of Treas.	W. G. McAdoo	1913
	Carter Glass	1918
	D. F. Houston	1920
Sec. of War	L. M. Garrison	1913
	N. D. Baker	1916
Sec. of Navy	Josephus Daniels	
Sec. of Inter.	F. K. Lane	1913
	J. B. Payne	1920
WOODROW WILSON *(cont.)*		1913–1921
P.M. Gen.	A. S. Burleson	1913
Att. Gen.	J. C. McReynolds	1913
	Thomas W. Gregory	1914
	A. M. Palmer	1919
Sec. of Agric.	D. F. Houston	1913
	E. T. Meredith	1920
Sec. of Com.	W. C. Redfield	1913
	J. W. Alexander	1919
Sec. of Labor	W. B. Wilson	
WARREN G. HARDING		1921–1923
V.P.	Calvin Coolidge	
Sec. of State	Charles E. Hughes	
Sec. of Treas.	Andrew W. Mellon	
Sec. of War	John W. Weeks	
Sec. of Navy	Edwin Denby	
Sec. of Inter.	Albert B. Fall	1921
	Hubert Work	1923
P.M. Gen.	Will H. Hayes	1921
	Hubert Work	1922
	Harry S. New	1923
Att. Gen.	H. M. Daugherty	
Sec. of Agric.	Henry C. Wallace	
Sec. of Com.	Herbert C. Hoover	
Sec. of Labor	J. J. Davis	
CALVIN COOLIDGE		1923–1929
V.P.	Charles G. Dawes	1925
Sec. of State	Charles E. Hughes	1923
	Frank B. Kellogg	1925
Sec. of Treas.	Andrew W. Mellon	
Sec. of War	John W. Weeks	1923
	Dwight F. Davis	1925
Sec. of Navy	Edwin Denby	1923
	Curtis D. Wilbur	1924
Sec. of Inter.	Hubert Work	1923
	Roy O. West	1928
P.M. Gen.	Harry S. New	1923
Att. Gen.	H. M. Daugherty	1923
	Harlan F. Stone	1924
	John G. Sargent	1925
Sec. of Agric.	H. M. Gore	1924
	W. M. Jardine	1925
Sec. of Com.	Herbert C. Hoover	
	W. F. Whiting	1928
Sec. of Labor	J. J. Davis	
HERBERT C. HOOVER		1929–1933
V.P.	Charles Curtis	
Sec. of State	Henry L. Stimson	
Sec. of Treas.	Andrew W. Mellon	1929
	Ogden L. Mills	1932
Sec. of War	James W. Good	1929
	Patrick J. Hurley	1929

Herbert C. Hoover *(cont.)* 1929–1933

Office	Name	Year
Sec. of Navy	Charles F. Adams	
Sec. of Inter.	Ray L. Wilbur	
P.M. Gen.	Walter F. Brown	
Att. Gen.	William D. Mitchell	
Sec. of Agric.	A. M. Hyde	
Sec. of Com.	R. P. Lamont	1929
	R. D. Chapin	1932
Sec. of Labor	W. N. Doak	1930

Franklin D. Roosevelt 1933–1945

Office	Name	Year
V.P.	John N. Garner	1933
	Henry A. Wallace	1941
	Harry S. Truman	1945
Sec. of State	Cordell Hull	1933
	E. R. Stettinius	1944
Sec. of Treas.	William H. Woodin	1933
	Henry Morgenthau	1934
Sec. of War	George H. Dern	1933
	H. A. Woodring	1936
	H. L. Stimson	1940
Sec. of Navy	Claude A. Swanson	1933
	Charles Edison	1940
	Frank Knox	1940
	James V. Forrestal	1944
Sec. of Inter.	Harold L. Ickes	
P.M. Gen.	James A. Farley	1933
	Frank C. Walker	1940
Att. Gen.	H. S. Cummings	1933
	Frank Murphy	1939
	Robert H. Jackson	1940
	Francis Biddle	1941
Sec. of Agric.	Henry A. Wallace	1933
	C. R. Wickard	1940
Sec. of Com.	D. C. Roper	1933
	H. L. Hopkins	1939
	Jesse Jones	1940
	Henry A. Wallace	1945
Sec. of Labor	Frances Perkins	

Harry S. Truman 1945–1953

Office	Name	Year
V.P.	Alben W. Barkley	1949
Sec. of State	James F. Byrnes	1945
	George C. Marshall	1947
	Dean G. Acheson	1949
Sec. of Treas.	Fred M. Vinson	1945
	John W. Snyder	1946
Sec. of War (See Sec. of Defense)	Robert H. Patterson	1945
	K. C. Royall	1947
Sec. of Navy (See Sec. of Defense)	James V. Forrestal	1945

Harry S. Truman *(cont.)* 1945–1953

Office	Name	Year
Sec. of Inter.	Harold L. Ickes	1945
	Julius A. Krug	1946
	O. L. Chapman	1949
P.M. Gen.	Robert E. Hannegan	1945
	Jesse L. Donaldson	1947
Att. Gen.	Tom C. Clark	1945
	J. H. McGrath	1949
	J. P. McGranery	1952
Sec. of Agric.	C. P. Anderson	1945
	C. F. Brannan	1948
Sec. of Com.	W. A. Harriman	1946
	C. W. Sawyer	1948
Sec. of Labor	L. B. Schwellenbach	1945
	M. J. Tobin	1948
Sec. of Defense (Est. 1947)	James V. Forrestal	1947
	Louis Johnson	1949
	George C. Marshall	1950
	Robert A. Lovett	1951

Dwight D. Eisenhower 1953–1961

Office	Name	Year
V.P.	Richard M. Nixon	
Sec. of State	John F. Dulles	1953
	Christian A. Herter	1959
Sec. of Treas.	George M. Humphrey	1953
	Robert B. Anderson	1957
Sec. of Inter.	D. McKay	1953
	F. A. Seaton	1956
P.M. Gen.	A. E. Summerfield	
Att. Gen.	Herbert Brownell	1953
	William P. Rogers	1957
Sec. of Agric.	E. T. Benson	1953
Sec. of Com.	Sinclair Weeks	1953
	Frederick Mueller	1959
Sec. of Labor	M. P. Durkin	1953
	J. P. Mitchell	1953
Sec. of Defense	Charles E. Wilson	1953
	Neil H. McElroy	1957
Sec. of Health, Ed., & Welfare (Est. 1953)	Oveta C. Hobby	1953
	M. B. Folsom	1955
	Arthur S. Flemming	1958

John F. Kennedy 1961–1963

Office	Name	Year
V.P.	Lyndon B. Johnson	1961
Sec. of State	Dean Rusk	1961
Sec. of Treas.	C. Douglas Dillon	1961
Sec. of Inter.	Stewart Udall	1961
P.M. Gen.	J. Edward Day	1961
Att. Gen.	Robert Kennedy	1961
Sec. of Agric.	Orville Freeman	1961
Sec. of Com.	Luther Hodges	1961
Sec. of Labor	Arthur Goldberg	1961
Sec. of Defense	Robert S. McNamara	1961
Sec. of Health, Ed., & Welfare	Abraham B. Ribicoff	1961

LYNDON B. JOHNSON		1963
V.P.	Hubert H. Humphrey	1964
Sec. of State	Dean Rusk	1961
Sec. of Treas.	C. Douglas Dillon	1961
Sec. of Inter.	Stewart Udall	1961
P. M. Gen.	John A. Gronouski	1963
Att. Gen.	Nicholas Katzenbach	1964
Sec. of Agric.	Orville L. Freeman	1961
Sec. of Com.	John T. Connor	1964
Sec. of Labor	W. Willard Wirtz	1962
Sec. of Defense	Robert S. McNamara	1961
Sec. of Health, Ed., & Welfare	Anthony J. Celebrezze	1962

Chief Justices

John Jay, N.Y.	1789–1795
John Rutledge, S.C.	1795
Oliver Ellsworth, Conn.	1795–1799
John Marshall, Va.	1801–1835
Roger B. Taney, Md.	1836–1864
Salmon P. Chase, Ohio	1864–1873
Morrison R. Waite, Ohio	1874–1888
Melville W. Fuller, Ill.	1888–1910
Edward D. White, La.	1910–1921
William H. Taft, Conn.	1921–1930
Charles E. Hughes, N.Y.	1930–1941
Harlan F. Stone, N.Y.	1941–1946
Fred M. Vinson, Ky.	1946–1953
Earl Warren, Calif.	1953–

Reading List

The reader interested in a larger collection of basic documents will find many to choose from. Among them are *Documents of American History,* and *Living Ideas in America,* both edited by Henry Steele Commager. A handy pocket volume is Richard D. Heffner's *A Documentary History of the United States.*

Inexpensive one-volume encyclopedias of great value to the student and entertaining for the general reader as well are Gorton Carruth's *Encyclopedia of American Facts and Dates* and Richard B. Morris's *Encyclopedia of American History.*

Narrative histories of the United States run into the dozens. A convenient volume written by two of America's leading historians, Allan Nevins and Henry Steele Commager, is *The Pocket History of the United States.*

For those interested in the modern period of growth and reform, there are such books as Richard Hofstadter's *The Age of Reform* and Eric F. Goldman's *Rendezvous with Destiny. The Autobiography of Lincoln Steffens* is by now a classic personal statement on this period.

Two books with a special view are John Hope Franklin's *From Slavery to Freedom,* perhaps the best history of the Negro in America, and Roger Burlingame's *The American Conscience,* in which our behavior over three centuries is seen through the moral judgments we made upon ourselves.

The history of ideas in America has been traced in several outstanding works: *The Growth of American Thought,* by Merle Curti; *Freedom's Ferment,* by Alice F. Tyler; and Harvey Wish's two volumes on *Society and Thought in Early America* and *Society and Thought in Modern America.*

The reader may find special pleasure in biographies of some of the shapers of democratic thought whose works are reprinted in this book. A few suggestions are Dumas Malone's *Jefferson and His Time,* Irving Brant's *James Madison,* Arthur M. Schlesinger, Jr.'s *The Age of Jackson,* Henry Steele Commager's *Theodore Parker,* H. S. Canby's *Thoreau,* Ralph Korngold's *Two Friends of Man: William Lloyd Garrison and Wendell Phillips,* and Carl Sandburg's *Abraham Lincoln.*

Several of the books mentioned are now available in paperback form.

Places to Visit

The largest collections of major documents in American history can be seen in Washington, in the National Archives building and at the Library of Congress. Some are on permanent display, and many others are shown to the public on occasion as part of special exhibits. A visit to both places is always worth including during a tour of the nation's capital.

Documents related to the administrations of some of our presidents can be seen in special libraries which have been established for both the historical researcher and the more casual tourist. Even more interesting, perhaps, are the homes themselves, restored as closely as possible to their appearance during the residence of their famous occupants.

The traveller should not miss an opportunity to visit Monticello, Jefferson's home in Virginia, and nearby Charlottesville, the site of the University which he designed. On the same trip one can take in Mount Vernon, Washington's home, and Colonial Williamsburg, the extensive reconstruction of the capital of the Virginia colony, once the theater of political operations for George Mason, Patrick Henry, James Madison, and James Monroe, as well as Jefferson.

In Philadelphia there is Independence Hall to see.

Boston's Historical Trail takes the tourist on a round of several sites vital to our past and in nearby Lexington and Concord are the first battlegrounds of the Revolution. Concord has the homes of Emerson and Thoreau, who are represented in this book, as well as those of Alcott and Hawthorne. North of Boston, in Quincy, is the home of the Adams family.

Near Nashville, Tennessee, is Andrew Jackson's Hermitage, and westward in Springfield, Illinois, is Lincoln's home. At Hyde Park in New York is the Franklin D. Roosevelt Memorial Library, next to the President's birthplace.

Picture Credits

Key to picture position: t-top; c-center; b-bottom; l-left; r-right; combinations: tl-top left, etc.

The following are abbreviations used for picture sources:

BB	Brown Brothers
CS	Culver Service
FDRL	Franklin D. Roosevelt Library
LOC	Library of Congress
MM	author's collection
NA	National Archives
NYPL	New York Public Library
NYT	New York Times
UPI	United Press International
WW	Wide World

page

2 NYPL
3 tl-NYPL; tr-NYPL; b-NYPL
4 Boston Athenaeum
5 NYPL
6 NYPL
7 tl-NYPL; tr-NYPL
8 LOC
9 t-NYPL; b-NYPL
10 l-NYPL; r-NYPL
11 Harper's Magazine, 1895
12 t-NYPL; b-NYPL
13 t-NYPL; b-LOC
14 LOC
15 NYPL
16 NYPL
18 Virginia State Library
19 Virginia Museum of Fine Arts
21 LOC
22 LOC
23 NYPL
24 LOC
25 LOC
26 NA
27 LOC
28 NYPL
29 NYPL
30 NYPL
32 t-*American Gleaner;* b-NYPL
33 NYPL
34 NYPL
35 NYPL
36 t-LOC; others-NYPL
37 NYPL
38 NYPL
39 LOC
40 NYPL
41 NA
42 NA
50 t-NYPL; b-NYPL
51 Pennsylvania Historical Society
52 LOC
53 NYPL
54 NA
56 NYPL
59 t-Boston Public Library; b-Vermont State Capitol
60 t-NYPL; c-NYPL; b-NYPL
61 NYPL
62 t-NYPL; b-LOC
63 LOC
64 University of Virginia Library
65 Boston Museum of Fine Arts
66 l-Virginia Historical Society; c-NYPL; r-*Portrait Gallery of Distinguished American Citizens*
67 NYPL
69 NYPL
70 NYPL
72 Fogg Art Museum, Harvard
74 t-Southern Methodist University, Bridwell Library; b-NYPL
75 NYPL
76 t-NYHS; b-Metropolitan Museum of Art
77 tl-NYHS; tr-NYHS
78 t-*Illustrated London News,* 1861; b-*Harper's Weekly,* 1862
79 The Hermitage, Tennessee
80 American Antiquarian Society
81 LOC
82 NYHS
83 American Museum of Natural History
84 American Antiquarian Society
85 NYPL
86, 87, 88, 89 *Christopher P. Cranch and His Caricatures*
91 Boston Public Library
92 NYPL
93 *With Thackeray in America*
94 *Christopher P. Cranch and His Caricatures*
95 NYPL
96 b-Essex Institute
97 l-NYPL; r-NYPL
98 t-NYPL; bl-Chicago Historical Society; br-*Woman in the Nineteenth Century*
100 New Jersey State Hospital, Trenton
101 t-CS; c-CS; b-CS
102 NYPL
103 NYPL
104 t-NYPL; b-N.Y. State Historical Society
105 t-NYPL; b-NYPL
106 t-Harper's Weekly, 1871; b-NYPL

107 *Common School Assistant,* 1839
108 t-Massachusetts Historical Society; b-*Pennsylvania School Journal,* 1835
109 t-Lexington Historical Society; b-NYPL
110 NYPL
111 NYPL
112 NYPL
113 Concord Public Library
114 NYPL
116 NYPL
117 *Leslie's Weekly,* 1876
118 t-CS; b-*Leslie's Weekly,* 1860
119 t-The State Street Trust Company; b-*Harper's Weekly*
120 NYPL
121 Maryland Historical Society
122-126 MM
127 LOC
128 tl-*New York Illustrated News;* tr-*Vanity Fair*
129 LOC
130 LOC
131 LOC
132 *Harper's Weekly*
134 LOC
135 LOC
136 MM
137 LOC
138 LOC
139 NYT
140 LOC
142 CS
143 BB
144 BB
146 BB
147 l-*Harper's Weekly;* r-NYPL
148 BB
149 NYPL
150 NYPL
153-156 MM
157 NYPL
158 NYPL
159 t-BB; b-BB
160 BB
161 t-BB; b-BB
162 l-NYPL; r-BB
163 MM
164 *The Century,* 1902
165 *Punch*
166-167 *New York Journal*
168 *New York Journal*
169 MM
170 NYPL
171 NYPL
173 *Puck,* 1889
174 l-*New York American;* r-NYPL
175 t-*McClure's Magazine;* b-NYPL
177 NYT
178 BB
179 WW
180-181 b-NYT
181 t-BB
182 BB
183 BB
185 b-BB
187 WW
188 t-WW; b-WW
189 Culver
190 BB
191 t-NYT; b-BB
192 NYT
193 t-BB; b-WW
194-195 FDRL
196 FDRL
198 Walter Lippmann
201 t-NYT; b-FDRL
202 BB
204 FDRL
205 NYT
206 NA
207 t-NYT; c-UPI; b-UPI
208 UPI
211 UPI
213 UPI
218 UPI

Index

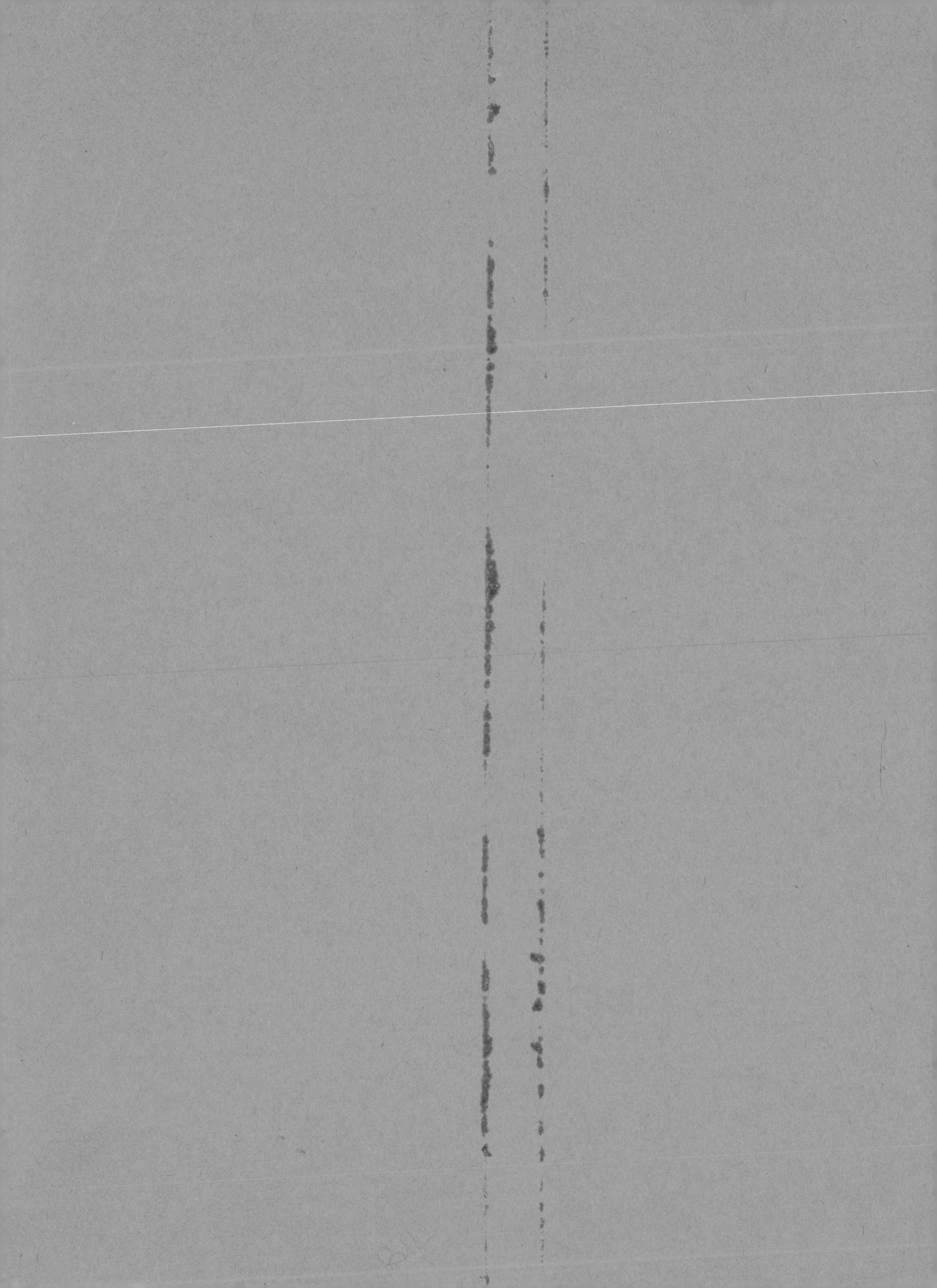